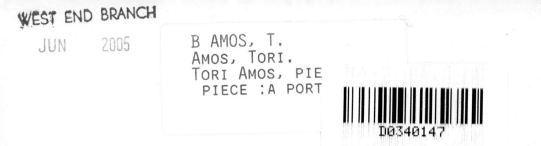

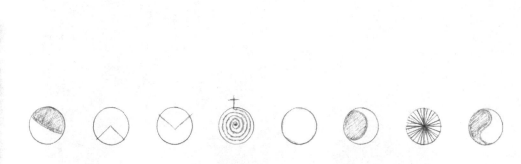

TORI AMOS piece by piece

TORI AMOS

piece by piece

A PORTRAIT

OF THE ARTIST:

HER THOUGHTS.

HER CONVERSATIONS.

TORI AMOS and ANN POWERS

BROADWAY BOOKS New York

PRINTED IN THE UNITED STATES OF AMERICA

BROADWAY BOOKS and its logo, a letter B bisected on the diagonal,
are trademarks of Random House, Inc.

Visit our website at www.broadwaybooks.com

First edition published 2005.

Book design by Marysarah Quinn

Page 353 constitutes an extension of this copyright page.

Library of Congress Cataloging-in-Publication Data
Amos, Tori.
    Tori Amos: piece by piece : a portrait of the artist : her thoughts.
her conversations. / Tori Amos and Ann Powers.—1st ed.
        p.   cm.
    1. Amos, Tori.   2. Rock musicians—United States—Biography.
I. Powers, Ann.   II. Title

ML420.A5874A3 2005
782.42166'092—dc22
[B]   2004057538
ISBN 0-7679-1676-X

10 9 8 7 6 5 4 3 2 1

Dedication

Tori:

This book would not be what it is without my daughter,

Natashya Lórien Hawley, who has taught me to laugh . . .

   and who better not read this book before she's sixteen . . .

Ann:

For my daughter, Rebecca Brooklyn Weisbard

(To quote my friend)

Where the words jump off my pen and into your pages

Pick out your cloud . . .

contents

THE CREW

John Witherspoon, *Manager*

Chelsea Laird, *Manager*

Mark Hawley, *Studio and Live Sound Engineer, Husband*

Marcel van Limbeek, *Studio Engineer and Live Monitor*

Andy Solomon, *Production Manager*

Matt Chamberlain, *Drummer*

Jon Evans, *Bassist*

Dan Boland, *Lighting Designer*

Joel Hopkins, *Security Director*

Duncan Pickford, *Chef*

Alison Evans, *Tour Documentarian*

Karen Binns, *Stylist and Friend*

Dr. Marie Dobyns, *Internist/Sister*

Loren Haynes, *Photographer*

The first time I met Tori Amos, during one of her promotional whirls through New York nearly a decade ago, I thought we might continue talking forever, given the right cushy sofa and all the green tea in the world. As it was, we had barely over an hour until I had to hand her off to another journalist. I'd always heard that Tori was a talker, the rare sort of artist who really connects with each interviewer. Much later, I would learn she's the same effusive, engaged person in the presence of her road crew, her daughter's nanny, or the fans who faithfully gather before every show on her endless touring schedule. Yes, this woman is a talker, but never in a frivolous way.

Tori is one of those people whose life unfolds in conversation. Her main interlocutor is herself: she understands that each human's way of being evolves through the interplay of many different soul elements, and she knows how to make her own inner voices meet, fight, love and co-create. She is also one of the most open collaborators I've known, not only in terms of her music, which she fully claims for herself in order to better welcome key players eventually, but in her daily existence. Tori is the woman in your neighborhood who stops by your garden, pauses, and gets you going for three hours on the topic of lilies that grow best in winter sun. Later, you'll walk by her pea patch and discover the most spectacular flower, not exactly what you planted, but something that shows the influence of the tips you shared. That's Tori—open to the world so that she can better create a microcosm of her own.

When Tori asked me to work on the project now crackling across these pages, we immediately agreed that a typical star memoir didn't make sense. Autobiographies imply finality. You're not dead yet, but you've finished enough of yourself to draw conclusions. Tori knew that her creative life is still unfolding, absolutely. Besides, in her communicative way, she wanted to offer a book that would begin an exchange of ideas, not about her career alone, but about the artist's role in general, and how muse and music survive in circumstances both hostile and ideal. Tori's process, it turns out, is a way of formalizing the push to create while still keeping its mystery alive. She has also confronted the common problems all artists face in a society that both deifies and undervalues that role— thorny matters of image, business practices, working with collaborators, and balancing a personal and a public life. We wanted to find the places where Tori's experience connects to the larger community doing what some theorists fancily call "symbolic work."

We hit upon the scheme of an ongoing conversation about Tori's artistic life and how it relates to the larger matter of creativity, especially women's creativity, in a historic moment of great potential and risk. The chapters here emerged first through face-to-face dialogue, then in cyberspace exchanges, where they were challenged and honed by both of us. Some passages are pure Tori; others come from talks edited by me; still others are a mix of her vision and my revision. I've provided a framework that moves beyond personal views, into the realm of myth and archetype, a territory where both of us like to roam. And there are other voices—Tori's inner circle, providing context and perspective.

This is not your standard rock star's I-was-born-a-poor-genius self-deification, nor is it the opposite, an attempt by an exceptional person to convince people that she's just folks. Tori Amos is not your ordinary girl, but she has much to say to all of us interested in what it means to be a woman, a creator, a nurturer, a fighter, a part of all the universes that merge into a life. I am honored to have been her talking partner, and we both hope that you will find your own voice in the spaces between our words.

—ann powers

INTRODUCTION The soul's dance

ANN: *There is no way to capture the image of the spirit that moves creation. The photographer's shutter cannot move fast enough; the writer's pen does not hold enough ink. Men might reduce her to a romantic notion of "the muse," art's glorified office assistant, but she demolishes those set notions with a single swoop of her hand. Look at her for one moment and see a flash of teeth: a lioness. In the next, she becomes a beautiful dancer, laughing with a lute in her hands. She can be as huge as the earth itself, or as quiet as the underworld. She wanders like a mother searching for her lost child, like a lover seeking her mate, like a woman made mad with wine and her own power, free in ecstasy. The force of creativity manifests in innumerable ways, and those who serve her as artists give themselves over to her constant transformations.*

Systems have been devised over time to describe the dazzling change and deep consistency that combine to form the human soul. In ancient days, people spoke of gods and goddesses; today, psychological jargon often substitutes for belief in divine rock stars. Call them archetypes, icons, or avatars—these modes of being lend order to existence and character to artistic expression.

As part of a long tradition of artists, Tori Amos calls the path of archetypes her way. In her songs, she draws the thread between her own life and the stories she draws from the underground river of myth; through her voice and her piano, she connects with the music, celebrates. Amos has found a way to sustain herself and her work, despite the lousy odds on the pop music betting floor. Since childhood, over four decades of composing and performing, Amos has scrutinized and renewed herself, piece by piece. She has been that feline queen, that graceful dancer, that sorrowful matriarch. Through it all, she remains somehow herself. This is the story of her unfinished evolution.

CONVERSATION BETWEEN TORI AND ANN:

I've always told you the songs are separate from me. Yes, I write them; I gather the elements. But I do so by going around and listening to other people's stories. I watch the audience; I study how people react to what I've already created, and that also goes into new songs. It's like being a chronicler, instead of just somebody who invents. I research and put what I discover together in a form—which is what every artist really does. In every songwriter's suitcase there is a kind of musical paint box that we take with us everywhere we go.

The romantic myth of the artist says that you are the Source. I have no illusion about that. I think this goes back to my grandfather. That was his great gift to me—Native Americans don't believe they are the Source. They have *access* to the Source. Endless access. But don't get confused.

I can access, but so can a librarian. They can tell you what you'll find in the seventeenth aisle. It took me years of figuring out how my own creativity operates until I finally realized that it is what I'm comfortable with, and that's my role.

Another way I often think about creation is in architectural terms. We say archetype, and that makes me think of architecture. The songs don't spring whole into existence; they are built. It's a structural process. A life is structural too, or at least the story we construct from our lives as we go along. In my music, I use texts—history, mythologies, my own stories—to construct other texts. I go to something very tangible, like a book or a visceral experience, to create something intangible.

Since recordings have existed, it may seem that music is as tangible as anything else, but in its essence music is ether. Before writing existed, people had to sit and listen; you couldn't bottle it up and take it with you. Songwriting is, in a way, a return to that state, through the maze of texts that define how we live. You make something ethereal out of materials that are often all too solid.

So I am immersed in the architecture of texts. I came to this place very young. When I was a child, my mother would read to me every morning. Children's books at first, but then there was a point, and I wasn't that old, when she would read her favorite poems and short stories—Edgar Allen Poe, Robert Browning, William Faulkner. She had been a literature major in college and stopped after two years to become a minister's wife. She transferred that love of the book to me. As a minister's wife she was surrounded by the Good Book, but Eastern Cherokee was very much in her soul and she was inspired by my grandfather Poppa's stories. And then my father was a preacher, a man of The Book, working in an oral tradition. My mother gave me the text and my father gave me theology. I often think that if I'd been stolen and brought up by somebody who didn't read to me, I might have music, but I might not be a songwriter. I needed my mother to give me the keys to the library.

The root or the structure of my songwriting is the voice that comes out of the piano, and, of course, my mother's books. She was reading me stories that were fairly airtight. I mean, talk about structure. Take a look at Poe's "Telltale Heart." So the structures of the Western musical tradition were imprinted on my brain in tandem with the structures of fiction and poetry. The literary tradition may now commonly be viewed as separate from music, but I didn't experience them that way. Instead I was taught to build bridges between them—no musical pun intended—early on.

When I try to define my work, I keep going back to the language of architecture, because it is multidimensional. I've always been drawn to books by architects; I try to look at building plans, to discover the secret passageways architects devise to allow entry and exit, to understand how they might create solidity or flow in a building. These choices resemble those that songwriters must make. When I want to learn from other writers' songs, I spend a lot of time examining their frameworks, stripping them down in my mind, listening over and over. I feel as though I'm sitting with another architect's blueprints. I see the patterns within the songs, the word choices they make, the voicings within the arrangements, all that. The most important ingredient might not be the most obvious. An incredible melody might be hidden within a distracting arrangement, or by a dissonant chord structure.

Houses, pianos—these inanimate objects are alive for me. They are made of primal materials: wood, stone, metal. Within such objects you can find an animate soul. If you gathered together a geneticist, an architect, a physician, a historian, a geologist, an archaeologist, and somebody who works with the psyche and said, "Define the Wailing Wall in Jerusalem," what would they say it's made of? Is it only the mortar and the stone, or does it contain what people have projected onto it? It has taken something on. It has taken something on that cannot be defined just by using visual perception. You can "put it under a microscope" and you still won't be able to prove scientifically what it is that people are feeling when they stand facing this Wailing Wall in Jerusalem. I'm interested in the composition of an object as it goes beyond the obvious. I feel the same way about musical composition. Songs, texts, are alive. I'm not saying they have two arms and two legs and a head like an alien. But there's a consciousness there, an autonomy. I'm a co-creator, of course, but this hubris that a lot of writers have in which they think that they're the Source—that's a lie.

This is one reason I'm so drawn to a song's architecture, to studying what a song is made of and why it works, how a sonic space is created that invites people in, what makes a listener start to listen. I'm interested in the moment in which a creation begins to live.

CHELSEA LAIRD:

There's a kind of enigma that people pick up on surrounding Tori's aura, her presence, and some people get it and some people read it wrong. She's very spiritual—not necessarily in a religious sense—and it's more for strength and inspiration. Doing this day in and day out, writing hundreds of songs every year, you have to have a source for inspiration. She got labeled a fairy princess early on, which she finds amusing. That has influenced, not to mention limited, how people choose to see and hear her. Don't ask me where that came from: some journalist decided they couldn't define Tori's relationship with certain theories, gods and goddesses, and yes, fairies? Not sure. I suppose it was easier for people early in her career to label it "freaky" so they didn't have to admit they didn't understand. But seriously, have you listened to the lyrics? Are you having trouble with them? Don't worry, so do I. But do your research. It's really this sort of odd thing for me, knowing her as well as I do, that people really have some interesting explanations of who she is and what she's writing about. As a result we have gotten every single frickin' fairy trinket you can imagine.

ANN: *Through sometimes irritating experience, Amos has come to understand how reductive most contemporary forms of expression can be when it comes to archetypes.*

CONVERSATION BETWEEN TORI AND ANN:

In the West, we have a culture that's unaware of myth; it's not really taught, though it's ingrained on some level. In so many films and so many books, the same stories are told over and over and over again. These are just different patterns from which artists pull. But in every case, myth is the blueprint. Tori Amos is not the blueprint of a nurturing mother. That archetype already exists. Myth is the fabric of our psyche. It's our cultural DNA.

In the space of performance and composition, I am not above the law. I follow strict law. I've done a lot of reading and studying, and the Jungian way was my way. That's the way that worked for me, with shadow. Taking on some of these different myths, I create a space for them to enact something. I'm in service to them. What do I say to people who don't know how to interpret my songs? You don't read the Bible literally. I thought parables were very clear, yet a lot of people have problems with them when they pop up today. I can't tell people that maybe they need to read some books, brush up on their archetypes. They could probably go on a web site and figure it out. But literalizing is very much part of the patriarchy. If you want something made concrete, I'll give you some shoes and pour some cement in them and we'll drop you off in the river.

Are there new archetypes being created every day as a result of new developments? Things have changed in a way. I understand that certain things haven't existed before as we know them on this planet, stemming from technological advances, for example. And it'll be intriguing to see how it plays itself out. Maybe in a few hundred years we'll see what new myths arise from the experience of computer viruses, for example, or biogenetics. But what, as a songwriter, I see now isn't a new paradigm; it's combinations of the old stories. And those combinations can be endless.

We have pop stars, actors, and rock stars who become the modern archetypes, but neither the artists nor their fans necessarily integrate what they're bringing into play. They don't always explore the depth of the patterns that operate in the specific archetype they are "dancing" with. Sometimes an artist is dancing so intently with an archetype that they have one foot on the curb and another foot in the air. If as an artist you forget to disengage with the archetype, then when you "come back down to earth" you can fall off that curb. Falling off the curb is not impossible for any artist, and it's a scary prospect. We all know artists who have fallen off that curb and self-destructed. The fatal thing artists can do is to begin believing they are these archetypes, even if the press does and even if the public does. These archetypes are beyond time, are beyond the rules of life and death. We will die and Aphrodite will live on as we are decrepit; the next young piano player a hundred years, two hundred years, three hundred years later, will sway her own hips, sing her own song, and dance the timeless dance with Aphrodite.

Some women performers are playing with one archetype; some play with a combination of quite a few. The combinations are endless. It can range from Hathor to Freya to Queen Maeve to Shakti to Athena to Diana—the list goes on and on. However, Aphrodite is one that is consistently chosen over time. And when a female artist embodies this archetype and can really pull it off—you look at her and you can feel that she emanates a supernatural presence. An obvious example is Marilyn Monroe. There was no mistaking: it's almost as if she were carrying that Venus lineage with her and stepped into it and realized it, and the people around her needed to keep her there. Ultimately she couldn't separate from the otherworldly. Some performers take an archetype on board with that intensity when they're onstage; the show depends on the audience believing the myth. But then, sometimes, they die. Or they get old, and they can't really do it anymore. Others transcend; they're the performers who ultimately have to tear down the altar of themselves, by themselves.

You have to be careful not to buy into that moment of projection, the idea that forms when all these people are having a relationship with the songs, with your shoes, with themselves. This is where working with archetypes is different from thinking you are one. When you start believing you are Aphrodite, or believing you are the Dark Prince, first of all, you have offended the Divine. And I find you don't know how to access it anymore. The true Shamans are the ones who have had to eat some humble pie and realize that they are only a part of the creative process. What an honor. What a privilege to be a part. But there is the Divine. And I'm not the Source. You're not the Source. Tash is not the Source. But we can all tap into the Source.

If performers get too wrapped up in their own personalities, I say they didn't feel it. They never truly connected to what was giving them their power in the first place. You might try on an image that people are projecting onto you, with the frequency and ease with which you try on a pair of sandals. I did that for a while, but I had to get out of it really quickly. In *Under the Pink*, my image was at its zenith, and I was feeling completely empty. But that's because I was taking the image on board rather than letting the songs energize me. I got out of that while making *Boys for Pele*. That's when I ditched that.

The idea that some musicians pass around is that other people don't have access. But I know my audience has access. I'm trying to encourage them to find their own—I talk about soul blueprints. Their own autonomy, their own sovereignty. Their own creative calling. It could be gardening. I can't do that. There are so many things I wish I could do that I can't do. It doesn't always have to be singing; some people are tone-deaf. That's a bit of a minus ten if you want to write songs, although it doesn't make it impossible.

To bring myth into your life, you don't have to dress in a purple and blue robe and wave a wand. You can if you like, but you could also be a waitress somewhere and inhabit an archetype. In today's world, we put entertainers on this kind of archetypal pedestal. In the old days, it was royalty. In the 1930s and '40s it was the movie stars' role, then it belonged to rock stars, then sports stars, then the celebrity phenomena, and now it's a mixture of all of them. These people are playing it out, just as the Greek gods and goddesses and their representatives did in ancient times. What Joseph Campbell was trying to tell us is that modern-day humankind shouldn't feel that these stories merely happened to anybody and everybody in every other era, but that they are also happening to us. We don't often see our own stories. Good artists are the ones that whisper our own stories back to us.

ANN: *What makes an artist? Talent, yes. But mostly, curiosity.*

ANDY SOLOMON:

Tori would have been accomplished and renowned, known and respected, as a musician in any time—the forties, fifties, sixties—I really think she would have found her audience and her voice. Why? Well, there are not many people out there who can play three keyboards at the same time in seventeen-inch heels. And exorcising her demons publicly—that I think is really what catches people. Man, that chick's got *balls*, you know? I think she was born to do just what she's doing.

CHELSEA LAIRD:

She's just so interested to learn. On tour, everywhere we go she asks questions, her radar is out. She buys books, gets the papers, wants to talk to the locals. She just wants to learn everything about the area and the people. Not to mention the traveling library that tours with us—it sits in one of the bunks on her bus. It's a collection of some of her favorites and some we've picked up along the way, but all are points of reference.

CONVERSATION BETWEEN TORI AND ANN:

All creators go through a period where they're dry and don't know how to get that plane ticket back to the creative source. Where is that waterfall? At a certain point you say, "I'll take a rivulet." And you find a place. When I hit a wall in my mid-thirties, I went back to story. And I began to see the pilgrimage that our hero or heroine would have to make, then, to get the oracle to speak to him or her again.

As a songwriter, if you're honest, you begin to find the qualities you scorn within yourself. When you are able to crawl inside and stop judging for one second and just find that place within where you could do that thing that horrifies you most—you need to find the incest victim in you, the perpetrator of incest in you, the killer and the killed: you need to find all those places. You have to get the ego out of it to do this exercise, because if you don't it will make you very, very uncomfortable. Have you never had a vision of something that abhors you? That you would do, or have done, to yourself? Of course you have. We do have murderous thoughts; in our minds we have done things that are violent. We've had things done to us, too; not just in dreams, either. This is what art is for.

When you choose your character, you're stepping into fact. This is who you are. In "Me and a Gun," I'm the girl who's raped. That is the ground that I covered. I did not cover the rapist's point of view. Now, if I were a guy, I'd cover that song from the rapist's point of view or from that of the victim's husband. If I were somebody who hated women, I'd cover it in one way, and if I were somebody who loved women, I'd cover it in another way. My having lived and survived this experience in real life wasn't the only reason that I could write and perform from that perspective. I could do it because I could walk back into that violated space and sing it from that space without wavering.

All artists will be faced with having to play cat and mouse with themselves on what they're doing. You can live the artist's way, you know—you can say it's not a job, it's what I'm doing. But if you start believing, sometimes you start taking on board these projections people offer you. You begin to take on the fantasy world that you created, and—this is the hubris of it—you also start taking on what the Divine has given you and not giving the Divine credit. Listen—when you're on the toilet, from the point of view of the toilet, you are not an icon taking a crap. You are a bottom taking a crap. If you can get that, you're going to be okay.

When I spoke to the Dark Prince in ceremony, he told me, "As soon as you stop being humbled by the creation process, Little One, it is so much bigger than you are. And when you think it is you and you are it, it will drown you or burn you alive."

MATT CHAMBERLAIN:

Tori's been so good at establishing a strong image, and a lot of people perceive her as the fairy princess or the wacky one. But they see her more than they hear her. That's the case with many pop musicians. You hear or read really great interviews with them and they say really cool stuff and you see their picture everywhere and they look good, and then maybe you hear one song. Maybe it's not the song that best represents them. That's the case with Tori. Friends I've known for years would come out to a show on this tour, and they'd be like, "Wow. I had no idea!" One friend of mine who's an avant-garde jazz saxophone player came out in Kansas City and he said, "This is like high art pop music." She's just one of those people who will keep doing her thing and people will really get it—maybe not now, maybe in twenty years.

ANN: *An artist is also someone who accepts struggle. Amos views her own career within the larger framework of a time in which creativity, and particularly the feminine spirit, has been pushed to the culture's margins. Sexy girls may be everywhere on our billboards and television screens, but real women still have to use all the strength of their voices to be heard.*

CONVERSATION BETWEEN TORI AND ANN:

We're in a Dark Age for artists. People are being threatened, accused; they're taking the microphone away; or you won't be on the radio; or you have to find your own way to get to the people because the powers that be won't help you. Unless you fly under the radar, unless you use symbology. Because sometimes we give a bit too much credit, thinking that the people in charge are very intelligent. Sometimes they don't even know you're referencing them.

I was born a feminist. And then at age five, when my strict Christian grandmother punished me, I realized, I'm not penetrating here. I'm just pissing people off. So I had to find another way to penetrate. I had to re-define what that word means. That word now is really about an opening, an entering into a separate space. And after the first phase of my life, I realized that it was okay to enter that space without having to be invaded.

How does a woman penetrate? It's a beautiful paradox. We don't have that organ. Fundamentally, we don't pee standing up. And that changes your view of life, from the beginning. The figure of Mary Magdalene stands for the earth: a seed can be planted within her, whereas seeds can't be planted within men physically. But there's another way to think of it, as a joining, where they're entering each other, you know. Because ulti-mately human life is not about sperm dominating eggs. I like the idea of just being able to be inside. Not using *penetration* as a violent word. The idea of being able to find keys—we're back to music, using keys to get into a space that we couldn't before.

I choose to fight my battles through my music, and if I'm misunderstood, well, I've done my best. I've gotten some good advice from people, some wise old people; you can call them medicine women if you want. And they said to me that it is not the right use of energy to try to get people to see who you truly are if they cannot see that. You can't control it, and why would you want to? Where will it stop? With one journalist? With France? With a generation?

So I've reached a level of containment with my energy. I can sit like the Sphinx and watch people say stuff about me and whip it up. Some of it's true. The funniest thing was, once I had a bad encounter with a radio person, and this interviewer turned around and, after having made some malicious, below-the-belt comments to me, pronounced at the end of the interview, "Wow, you can fight back. I thought you were supposed to be spiritual." I said, "What is your definition of spirituality?" All this guy knew how to do was be completely offensive. What did he think: I was going to bring out the prayer book and sage? The only thing this guy responded to was a firm line drawn in the sand. I just looked at him and said, "Cross this and we'll be having radio person medium rare for dinner."

This goes back to why I'm still around. Usually I'm a pussycat, but pussycats can become big kitties really fast if necessary. People always think there's this Svengali behind the scenes. Well, then, there are many. There are a hundred. Karen Binns is one of them. John Witherspoon. Matt Chamberlain. Neil Gaiman. Duncan Pickford. Mark Hawley. Chelsea Laird. Marcel van Limbeek. In the end, there are thirty people who are very instrumental, but people change, the lineup often changes, and I'm still able to sell out three nights at Radio City. So then when somebody still says, "Oh, I wonder who's figuring all this out for her," I say, "Tell me who it is, so I can call them and get a night off."

JOEL HOPKINS:

The main thing with Tori that I've seen from day one is that she's been entirely consistent in what she wants to do and what she wants to put out there, and the kids have never felt alienated. And we've gone from one generation to the next among her fans—now we have the original cohorts' little sisters. The older ones may have moved on, but they have passed the torch. Tori is always planting these seeds for the next kids that come, and we've seen that happen: we're seeing the little kids coming out now.

KAREN BINNS:

Tori represents the woman who fights for the world. She fights for her children or fights for her man; she fights to make sure everybody's eating okay; she fights for the words that need to be said. She's always fighting. And if she's fighting, that means she has to be in touch.

TORI:

Sometimes you are forced to defend your beliefs. Sometimes you are forced to look at relationships that aren't positive anymore. There are times when I have had to make peace with the fact that I am at war. And sometimes you have to fight those who do not want love to conquer all.

Now, backstage at an undisclosed arena where the sweat of athletes is still perfuming my makeshift dressing room, my many conversations with Ann Powers have begun . . .

"Ann," I said, "if we are going to spend two years working on a project together, we need to get a few awkward conversations out of the way."

"Tor, I've been dealing with awkward conversations professionally for twenty years. Have you ever tried to get something quotable from an exhausted lead guitarist after a three-hour stadium show, when he's got a seventeen-year-old groupie waiting for him in the back of the tour bus? Whatever you have to say can't be harder to take than that. Proceed."

I did. "You come from the journalist side. I come from the artist side. It can become offensive. I'm sure from your side as well as from mine."

"Well, it's true everyone expects us to be enemies. And in some ways we are. My job is interpretation. Yours is art, which often benefits from mystery. And while I've met many very articulate musicians, most seem almost threatened by detailed questions about their work, which makes interviewing them frustrating. It's as if they expect me to misunderstand them."

"No arguments here, Ann. Likewise, I may have spent only forty minutes with a journalist, but in that time I will have tried to open up the shutter—undress the obvious answer to get a more compelling response that will jump off the page. And then what happens? The article comes out and I can't even recognize the journalist that I met from the biting, vitriolic person that is writing about our time together."

"Well, some writers *are* just nasty—not unlike that charmer with the groupie on the bus. And even the nice ones have egos. We view our work as a creative process, too, and sometimes the artist's process gets in the way of ours! If I've decided a song means something—say, that "your cloud" is about your Natashya—and you tell me something different—that it's about Hamlet's ghost—I might just want to contradict you. I can't just assume you know everything that the song's about, either. As you yourself have said to me, meanings can change and emerge over time. Maybe I *am* right . . ."

"You know the funny thing is, Ann, whenever I start asking a journalist questions, they either start to cream in their pants or run out of the room."

"Hey, it's more fun for me if we're friends, and friends don't just nod and agree. But let's be absolutely clear. I'm the one opening up the drawers here. And you realize, we will have to discuss some painful events in your life. I can't be my usual, sweet interviewer self all the time if I'm going to get—or help you get—what we need for this book."

"Look, Ann, I know you're going to probe. Rather you than a proctologist."

She laughed and I continued, "Or a shitty rock journalist."

"Fair enough, Tori. And I thank you for not being a boring rock star."

Ann and I decided to strip our roles back to basics. We are both women born feminists in the 1960s. We are both married. We are both mothers. We are both in the music industry. Traditionally we are enemies. But for this project to be effective, I had to allow Ann to expose Tori Amos. And Tori Amos's inner circle. And me.

chapter one
corn mother: genealogies

ANN: *Our mother is the ground we stand on, and the earth itself is our mother. How many people have believed this, over the centuries? Society itself began with kinship, lineages marked by blood and love, while civilizations took root in relationship to the places where people settled and learned the land. The idea that the world was born of a woman is common in myth, across continents: in Africa, Asia, the Mediterranean, northern Europe, and the Americas, such stories abound. The Genesis story of a lone male God making life with a lift of the finger has achieved cultural dominance, but beyond that bragging tale of six days' labor are others that present Creation as an ongoing process, undertaken by a matriarchal force nourished by her family's respect and love.*

Throughout the ages, people have chosen gods to suit their apparent needs; similarly, an artist can view her personal acts of creation in light of various sources. She can thank her ego alone, but that is dangerous—the limits of an individual's personality can quickly turn genius into a dry spring. She can acknowledge her peers as inspiration, cite the demands of the marketplace and the influence of various schools, but influences not so carefully chosen also cannot be avoided.

Every artist is born in a place, within a family, and though she may leave those sources far behind, they remain within her. The achievement comes in acknowledging those origins without being devoured by them. The Cherokee have a story that relates to the need to find balance between personal ambition and accepting life's offerings:

Selu, the Corn Mother, lives with her grandsons in the mountains. The young men are hunters, and Corn Mother provides the staples that round out their meals. The men want to hunt and hunt, and this greed for meat makes Corn Mother sad, yet she loves her descendants and does not challenge them. One morning her grandsons spy on Corn Mother as she makes the corn, which falls

from her body whenever she slaps her sides. This terrifies the men, and they re-
ject her. She withers, but before dying instructs them to bury her in the earth and
tells them she will arise again as a plant that will need to be cultivated. Corn
Mother does as she promises, but in her new form she cannot be blithely gener-
ous. People must learn to cultivate her; they must earn her fruitfulness. With this
lesson Corn Mother teaches humankind the need for balance and the love of na-
ture's gifts.

Tori Amos heard the story of Corn Mother from her grandfather as a girl,
during summers spent with him in North Carolina. The love of the earth was in-
grained in her, along with an awareness that her own talents were a blessing she
could not take for granted. Her Cherokee blood is one element in the complex
weave of influences that created Amos as she grew toward the moment when she
could begin, respectfully, to create herself.

TORI:

"The grass. The rocks. The trees. Don't care nothin' about who ya are or
who ya think ya are or who ya pretendin' to be." Poppa would be in fits of
tickles by that saying. "And Shug . . . [what Poppa called me—short for
Sugar Cane and Shush all mixed up], Shug, when ya think yer mighty like
a mountain ya might wanta think of being a Rock Nurse. You didn't hear
yer Poppa say Rock Star. Or Night Nurse. I'm sayin' Rock Nurse, Shug. Ya
know what that is? That's somebody who's needin' to take care of a rock
for a year before they go and hurt themselves tryin' to move a mountain.
And after a year of being humbled by how much more a rock knows than
Jack's Ass, then they'll be seein' stars. The real ones, Shug—remember
those?"

CONVERSATION BETWEEN TORI AND ANN:

My mother's father, my Poppa, had perfect pitch. He rocked me to sleep
ever since the day I was born, singing with a tone that reminds me of sun-

light shining through black strap molasses. It was a pure velvet tenor voice. He and my Nanny had a town life—he would shoot pool, they had culture. I remember every Saturday Poppa and Uncle John would bring home chili dogs from the pool room so that Nanny would have a break before the big Sunday family dinner. Nanny was a four-by-four. Four foot eleven inches and 214 pounds. Poppa would say there could never be too much of Nanny to love. When no one was looking, he would bring her a flower that he picked up on his storytelling wanderings, give her a kiss on the cheek, and say, "This flower wished it was as perddy as you, Bertie Marie."

Nanny grew the garden. It was tiny, but it enticed me because of the begonias and the honeysuckle. It was wedged up against the Lutheran church parking lot. Nanny didn't want to unravel the covert darkness of a small town. She just wanted to uncomplicate everyone's life once they came into her home and sat at her table. Nanny's table would wrap its arms around you with soul food. The biscuits, the creamed corn, the corn on the cob, the corn pudding, the corn bread in the skillet, the whole thing. Fried okra, pinto beans, turnips, and mustard greens—"Sweeter than collard greens," she would say. And in a way, Nanny's love was in the food. It was very much that kind of twelve-people-for-lunch-every-day kind of thing. She was this warm, warm creature who wasn't overly educated. When Poppa died, when I was nine and a half, she started to lose her mind. Patsy Cline's "I Fall to Pieces" finally started to make sense to me then.

Poppa was born Calvin Clinton Copeland and answered to C.C. or Clint as a boy. But I only heard most people call him Poppa—at the shops in town, at choir where he sang every Sunday and collected pieces for his stories—whether inspired by the organist making eyes at the minister or the manager of the hardware store running off with the pharmacist's wife . . . Poppa, unlike Nanny, did want to unravel the covert darkness of a small town while we all sat together on the porch snapping beans— Nanny, Granny Grace, Aunt Ellen, me, and my mom, Mary Ellen.

Nanny and Poppa each had a full-blooded Cherokee grandparent who was on the Eastern Cherokee tribal rolls. They were spiritually drawn to the old ways and chose to stay on their native ground. From the Smokies of east Tennessee to east of the Blue Ridge Mountains in North Carolina, they settled on old Cherokee ancestral land. They understood that this ancestral land was their sacred spiritual source, just as the Lakota will say the Black Hills are theirs. This is where I spent all my summers as a child.

TORI:

Poppa wouldn't give up on me.

"Focus on that tree, little 'un," he would say. We're talking around 1967, when I was four.

"Come on, Poppa, I'm hungry."

"You almost have it. You can get this. Feel her strength. Let her tell you her story. Now sit still and let her play you like you play that piano."

As I got older Poppa would push me.

"Can you hear the ancestors, little 'un? They are not happy today."

"No, Poppa, I can't really hear them."

"Then ya just aren't listenin', are ya? Now don't you roll those eyes at me. Yer gonna needs to know this one day."

"Know what?"

"How to tap into a place's power spot." He would bend down with his hand, touching that sandy Carolina soil.

"What are you talking about?"

"Hum. Ya gotta hear the hum." He looked straight at me as if I were being told the most important piece of information ever.

"The hum?"

"Yes, the hum of the Great Mother. Let this sink in. Every inch of this land has been walked on by somebody's ancestors. That means there are events, conversations, killins', singins', dancin'—Lord almighty—

squabblin', you name it. It has happened. So ya decides first what ya needs to tap into. Find the way in. Ya must hear the tone. Follow it and yer probably at a vortex."

"You believe this, Poppa?"

"I know this, Shug: the white man don't know."

"Careful, Poppa, Dad's white."

"Hmm. He's Irish-Scottish. That ain't white. They been fightin' the white man who takes the land—takes the land till the Grim Reaper comes up and taps the white man on the shoulder and says, 'No weaslin' outta this one, yer time has come.' It used to tickle your old Poppa to see a white man turn white as a ghost."

"Okay, in English."

"Most people nowadays, Shug, don't see. Don't feel. Don't hear anythin' that science can't prove. A hundred years ago people said a man would never fly."

"But he couldn't."

"Yes, granddaughter. Yes, he could. He just hadn't figured out how. The Eagle Dancers knew man could fly. It was only in this dimension that the mechanics hadn't been worked out."

"So now we know how to fly."

"Only in the physical, granddaughter, not in the spiritual. Back to your studies, and find me a vortex before lunch."

"Does my hungry tum-tum count?"

"Nope."

I somehow knew that this was where I had to learn and train. Poppa would talk about shape-shifting, the practice of shifting the containment of the human condition in order to open it up to other forms of consciousness. We'd take walks every day, and he would communicate the way he saw the world, which was that there was life in all things, that there was a kind of knowing in all things. Like anyone, according to Poppa, I'd have to retune my own receiving information system, in my own being, to be able to hear the unique harmonics—thereby understanding the language of the spirit world. What I do know is that he knew this language. I cannot tell you I quite understand how he did, but I watched with amazement as he would communicate with nature, and he seemed to understand it—he seemed to bask in his relationship with it.

I did not have this ability and somehow I knew I never would, but at age four I began to feel something else. I began to feel the music inhabiting me. I'd say to Poppa, "Songs are chasing me," and he would say, "Shug, slow down and let the song's stories talk to you. Tell them ya've got room around the fire for 'em and their friends. And ya listen to 'em, Shug, ya listen up now, and they'll teach ya things ain't nobody on this earth can begin to think about even tryin' to blow in those kind of trade winds." He'd say, "Don't be afraid, Shug, my grandmother Margaret Little told me the same thing when the stories started bendin' my ear as a little rascal. She'd say, 'C.C., if the stories don't knock the fire out of ya, then they just might warm that little rascal heart of yers.' " He told me from the beginning, "The stories have always come a visitin'. And the stories have always said, 'C.C., this is who we are and you'll use your own language to tell folks about us, but this is our framework.' " And he said he could see them. I have the same experience, even to this day—I can tell you how I see mine. I see the songs sometimes in light filaments. It's a light filament of architecture. The light resonates with a musical tone, but it is a definite structure. Then I translate the light structures into a musical form.

Poppa would talk to me about how there were just certain places that we are called to, all over and around the world. You can't explain it, but you just feel for whatever reason that you have access. You know when you're comfortable walking down those streets and knowing you're not going to get mugged. The place knows the codes that you carry. And your codes know the place instinctively. So point being, when Poppa was learning how to access different vortexes, he was in his power center. He'd learned the power of embracing the land from his own grandmother, who had insisted that they stay within Cherokee land, which was thousands of square miles. So her whole life she spent circling Cherokee land; that's where her turbulent yet compelling story broke away from the root, in north Georgia, north of the Cherokee capital, Echota. It's still there.

Both Nanny and Poppa inherited colorful but complicated and difficult family histories. Poppa's grandmother Margaret Little survived the Trail of Tears. In 1838 and 1839, she was hearing about the roundups of Cherokee families whereby they would be taken to internment camps. This devastation of the Cherokee and other Eastern tribes had been cemented in 1830 when President Andrew Jackson signed the Indian Removal Act. Chief Junaluska of the Cherokee tribe pleaded with Andrew Jackson, yet even though that chief had driven his own tomahawk through the skull of a Creek warrior and saved Jackson's life at the Battle of Horseshoe Bend in 1813, Jackson's greed for Cherokee land was stronger than any sense of debt or moral or ethical principles. The modern Cherokee Nation had founded its own constitution in 1827, after Sequoyah (also known as George Gist) had officially written down their oral constitution and official records, using a syllable-based lexicon consisting of eighty-five characters.

By 1828, the first Cherokee newspaper, the *Phoenix*, was publishing articles. The Cherokee people believed they had built the necessary bridges to integrate into the modern world, but white soldiers and civilians soon began to destroy everything that the Cherokee had created. Once gold was discovered near Dahlonega, Georgia, white folk exhibited a lascivious desire for Cherokee property. An ethnic cleansing that had been looming for the past two hundred years was now on Margaret Little's doorstep.

The *Cherokee Phoenix* was burned to the ground in 1834 because its editors were speaking out against Jackson and the Indian Removal Act, and so the oral history that Poppa passed down came from Margaret Little, who knew at sixteen that she had to flee. In Poppa's words, "Certain animals know before there is an eruption of a volcano, it's time to run for yer life. Margaret Little said, 'The white soldiers called us Indian dogs; better the instincts of a dog than a white man. That's what saved my life and why yer here eatin' up my vittles today, C.C.' "

Poppa was brought up by Margaret Little because his mother had a stroke at a very young age. Poppa only ever referred to her as Margaret Little, never Grandma Margaret, never Granny Maggie. She would tell Poppa, "Some of the older Indians would be arguin' that we should give the white man the benefit of the doubt. Now, unfortunately the ones who did ended up walkin' the excruciatin', torturous eight-hundred-and-fifty-mile walk to the dust bowl—where there were no green fields, no Corn Woman, no lakes, no mountain streams—toward what the white man called Indian Territory, now Oklahoma. That was the white man's idea of a fair trade; their 'God has given them this land,' that's what they kept sayin'. Did their God have the right to give them this land? Did their God give them the right to subjugate us? Who is their God? It cannot be the one called Jesus."

Poppa continued weaving the tale. "Margaret Little went up into the Smoky Mountains and hid for nine moons, livin' on nuts and berries, and whatever she could catch with her knife and tomahawk. She's never spoken about anybody bein' with her durin' those nine moons of hidin' like a fugitive. She always said she could smell a Bluecoat soldier a mile away 'cause her tomahawk would start singin'."

Margaret Little survived with the help of Corn Woman and the Great

Mother. She firmly believed in the power of the ancestors to protect her through her dreams, which became her guiding light. So one morning, knowing that soon she would starve to death or be captured, because the tomahawk had started to hum, she trusted her instincts and made her way down from the Tennessee side of the Blue Ridge and Smoky Mountains onto a large farm in North Georgia, where she signed on as an indentured servant. There she worked, and there she caught the eye of Granddaddy Rice, as Poppa called him. According to Poppa, Margaret Little wasn't very popular with Granddaddy Rice's grown-up sons, who still mourned their mother, who had passed away. Because Granddaddy Rice could still feel the steel in the tip of his boots, as Poppa phrased it, he had a very different idea on what should be done with the question of Margaret Little than his grown-up sons and their wives had. After Margaret Little had a wedding ring on her finger and a bun in the oven, possibly simultaneously, the grown-up sons tried to run her off. But, as she would say to Poppa, "If I could stand up to a whole army of Bluecoats, I could handle a few hateful, greedy white boys." So on the day that the two grown sons showed up to threaten the life of Margaret Little and her unborn child, while Granddaddy Rice was away on some trip, they were met by one of Margaret Little's best friends.

Poppa would say, "I've met Margaret Little's best friend, and she keeps her underneath the tie of her apron." The two sons stood in the doorway with a shotgun, telling her that if she didn't get her savage squaw ass on the next mule out, then she and her little brat would be found dead in a hunting accident. She turned her back to them and they let their guard down, thinking she had acquiesced. That's when Lady Tomahawk, Margaret Little's best friend, sliced through the air between the bodies of the two hateful sons, splitting the wooden doorstep in two. They literally did not know what in God's creation had just hit them. A ranting

Margaret Little ran up and retrieved her tomahawk to place underneath the tie of her apron, with the warning, "Next time I won't miss, boys." When Granddaddy Rice made his way back home he was met with the news that his sons and their wives had relocated to Texas to try their hands at ranching. Over the years Margaret Little and Granddaddy Rice formed a kind of partnership in order to keep the farm going through good times and bad. In 1861, Granddaddy Rice was an old man and Margaret Little was somewhere around her late thirties. The Civil War began then, bringing the South to her knees.

I remember being at the Sunday dinner family reunion—that would happen every weekend in the summer—and when someone would mention "the Wahr" I began to realize that rarely were they talking about World War II or even Vietnam. Because so many families fought against each other, cousin against cousin, father against son, the schism that tore through the land, up and down the young American coast, was still trying to heal when I was born in 1963, more than a hundred years later. That many southerners in our modern-day society, as rockets were beginning to go up to the moon, were still not over this particular wounding shows in some way the extent of this physical and spiritual bloodbath.

As Poppa always said, Margaret Little never agreed with the idea of slaves, African or Cherokee, but like a lot of other farmers in the South who didn't have slaves she was just defending her home at a certain point. He would say to me, "Imagine a world, Shug, with no radio, no tell-e-vision, so it's hard to even know what kinda crazy makin' those polly-ticians were drummin' up on both sides of the Mason-Dixon. People could get all worked up—just hearin' the preacher talkin' about losin' everythin' to them greedy Yankees. It got folks all suspicious and scareder than scared, and they wasn't wrong to be scared . . . So it's awful easy for this sixties generation to think they know so much about what they woulda done. They didn't even have them a gee-tar that plugged in back then to make all that racket at some protest rally for the good guys. See, the crazy thing was, was that we didn't see we was the bad side, 'cause we didn't have slaves or wanna be slaves, and by the time it got to us, the average pappy-tryin-to-put-food-on-the-table-for-his-youngins, we was just a voiceless majority of a piece of the South." As Margaret Little told him, "When it all started gettin' heated up, the farmers' wives thought they'd just take care of the crops, do the farmin', and those polly-ticians can set-tle this thang and everybody's gonna be aww-right, the God Lord willin' and the creek don't rise."

By this point in the story, I'd already snapped my beans and gone to sit on the porch steps just downwind of Poppa's apple-smoked pipe tobacco and his hypnotic tenor voice. "So y'all can guess," he would say, "the cha-grin of Margaret Little when in 1864 she heard that the Bluecoats were comin' her way . . . Burnin' everything down, stealin' all the livestock, folks, youngins and kinfolk, whose hearts are already halfway to heaven dyin' of hunger and brutality. Yep, all the stories that were spreadin' like wildfire she'd heard before. She'd heard all about the roundups when she was a young girl, son taken from his momma by the Bluecoats, makin' all those people walk on foot, gettin' gangrene rotted feet. Hell, they treated pigs better than they treated her people who were dyin' on the way to Indian Territory. This was one woman who was not in a state of disbelief about what the Bluecoats could do, so she made up her mind. She didn't listen to the preacher or the other farmers' wives sayin' that their God would protect 'em. Stands to reason that a woman like this, whose people had been subjugated, while lookin' at those Christian graves starin' out at her with so much superiority, would realize she'd had about enough. And she had. So she came up with an idea. Turns out, about a week later, Bluecoats came and sure 'nuff burned the house, burned the barn, burned the fields, mammas and daddies even, everythin' they could burn they did. They took the livestock for eatin' and left Margaret Little's family to starve to death. Now ya gotta understand when I say this—there was *no* freeza full of food or a Winn-Dixie down the street, or another farmer who had a country store a mile away. No suhree, the South was in cinders and ya could even hear a mamma cryin', 'My God, my God, why has thou forsaken me?' as she cradled her burned baby in her arms."

By this time in the story Nanny would be snoring—after all, she's been up since four-thirty a.m., getting the homemade biscuits and the skillet-fried cornbread prepared for the army of people she would be feeding through the day. I, on the other hand, was transfixed. Poppa's drawl drew me back in. "Shug, now be honest, now: have ya figured out how Margaret Little outfoxed the Bluecoats?" And, as always, I said, "Poppa, tell me. My memory isn't so good." He would look at me and say, "Yer only six and a half, Shug. Ya betta have yerself an extra helpin' of mustard greens every day so yer mind don't turn hollow, like them Bluecoats in their grave. Shug, that like to tickle me to death, yer memory ain't good. Well, if you'll listen I'll tell ya again. Margaret Little would say to me, 'Ya gots to know your enemies, C.C. To figure out how yer enemy thinks, ya gots to crawl inside his blood, inside his veins. Now ya look into that fire and ya picture yer enemy and ya feel his breath in yer lungs. Now ya walk 'round like this and shur 'nuff, perddy soon ya'll be thinkin' like your enemy, and then ya know what's gonna happen? You, C.C., will know exactly the next move yer enemy's gonna make.' "

Poppa about now would inhale from his pipe, and I would crane my neck to try to get a whiff of the apple-sweetness. "Shug, have ya ever de-filed a Christian grave?" "What are you talking about, Poppa?" "I said, de-filed a Christian grave, Shug . . . I can see by the look on yer face, I need to explain. Ya see, Margaret Little knew how the Bluecoat thought. She knew that nothin' was sacred to the Bluecoat down South. But, ya see, the Bluecoat's God was not Southern, but he definitely was Christian. So Bluecoats, as well as any other God-fearin' Christian, all got buried in white Christian graves. Yep, even the Bluecoats as well. So, turns out, Margaret Little pinpointed the only piece of land that wouldn't get burned. That wouldn't be drenched in blood. And ya know where that was? Yep, them white Christian graves. Margaret Little knew that she was never gonna be allowed to be buried in a white cemetery. Ya see, Shug, there was white churches and black churches back then. And ya wasn't allowed to mingle socially. While Granddaddy Rice was alive, which wasn't for much longer, the church wasn't gonna say no to Granddaddy Rice and his money. So Margaret Little accompanied him to church sometimes, but mostly she had her church in the woods surrounded by the kingdom of the Great Mother.

"She'd say to me, 'I saw me some fresh dirt, and the word was, Bluecoats was tryin' to bury their friends if they died. So I went into this Christian cemetery and dug me some graves m'self. I'd taken all our seed, put 'em in as many bundles as I could, and dug fresh graves for my seed all 'round these fresh Bluecoats. And I even thought to m'self, bein' since they'd slaughtered all our livestock, I was sure I could come up with a recipe for Bluecoat stew. But ya see, my seed wouldn't be harvested till after the Bluecoat turned into a No-coat. I also had me some dried beef and enough eatin' for me, Granddaddy Rice, and the youngins for at least a couple moons. I had it wrapped in such a way that would discourage any vermin from gettin' to it.' " Poppa's eyes would shine when he said, "And the Bluecoats came and, likes I said before, left nothin', just a wasteland, but shur 'nuff Margaret Little was able to feed her family with the dried food she had hidden in the fresh white Christian graves. I asked her how in the world she planted the seed. And she turned and looked at me and gave me a look that could freeze the sun. 'C.C., I'll tell you what I did—since they butchered our oxen to eat for themselves and took our horses, there was only one thing left to do—I got me a young lad from the village and had him steer me as I became the oxen m'self. I strapped that harness on and plowed the fields with my body. When harvest time came, it wasn't a lot, but it was more than enough for Granddaddy Rice and the youngins and the young lad and his family.' "

I looked over at Nanny and realized her people were on the Eastern Cherokee tribal rolls also. That's one reason Nanny and Poppa joined forces. They were both called half-breeds.

CONVERSATION BETWEEN TORI AND ANN:

On Nanny's side, her grandfather, who had also tried to escape the Trail of Tears in 1838–39, had been murdered. Many of her family's stories were lost. Her grandfather was known as John Akins. John had married a white woman who remarried a white man soon after John's murder. The white woman's new white husband didn't want anything to do with her "savage brat," and so she gave up her son. At just around two years old, little John Akins, named after his daddy, was abandoned.

Nanny always referred to her daddy, my great-grandfather, as Poppa John. He was reared by former slaves who had just been freed. He was a half-breed; his mother was German, and his father, a Cherokee man, was dead. Nobody would take him, so this black family with few material possessions nurtured him with love. As far as he was concerned, this was his family. Eventually, Poppa John's biological aunt pieced together what had happened to her nephew and made contact. They developed some semblance of a family connection, and much later on in life, after Poppa John had created many children who loved him with a wife he adored, named Ellen, his little German mother reentered his life. Because not one of her white kin would take her in, this tiny woman in her eighties, standing four foot nine inches, demanded a room at Ellen and Poppa John's. When Poppa and my mother would start giggling up a storm, I would hear my mom say, "Oh, Poppa, you shouldn't say that." And I always knew they were talking about that mean little woman. At that point Nanny would join in the giggling and say, "Mary Ellen, I know it's an awful thing to say, but what Poppa says about old Granny is the truth, but I'll let him say it 'cause he's a goin' to hell anyways." Poppa would chirp right up and look down at the ground and say, "I'm addressin' you, Granny, where I think ya gone. Ya was as mean as a snake in life that even the snakes won't take ya now. I'm tellin' ya the truth, Shug. I was sure she was that mean old biddy from 'Hansel and Gretel,' and I never let yer mama anywhere near Granny because I knew she'd likely turn her into Mary Ellen pie."

Poppa John was a woodcarver and made furniture. The chair that old Granny sat in all those years ago, having been taken in by the little boy she'd abandoned, sits in my beach house. It was lovingly made for her little size by Poppa John. This was in the Carolinas, near the Eastern Cherokee Nation. They all eventually settled right outside Charlotte to work in the mills in Catawba County, ancestral land of the Catawba tribe. I was born in Catawba General Hospital.

The Cherokee land . . . I heard about the broken treaties all my life, from my grandfather, and then my mother, who can go on and on and on concerning the details; she knows a lot about it. The idea that your possessions can be taken, your land can be taken from you, has been fundamental to me and has made me very clear about what I own spiritually. And I refuse to let anybody be able to take my sacred ground. You can take my land, but not my sovereignty, my inner sacred ground. That's what my grandfather held on to with his stories; what my mother kept with her books that she memorized, so that if they were taken from her, or burned, the words would be emblazoned across her heart. Words by Emily Dickinson, by Elizabeth Barrett Browning, by Robert Frost, wove an invisible gown for my magical mother. My mother's family learned through the hardest experience that you must preserve the realms within.

SONG CANVAS: "Ireland"

Hazelnut, the village mutt, lives in a call box in Timoleague, Co. Cork. Two buckets of rose hips sit next to the Aga rangecooker for Dunc's special syrup. Ireland in the summer . . .

Here is where I seem to remember slices. Here is where I've come to remember Poppa's stories of the Cherokee Nation. Go figure. The Cherokee and Irish have both had their cultures invaded, and maybe that's why they have bonded within my family bloodline—but it's more than that. I don't know if there is something in the water, something in the rain. And jeez. It's been raining. The August fires are burning steadily here in the old Irish house. The tank tops we all brought are whispering warm-weather chants under cardigans. The guys have gone down for a Murphy's or a Guinness on tap, down at Paula's place. It doesn't matter if she hasn't seen us in a year; she always acts like we're regulars. Maybe that's just the Irish way, but it pulls me back time and time again. When I was writing the song "Ireland," I was reading some book a journalist had given me on James Joyce and I was drawn into the fabric that made up his tapestry, his life. There was a spoiled nun who taught him the names of the mountains on the moon . . . I figured if "Ireland" was referring to James Joyce, then it needed to have nuns, and if it had nuns, then it needed to have white-collar sadomasochists from Wall Street, and if it had that, then it needed to have Vikings, since anywhere you go around Ireland their presence is still felt. And if you had

Vikings, then you needed to include the ancient Irish legends, which are usually divided into four cycles. The first one is the Mythological Cycle, whereby the Tuatha Dé Danann, who are descendants of the goddess D'Anu, known as the divine people, begin the richness of Irish mythology with stories that tell of their origins and their ways. Stories of the malevolent Fomorians, who battle the Tuatha Dé Danann for control over Ireland. Tales of the Sídh—a term for an otherworldly being, or a place—a mound where the Sídh live. The Tuatha Dé Danann were defeated by the Milesians by the end of the Bronze Age (circa 300 B.C.), and their otherworldly presence took the form of the Sídh in the legends. After their defeat, writes their contemporary chronicler Eithne Massey, the Sídh "took refuge in the world of hollow mounds and magical islands far out to sea, but often used their otherworldly powers to help or hinder mortals."

The Sídh's historical myth is the source of the bastardized concept of a fairy—as if anyone gives a rat's ass. But for all those fairy haters out there, at least now you'll know the origin of that which you hate.

Next up comes the Ulster Cycle, then the Fianna Cycle during the Celtic Iron Age, and then the Cycle of the Kings during the early Christian era. "Ireland" incorporates the story of Macha, a goddess of Motherhood and Blood, who was nine months' pregnant when she was forced by her husband to race against the king's horses to fulfill a boast he had made. Macha did in fact run faster than the horses—and cursed the sons of Ulster after having given birth to her twins. Late at night in pubs in Ireland, sometimes you will hear a reference to Macha and her curse, which many believe can still befall you when you least expect it.

Queen Maeve and the warrior Cú Chulainn are the main characters in the Cattle Raid of Cooley, also known as the famed Táin Bó Cuailgne. The Morrigan embodies one of the triple battle fairies. The desire men felt for the beautiful Deirdre was what ended her life, as far as I'm concerned one of the saddest stories of all time. Eithne Massey's book *Legendary Ireland: A Journey Through Celtic Places and Myths* is where you can dive into more on this.

TORI:

Okay, so here I dive. I dive into my father's side. In Co. Cork I find the Irish-Scottish Rib and jump on. The whole Irish-Scottish part of my culture has never been a problem, for chrissake. I mean, come on, I bought a house in Ireland in 1995. The Irish, the Scots in the family, you know how that can be—for sure there was the usual family stuff, but not usually much of a problem. But there was one person. The Puritanical. The Shame Inducer. I was five. She was and always has been my greatest adversary and challenger. She was my grandmother. My father's mother. I think she was made a saint somewhere in the hills of the Appalachian Mountains of Virginia between Fancy Gap and Galax. Galax—home of the fiddler's convention. I remember going when I was five, and there was a sign that read ACUPUNCTURE AND CHINESE MEDICINE, and my grandmother issued the edict that Chinese medicine was sent from the devil.

Can someone not be considered evil but do harm? Harm to those who serve the Great Mother, while Grandma herself proclaimed to be a feminist because she had a college education in the early 1920s . . . all the while preaching that women should turn over their virgin bodies to their husbands and their souls to our Lord and Savior Jesus Christ. Yes, Grandma was an ordained minister/missionary as well as a teacher. I would say to her, "Why do you have to bring Jesus into this, Grandmother? I happen to like the guy, so let's just leave him out of this." "I can forgive you for your sinful words, Myra Ellen," she would say. "I am just guiding your father on how you should be handled. How you should be molded into a respectful Christian young woman. Everything we do we do because we love you." Yeah, right. Barf. At around this time, as punishment, she had me in the corner, trying to pray the fear of Jesus into me after I "talked out of line," because I spoke out against the horrifying decision that she had made to put my brother in a shoulder brace in the hopes that he would hold his shoulders back. I felt I just had to unravel the way she planted thoughts in people. Soul-destroying thoughts.

The Irish side of my dad's family had been weavers, and that became my first clue into this. I made an oath in that corner: Grandma, I will weave myself into your ideology so I can hunt for the hidden codes of control that affect those around you who fear your judgment, even including, at times, my father. I will escape your grasp by holding your hand. And I will pray—take me to your God because this cannot be Jesus' loving Divine Father, so take me to your God, this control freak who makes boys think that their John Hancocks will grow boils if they let themselves spill their seeds into shy but friendly thighs. Take me to your God, this control freak that has suggested that Satan, with barracuda jaws, lives inside the petals of a girl so that if you let a boy between your jeans, then guess what? Grandma will be waiting with Bible in hand. If she could she would pull you in front of the judges at the end of days, during their roast lamb dinner, and make you drop your jeans so that they can extract a sample from your love stains—to prove what? The need to control . . . The need to dominate by subjugating others so they believe in your God, in your way. Where is emancipation in this kind of spiritual bullying? At five I knew I was at war with my grandmother. As far as I was concerned, she was masquerading as a feminist while jailing the Feminine. If a woman wanting to choose her own path, sexually and spiritually, went against Grandmother's puritanical belief system, then she would be treated—

I would be treated, or you would be treated—as a pariah. This made me close ranks within my Being. Close ranks so that my grandmother's methodology and orthodoxy could not filter the coffee out of this bean. The American Inquisition. It can be traced. And chased.

So, this was the Scotch-Irish grandmother who instilled the fear of God in me, in a very negative way. Yet I respected the mental capabilities of this woman, because she did recognize something. She knew that I was not one of them. In a way, she gave me a huge gift. Because of her reaction to me, I began to understand my path. I was given a clue: I began to see the burn-the-witch mentality of strict Christianity, and I began to recognize that I really needed to search out my spiritual family. Because her ideology wasn't part of it. Behind the Christian love-your-neighbor-as-yourself facade, there was another story. There was not a lot of compassion there if you had been deemed a sinner. There was not a lot of support for who people really were. But I realize, now that I'm older, that the Great Mother even encompasses the adversarial Grandmother. From the Beginning, from the myth of Sophia breaking away from the ancient Creatrix to find her autonomy, the Great Mother was forming herself. From the ancient Inanna forcing herself to the underworld to visit her sister, Ereshkigal—passing through the seven gates of the underworld and then being hung on a hook, rotting—where she had to look at her sister, and her sister had to look at her. Both needed each other to see inside themselves, to see inside their own shadows. To come to terms with who they really were, not who they thought they were. And again, the Great Mother was learning to relate to other pieces of the Feminine.

Many years after I faced down my grandmother as a child, the mythic astrologer Wendy Ashley told me that my chart contains a crazy number of planets in the house of religion. I mean, it's just there. It's part of who I am. I am a daughter of the Church. From very early on, I've seen how

Christians can manipulate people by manipulating Jesus' message, but I've also known loving people within the Church who walk the path of compassion. Either way, I can't fully get away from Christianity's influence, and I don't want to get away from certain aspects—the message to love your neighbor as yourself, the idea of resurrection—those aspects of Jesus' message. Many people believe in those principles though they are not practicing Christians. The truth is, I believe that if Jesus were alive today he would not be a member of a Christian church, because hypocrisy is at the center of many a church's crossroad.

ANN: *The oppositional elements among Amos's immediate forebears found a resolution in the marriage of her father and mother. The partnership flourished, though it had its costs. Amos grew up witnessing the dreams of her parents collide and transform, and she found both inspiration and much to challenge in their loving example.*

CONVERSATION BETWEEN TORI AND ANN:

My father was going to be the next Billy Graham. That was his inspiration, his calling. When I was a child, he was grooming himself for that. He was pastor at a really big church in Baltimore; I think at one time there were 2,500 members. He had his aspirations. But I'll tell you this, when somebody was on their deathbed, or a family had lost someone— and this could happen once a week in a big church—he always paid serious attention, whoever it was.

He says ministers and priests are the last ports of call. Doctors can explain what happened clinically, and say, "We're very sorry." But at that point the families are saying, "Where are the guys with the dog collars [our church slang for clerical collars]?" The family is standing there saying, "They've just sewn our daughter up and, you know, she's twenty-three years old, she has breast cancer, and it's taken over her body and we're going to lose our baby." Or, "She was in a car crash and is gone now, though she was perfectly fine an hour earlier." These people are looking death squarely in the face. And my father will sit there with them. In that hour, in that time of need, I've seen him show up time and time again. In our own family he couldn't always show up, even for a dinner conversation. But he fully understood his responsibilities in those moments of grief.

Sometimes all you can do is just sit and hold a space. It's the hardest space you'll ever hold. You pour the tea, you bring the food, you don't have to make silly talk. They'll talk or not talk. I watched him do that and began to see that there's a rhythm to it. And it's one that I have to find in performance, when people are bringing their grief to me in a similar way.

What I find really intriguing about my dad is that certain aspects of his character that he doesn't think are of value are his true gold. And I believe every person has their gold. It gets tricky when people put so much value on their gifts because it makes it hard for some of us, mainly because they don't give us much of a chance to value their gifts. Other people think their gold is something other than what it really is, so they keep their gift in the background. That was his reality.

In 1963 my father marched with Martin Luther King Jr., in the big March on Washington. He was always close with the African-American ministers in the conference. His best friend was a guy called Bobby Bishop. We would be sitting at the Orioles baseball game surrounded by black people. When Bobby would drop me off at school, the teachers would say, "Who was that black man who dropped you off?"—they thought he was a kidnapper. I'd say, "That's my Uncle Bobby," which he was. My father joined the civil rights movement because he'd seen how his friends had been in chains. And I think that is one of my father's qualities that people don't understand. He believed in education for women and he believed in civil rights all the way.

I think my father was so drawn to my mother because the distant Mormon side of his people, on his father's side, believe that the Native Americans are the lost tribe of Israel. So she was, in a way, part of something. And he didn't even know why he was drawn to her, I think. As for my mother, she thought she was marrying a handsome doctor. A healer. My dad was a premed student before he switched his focus and studied theology. My grandmother, his mother, wrote to him and told him that he needed to change his major. "How could I have five boys," she wrote, "and how could not one love me enough to become a minister?"

He bit the carrot. And he and I have discussed it. He'll turn the tables on me. He'll say, "Well, what would you be writing about if I had been a doctor?" And that's fair enough.

It was difficult for my mother, though. She dealt with it by pushing a Jackie O persona. Here was this woman who believed all these things—the Native American philosophy—and people at church had no idea who she was. She was the minister's wife: completely gracious, never said a peep. She played the wife to a T. I mean, the southern lady, polite, lovely, style, class, boom. Not a foot out of line. And yet something in her was dying slowly.

I was fairly young when I realized that I was compromising my mom by telling her certain things I'd seen happening in the Church. I began to see that she was in a really weird position. That's the word I would have used as a kid. For a while, my mom gave up so much to support my father that she lost pieces of herself. But she regained that as she dove into her Native American research years ago to prove that her people were on the tribal rolls. As my mother helped my sister get into the Indians Into Medicine program (INMED) at the University of North Dakota, she aligned herself with the Corn Mother and brought the compassionate heart into her Bible study. You will find that many Native Americans practice a form of Christianity, mainly because the one called Jesus, with his compassionate heart and constant love, reminded many Native Americans of one called the Great Peacemaker, recognized in numerous tribes as a spiritual prophet who lived before those who came and landed at Plymouth Rock. My mother runs my publishing company now. She and my dad. For her it's always been back to the texts.

What I began to see as a child was my grandmother's power over people. She was able to get my father to make the life change from being a doctor to being a minister—that's power. It's changing someone's life completely. It changed my mother's life as well. Hey, she went along with it. But she was going to be an English teacher married to a doctor. She then had to go to work to support the minister, and give up her education. This is not a small thing. I also didn't like the way my father's mother treated my mother. There was a distance. And my mother so wanted to be embraced by her. That was so important to her, and it never happened.

If these things hadn't happened, if my father had gone on to be a doctor and my mother had been able to follow her original path, we wouldn't be having this conversation. I would have been writing songs about God knows what. I wouldn't have learned the key lesson I learned from their hardship at the hands of my grandmother and the Christian Church. I wasn't going to let anybody have power over me like that, so I looked at her and I studied her, and I came to realize that she kept going back to the idea of the Word made flesh. And I said, *All right, the Word is going to live inside* my *flesh, and you will not have a library card to get into it.* So that's when I started making songs that other people couldn't walk into, and I discovered my creative spark.

ANN: *The intimate impact of her family on Amos's developing identity was soon joined, and sometimes countered, by another crucial source: music. The fledgling pianist's alliance with her instrument allowed her access to a new, self-generated world of secret revelations. At the same time, other artists' music transported Amos into realms she'd never imagined existed. Passionately, but carefully, she incorporated their spirit into her own forming imagination.*

CONVERSATION BETWEEN TORI AND ANN:

It's the kind of question one often gets asked, and I suspect most people faced with it simply make up an answer—but I do have a first musical memory. I remember looking up at this big black upright piano. It was old. There was a wind-up stool, and I remember putting phone books on the ground, trying to get myself on it. I was two and a half. I was stalking the piano, seeing it, warming up to it. I wasn't intimidated by it. I was checking it out and it was very welcoming. And so I began a relationship, which just seemed the most natural thing to do. And you don't question things at that age, really—it's just natural, you're drawn to certain things. My family encouraged it, which was great.

When I was five, I had begun going to the piano and composing little snippets, little songs to help me stay clear on what I was seeing and thinking and hearing. Especially within the Church, because people wouldn't openly discuss their perceptions or what was really going on. There wasn't a lot out in the open. This was before the dam broke on the abuses within the Christian Church. Whatever the extent of it for different girls, different guys, what they went through, I was there, watching, as the minister's daughter, and I was able to kind of clock it. My dad and I have recently had conversations about the shocking extent of these abuses within the Church worldwide. Some young people were sexualized and others were desexualized. I had my little radar up, because I was a composer. I mean, come on—it's like there is this big elephant shitting in the living room and everyone just looks around it to watch the football game. Later, when I went to the conservatory, my teachers told me that if I wanted to compose, I'd have to be a camera at all times. And as a child I created sonic paintings, so that I could walk into them without having to leave the house or leave the room. So I was able to chronicle what was really occurring but not being acknowledged.

After a certain point I didn't even feel the need to leave the Christian system because I thought nothing could get me. I was able to sit while my dad was reading the paper after dinner and create musical worlds, and sometimes they were encoded. It was all there for people to hear. Very much like the Renaissance painters who placed symbols within their paintings to be interpreted. I tried to follow their pattern and put sonic symbols in my work. I created musical codes from a very young age, so I could recall what was really happening in my life. I had to know where the knowledge was, so I stored it all in the songs. I store everything in the songs, everything. I'm leaving you clues and I'm giving you the chance to go on a little hunt.

Sometimes now, I go to the piano for a while before I do an interview or make a public appearance. I'm going back to the Source. This is how I figure out where I'm really coming from. It helps me decide what I will tell somebody, whose opinions I want to clothe myself in before I lie down under the microscope. This, at the piano, is where I chronicle everything. If I have a misunderstanding with someone, a falling out, I come here.

A time came later in my youth when I had to find the bridge between the aspects of playing music that constituted communication with myself, and performance. That's when I got a repertoire together, things that people would like. This is why I've done covers over the years. It's something that I started doing a lot of, while cutting my teeth as a lounge player, and after you do so many you see the songs you do well. I'd slip one of my songs into a set occasionally. But I understood that I was there to play songs that the customers wanted to hear, and so I learned a lot of material that maybe I wouldn't have chosen to learn. That's how I learned song structure; I've seen a lot of architects' blueprints, you could say. When you look through all those blueprints, then you begin to go, *Oh*, that's *how they solved that problem with the basement.*

These days, I do keep my specific musical influences private, somewhat, when I'm in the middle of a work. This is one thing that is sacred to me. What I'm listening to during my process, how I get my groove, that's private. Some journalists have asked, "Is there anything you won't talk about?" Yes—what I'm listening to. The Internet practically has my gynecological record, and I accept that. I'll also share information about some of the things I'm reading, and other nonmusical starting places. But if a text is a jumping-off point for me and if it's really part of my core process right at that moment, then no, I won't share it. I think that's very personal. And also, there are people who will penetrate the process for reasons that are not benevolent, that go beyond mere curiosity.

That said, I am happy to acknowledge certain artists who made a big difference to me when I was developing as a composer. As a pianist, my left hand was really kind of developed by listening to Stevie Wonder, along with the bass playing of Led Zeppelin's John Paul Jones. I remember just listening to "Superstition" from *Talking Book*, and the whole of the *Innervisions* album, and studying them, as a player more than a writer or a singer. My sense of song structure was developed by listening to Lennon and McCartney and Joni Mitchell. Or Gershwin, or Hoagy Carmichael, any of the classic songwriters of the early twentieth century. Now that's song structure. I really love that kind of structure, that older style of writing a standard. I was also influenced by the Negro spirituals my Poppa sang.

My mother had a huge record collection—she'd actually worked in a record store before meeting my father. She saved all her records, and when I was small, along with educating me through books, she'd play them for me. She's the one who played me Gershwin to Fats Waller, all the greats of the pre-rock repertoire.

Like everyone born in the 1960s, I heard the Beatles at a young age. My brother, Michael, is almost ten years older than I am, and he was bringing home music that affected him. I was able to hear *Sergeant Pepper* when it first came out, though I was only four years old. Michael was this huge giver of information. He was the messenger. He and his friends would borrow records from each other. He was studying the guitar, so he was drawn to guitar players. So my mom was bringing in one generation of music, and he was bringing in the next. And then, when I went to Peabody Conservatory, I began hearing the classics and getting the idea of discipline.

What the Beatles' songs did for me was create space. To this day those songs create worlds for me to walk into, or puddles—whatever it is, it's a space. And I don't feel I need to know what Lennon and McCartney were seeing. I don't feel I need to know them. I feel I'm given permission, and it's unspoken, to have my own—I don't like the word *journey*—but adventure, almost. And I'm allowed to walk and breathe in that space and have my own relationship with the song.

Then, of course, there was Led Zeppelin . . . Talk about a second coming. I just remember listening to them and feeling my body move and going to the piano and moving my body at the piano. And their music would transform into other music I was working on. What their work taught me was how to stay in a rhythm, feeling my body move to this rhythm and trying to create a continuation at the piano, just knowing that I had to take this power into my world. Realizing it would look different, because I'm a piano player.

I watch how Tash, her friend Emily, and Tash's cousin Kelsey make their creations. They have been inspiring me to pick up my pen. Writing a book and a record at the same time is not something I'd choose to do again. Nor is getting married two weeks before rehearsals began for a ten-month world tour. Why? Well, the upside is that they share the same breathing space, the same emotional house. Let's say they are like roommates. The downside is, they share the same breathing space, the same emotional house. Let's say they are like roommates. So in a way, yes, they breathe creative life into each other, but they also can steal breath from each other. Either way they share a bond. Similar to a marriage. If marriage works, it's because the two that have joined together as a force have discovered that when the well runs dry, there is a second well with an endless Source. But as we all know, the trick is to discover that second well.

There is no map you can buy to the second well; it can seem elusive. Yeah, yeah, yeah, I've been to the mountains, to the desert, to the sea, just like you, and for a moment it seems that, wow, here it is, the second well. And then no sooner than you think you've discovered it, it's gone. Then you find yourself following the "food change path": you know, change your food, change your path, you are what you eat, Eat Right for Your Blood Type, etc., etc. . . . we've all done it. But if you're like me, then you realize one day that after you've been doing this for a year, your actual blood type is A+, not O . . . Fucking great. Then you go to the philosophers and you read the Jameses—Hillman and Hollis. You read Hollis's *Swamplands of the Soul* and there is a glimmer. You devour Robert E. Johnson, Joseph Campbell, Marion Woodman, Jean Shinoda Bolen, the endless list of writers. You go to the ancient myths, including the Bible. You go to the Gnostics and discover that St. Paul, in all probability, was one. You study Elaine Pagels, all her writings on early Christianity: *The Gnostic Gospels, The Gnostic Paul: Gnostic Exegesis of the Pauline Letters,* and *Beyond Belief: The Secret Gospel of Thomas.* At a certain point you begin to bead a necklace, weighing what you have been taught compared to the information you've discovered yourself, and you realize all the contradictions.

While beading what may be truth, you bead that which may have been hidden from us. Truths that have been uncovered with the discoveries at Nag Hammadi in 1945 of ancient texts, even Gospels, that were written as early as the four Gospels that we live by—Matthew, Mark, Luke, and John. Discoveries including texts such as the Gospel of Thomas, the secret book of James, and the secret book of John—and all of a sudden there is a flash of light. And where has it come from? Watching Eddie Izzard do Ozzie as well as Ozzie does? Mixed with the love of a good man. Mixed with watching a transvestite perform "I've Never Been to Me" by Charlene, mixed with your mom barely surviving a cardiac arrest . . . and then *voilà.* There it is. Finally, you stumble upon the second well.

Tash said to me the other day,

"Mum?"

I responded, "Yum."

"Mum?"

"Yum."

"Mum, sometimes I'm stupid."

"Tash, don't be so hard on yourself."

"Mum, sometimes you're stupid, too."

"Hey, Tash, what are you getting at?"

"Sometimes, Mum, when you're cross and I'm Bombaloo." (She uses a word meaning how it sounds, from the kids' book *Sometimes I'm Bombaloo.*)

"Yeah, go on . . ."

"Well, we act stupid then, Mum."

"Maybe you're right, Tash. Maybe we do act stupid."

"I-got-an-idea . . ."

"You do? What's your idea?"

"Mum, you can be five in our game."

"Yeah, okay, and?"

"And I can be sixteen going on seventeen."

And I thought to myself, *I guess I've been five all week . . .*

ANN: *Amos's teachers came from everywhere: from within her family, from the radio, from the land itself. But Amos also famously gained a formal musical education. The years she spent studying at the Peabody Institute of Johns Hopkins University in Baltimore taught her both discipline and disappointment. She had other teachers as well: in piano practice rooms, and in the lounges she began playing in as a teen. And one teacher, her father, remained central.*

CONVERSATION BETWEEN TORI AND ANN:

I'd been dreaming through the night one night last fall, just kind of going back in time, and I woke up to a message: Husband said, "Somebody called yesterday." I was getting the tea ready that morning, getting Tash ready, and he just looked and said, "Now is not a good time to tell you this, but it came in yesterday and I didn't tell you then 'cause that wasn't a good time, either." He said, "Somebody called and your music teacher died." I said, "Which one?" And he wrote down the name and he showed me, and it was Diana Morrison, who was a voice teacher of mine when I was about eighteen, until I was twenty-one. She came to my shows up until a few years ago when she got a bit older, but she was one of those really vibrant creatures.

Colorful scarves, blond curly hair, older, though. From an earlier generation, but a feminist and a real force in music in the Washington, D.C., area. And very, very much a part of my music. She trained people for years, showing them how to not destroy their voices. I had gotten nodes like any other singer; I mean, I was singing six nights a week, five or six hours a night in the days when she was my coach. Knowing that she died put me in this place of going back. I've had so many teachers for different things, and it's important to acknowledge that.

Though I heard my brother's and my mother's records, in a formal sense I was exposed to classical music before pop. People always toss around the phrase *child prodigy* to refer to my years at the Peabody Conservatory, because I was so young, five, when I started there. It was assumed—by my parents, my teachers, and myself at that time—that I would go on to become a concert pianist. That's what you do if you're in a place like that—you're not just playing, you're there to be a champion. No different from a gymnast studying with Bela Karolyi: at a certain point you're daft to do it if you aren't going to win, and if you don't cut the mustard you become a teacher or just leave.

I had trouble reading music. My ear was good. I could hear and play things back, but I struggled with reading. When I say that, I mean I could read better than most people, I could read Debussy and Bartók, but not Chopin. At eight years old, I wasn't playing *Fantasie Impromptu*, and that was a bit young, but I should have been playing it, and other pieces on this level, soon.

I knew that I couldn't compete with the best in the world, and the clocks were ticking. Three years previous I'd been untouchable for my age, and then suddenly I wasn't. I sought out people at the conservatory who would be straight with me, other students, and I knew I was marked, just as I'd been marked by my grandmother at home. I knew I was a disappointment, and it was sad to not be the Girl Wonder anymore. My father, particularly, couldn't accept it. And in a strange way, it's a good thing that he didn't, because he never gave up on me. But I started to spend time with the composers at school and began to see that this was a very different endeavor. I was very humbled by the tradition of composing, but I also knew that, as a composer, I didn't have to achieve an apex when I was eleven.

I started to let people know that I loved this other kind of music. I think I was ten when I said to one of my teachers, "What about the idea of John Lennon? Lennon and McCartney as modern-day Mozarts." That was just blasphemous. There wasn't a place for the idea of being a contemporary composer, working in the pop idiom. Jazz was acceptable; in fact, it's a big piece of the Peabody program. And now I think they actually do have a contemporary music program—they've asked me to come and lecture, which is so funny. I don't know if I'll do it, or if I would be good at doing it. Maybe it's better for me to just teach by example.

By the time I left the Peabody, I was really listening to contemporary music. It was my life, my blood. I was composing a lot. At the insistence of my father I did continue to take lessons, under a Roman Catholic nun at St. Camilla's, a school close by. Her name was Sister Ernestine. I did it for my dad. She snoozed through our lesson usually, so I just composed instead of playing Rachmaninoff, although I love the Russians. I had romances with these composers in my head. Through the music I joined with them, coupling with their motifs in my left hand. I actually kept taking lessons on and off until I was twenty, because that's just what I did.

When I was around twelve I began to share the songs I was writing with my girlfriends. I even won the Montgomery County Teen Talent Competition with one of my own songs. I beat out a girl who was fourteen who went to my school. Wendy Nelson. She was just the coolest thing. She would talk about this guy called Bruce Springsteen and sing all of his songs at the piano. Later, when people would say, "You must have been inspired by Kate Bush as a teen," I'd say honestly I'd never even heard of her back then. Wendy Nelson was my inspiration.

At fourteen I started performing on the lounge circuit and learning my repertoire. That was my father's idea, and though it may forever seem strange that a minister sent his teenage daughter into gay clubs to sing and play, thank God he did. There was nowhere else that would accept me as a performer. The gay community embraced me just as I was working through my own sexuality and gave me a safe place to deal with that. One night someone came up to my father when I was playing at a bar called Mr. Henry's, and said, "How in the world can you bring your daughter into a gay club?" And he replied, "Well, she won't be going home with any of you!" He had the situation sussed out. He knew I needed to learn my trade and I could do it there. Sometimes the Great Mother visits us in unexpected ways. I remember the gay waiters, specifically one called Joey; he showed me how to dress, how to push a Joan Fontaine look, and how to give a blow job on a cucumber, swathed in cashmere, of course—this way he could always check for teeth marks.

As with every school I attended, I eventually had to leave the lounges. A friend of mine in D.C., Steve Himmelfarb, convinced me. Steve's dad was living in North Hollywood, and he moved out there to become a recording engineer. Then he came back to see me. One night we were having a coffee after I'd been playing in downtown D.C. and he said, "You're going to have to get out of here at a certain point. What is it going to take? You will be doing this at thirty, playing for these senators. They're going to give you a dollar in your tip jar, and you're going to get old. That's it." He could see the future. Soon after Steve's speech, I moved to L.A. He became an engineer at Capitol, and you know what happened to me.

At that point I had to leave the person dearest to me, my mother. I had to leave my father, my greatest teacher, behind. When you are twenty-one and making as much money as your father—ministers and teachers don't make much money (not that that's right, but that is what it is)—the curfews and the disagreements over whom I should date and how I should behave all got to be too much. He and I get along much better now, but at that time it was really overbearing, and I knew that I had to become a woman.

ANN: *Corn Mother's story brings to light the importance of honoring your origins, but it also makes room for humans to seize their own destiny. The earth goddess's grandsons create civilization with the hunt, and though they no longer live in an Eden, they inhabit the real world. An artist must also go beyond her origins to fully realize her vision. For Amos, this moment of separation began when she named herself.*

The sumerian goddess inanna

CONVERSATION BETWEEN TORI AND ANN:

People called me Ellen, my middle name, during most of the years of my apprenticeship. I was fifteen when I realized I needed my own name, but for a while I didn't know what it was. I went through tons of names, even Sammy Jay; there were a lot of different ideas floating through—I don't know if you can actually call them ideas, more like brain farts. Finally, when I was seventeen, somebody just walked in one night and revealed it to me. It wasn't someone close to me—just a guy my friend Linda McBride dated for a couple of weeks. They came into one of the lounges where I played, just to have a drink, and when she introduced him to me, he said, "You're a Tori."

And I just kind of went, *I think you're right.* Soon after that, a friend of mine who worked in the Reagan administration came to the piano bar. I told him my new name, and he said, "You can't be a Tory. I mean, it's like calling yourself a Republican, only British." And I said, "I don't care. I just don't care." I knew the spelling wouldn't be like that anyway.

When I consider why I took that name for myself, I realize that maybe I was trying to create another potential. Myra was my given name; the root of Myra is, of course, Mary. And I understand that I carry that. It was important to my father that all the women in his life, my sister and my mother and I, had forms of Mary. He was devoted to the mother Mary. There's a respect there, for Jesus' mother. The Magdalene, however, they didn't even call her Mary—she wasn't a consideration.

So in our family there was Mary Ellen, my mother, Marie Allen, my sister, and I was Myra Ellen. So I really felt I could not create my own destiny—it's almost as if I was given cement and told to build a cabin. I knew that certain controls were in place that I couldn't break. I could not break through the opinions of who Myra Ellen was and what was expected of her.

Again, we go back to the power of words and how they can make you feel. They bring liberation or stagnation, they're chains. I began to see the structure of Tori—there's conserva*tory,* and vic*tory:* you see that word in so many different other words—also anti-inflamma*tory,* but my favorite has to be Yakatori chicken. And I began to feel that the sound of this name was a window. Although I can't fly, it gave me access to go to certain subjects, to get into secret ideologies. To travel, which I've been doing ever since.

SONG CANVAS: "Mother Revolution"

There were two Jamaican nurses taking care of me. They were both deeply religious women. They believed in God and followed the Bible word for word. I would speak to them of the Great Mother; I would tell them that they reminded me of the depth of love that I felt from the Great Mother. When I would sit by the sea, so as to let the rushing of the winds and the salt clear the way—cleansing the thoughts that were pulling me down, I would reach for the hands of these two women. All three of us believed that there were forces that could pull you down. Pull you away from your center. They called it Satan. I didn't choose to disagree with that terminology. Satan means different things to different people, and a lot of people see it as an outside force working to recruit people into his army. Over the years I've chosen to see it somewhat differently. I believe that this force, called Satan, if you will, is a position from which you or I choose to act. This force takes no responsibility for the suffering it causes. Some people who need to have power over other people can't see that they are operating within the satanic framework. If you stop walking on eggshells and are honest about it—dominating another human being, needing to control another human being, even if it's in that person's best interest, treating someone like a possession, taking advantage of another human being because you can—all of this is what 666 really is. The misuse of power. Not all of us are willing to admit where we're misusing our power.

I would sit and speak for hours and hours with these Jamaican nurses, each of whom had had a child who had been killed, and they both chose to hold the space of the Great Mother. One of them lost her eighteen-year-old baby in a car accident and was sued by the so-called friends who survived, who were trying to eke out as much money as they could. Yes, of course the money was paid out by the insurance company, but not one survivor had any concern or compassion for their friend, who was dead, for the mother who had lost her baby. No, they cared about what they would get out of it, though their lives had been spared. Now that is satanic. Until each of us has the courage to look at our priorities . . .

The Apocalypse is not something out there that will eradicate everything on planet Earth. That would be far too simple. The Apocalypse is in each and every one of us. It takes courage to fight the beast. The beast is allegorical and rears its chameleon head when power is misused by each and every one of us. Sometimes we misuse power by not standing up for ourselves, by being powerless. That's the inverted beast—when you can't say no but you should because you're being asked to do something that you know isn't right for you, but you do it because you were never taught how to say no. You were never taught that sometimes the consequences of saying no are that the person that you've said no to will say you're not being a good friend, then will threaten to leave you or will just walk out on the relationship. So as they start to walk, then you start to buckle and you say, "No, don't go, don't go, I'm sorry—I just want to make it okay." That's another form of the Apocalypse. This is called spiritual slavery. You have just handed over an invisible leash that goes from your neck to their hands. Now, until we all have the courage to look at where we aren't choosing freedom for the soul, then we are out of alignment with the Great Mother and the Divine Father—whatever you want to call them. Sometimes the Great Mother seems to inhabit little people as well . . .

I have been writing about Grandma for days now. Tash finds me on the curve of the half-moon-shaped old Georgian stairs, sits down next to me, and says, "You need to stop work and come play now, Mum." "Yeah, but Tash, I have a deadline." "It'll be okay, Mum. Come on and play." "Okay, Tash, which animal do you want me to be in the safari?" We play—Tash, Emily, Kelsey, and I—down our hill on this huge rock in our garden that the kids dubbed "the safari." And out of the blue Tash puts her hand in mine and says, "Do you know who we are Mum?" And at that moment I just look into her blue planets for eyes, and she says, "We are Daughters of Song, Mama." And at that I jump up with new life, pick her up, and say, "Now let's go play."

mary magdalene:
the erotic muse

TORI:

"Jesus was a feminist, dear."

At nineteen years old I look up at my mom and with exasperation say, "Ma, I've got no problem with Jesus, okay? Always dug the guy—still do. Do you really think the Magdalene would have entertained the idea of them as an item if he weren't for women's rights and equality in the workplace?"

"Yes, dear, I understand all that, dear, but you do seem to be carrying a lot of aggression concerning the Church."

"Damn right I am, Mom."

"Please, let's not use *damn*, dear."

"Okay, Ma. Darn tooting I am. But I am harboring a lot of fucking rage over those Passive-Aggressive Manipulators of Authority that constitute The Patriarchy."

"That's better, dear. Articulate the breaking of the dam, the breaking of the emotional chains that have bound women for centuries—from your young feminist perspective. Use your music to tackle the infirmities of the patriarchal structure, which at its foundation has a cancerous moral flaw."

"Huh . . . ? Ma, are you all right?"

"Am I all right? Oh, darlin', I haven't felt so alive in years. Thank heaven your generation is rising to the call."

For a moment it seemed as if my mom were singing "Sister Suffragette," from the movie *Mary Poppins*. She was on a roll.

"In my own daughter, in other mothers' daughters across the land, there will be a thirst for knowledge. Yes, that is the way we will rattle the foundation of The Patriarchy's segregation. Their segregation of heart from mind, of actions from consequences, of man from woman, of power from imagination, and of passion from compassion."

"Jeez, Ma. I didn't know. I had no idea you still had it in you."

And she looked away. When she turned back she took my hand and whispered, "We all have it in us, but those voices can get lost and buried. Those thoughts you just heard have only been sleeping in me. And they sleep in everybody, dear. Don't let anyone tell you that these thoughts are dead. But they have been in a deep sleep. Your passion for the Magdalene is electric. So I don't want to discourage you when I say, a majority of the people in America are just not quite ready to open up to Mary Magdalene the way you have. But be vigilant."

"Why? What do you mean?"

"Be vigilant. Be vigilant against dangers. Be vigilant against the Magdalene's villains, against her vicious betrayers. And, dear, in most cases . . . they won't even know who she is or what she is. Some will, but many won't."

Why is my mind remembering this moment in time all those years ago? Like a film playing in my head as I sit here—sit here waiting. In the conference room at Doubleday. Jeez. It's easier to get into the Oval Office than to get into the military compound known as Doubleday Books. So here in the Broadway Division I sit, remembering my mother's monologue as Johnny and Chelsea do business in another room. Funny. I look up. I'm surrounded by point-of-purchase posters for *The Da Vinci Code*. Ah yes, *The Da Vinci Code*. The book, whether you like it or not, that struck a chord with the masses, whereby the public began to look up to the Magdalene, to open up to the Magdalene as a Being, not just as a demeaned prostitute. And yet, what is a prostitute? I know many businessmen prostitutes. What is a sacred prostitute? Do I know any? Could you be one? Could I be one? My mind wanders as I sit here . . .

ANN: *Rock and roll is an erotic art. That's a central truth perennially revealed, riding into the public consciousness on Elvis Presley's hips, Robert Plant's androgyne scream, even, though slightly degraded, Britney's stripper sneer. No one accepts, celebrates, and explores this given more keenly than Tori Amos, veteran traveler in the delicate areas where imagination meets the flesh. From her first days as a singer-songwriter, she has stood, eyes and voice open, before subjects around which other stars pole-dance. Speaking honestly of rape in "Me and a Gun," sexual dissatisfaction in "Leather," or masturbation in "Icicle," Amos undertook the feminist task of speaking women's truth to patriarchal power. Later, her investigations became both more personal and more enigmatic. Blunt lines edging toward obscenity shoot through songs like "In the Springtime of His Voodoo" and "She's Your Cocaine"; more mature statements like "Lust" and "Crazy" gain both tenderness and richness from an underlying heat. Like desire itself, deeply and often bafflingly individual, Amos's songs communicate a palpable rush through unexpected words and music.*

The voluptuous lexicon revealed in Amos's songs finds a counterpart in a performance style based in bodily yearning and release. The joy of sex moves through Amos when she sits and moves at her Bösendorfer, as does its agony. Yet too many observers have reduced her onstage behavior to an undignified phrase, "humping the piano," just as too many have read her lyrics as just a lover's diary. The truth is deeper. Amos is indeed playing a game with Eros when she gyrates aboard her instrument, but to comprehend it one must go beyond biography and the pleasures of the moment to grasp a very old story.

She states it outright: "I serve the Magdalene." Now that Jesus' mythical (and likely historical) consort is the stuff of a best-selling thriller, it may seem as if Amos is simply seeking the hottest spiritual avatar when she declares this loyalty. In fact, her life's work is grounded in the pursuit of reconciliation between this maligned priestess of sexual healing and her virtuous counterpart, the mother Mary, otherwise known to Amos as culture and Earth itself.

As with so much that informs her art, Amos first heard the Magdalene legend in church. But she's followed it much further, to the very base of her artistic self—the musician as a channel for a spirit as impious as it is blessed.

TORI:

"For good or ill," my father would sermonize to me, "you are a daughter of the Christian Church." And you know what? That's probably the most accurate statement my father has made in respect to who I am as his daughter and my relationship with the Christian Church. I'm remembering the different bishops of the Methodist church, sitting around my mom's Sunday dinner and expounding on Jesus. Similar to Paul, known as St. Paul, these bishops were preaching their own theology, in Jesus' name. They, with their theological degrees, there with my father—who subsequently was to receive his doctorate from Boston University. Yes, we had quite a group discussing the Gospels around the dinner table. Were they preaching Jesus' message of gender equality? No. But probably the most glaring omission, to me, was when they would refer to Jesus as the Bridegroom.

So, stay with me here a second. Be with me at that Sunday dinner way back when, and hear the reasonings I was given. "We think of Jesus as the Shepherd, and we are the sheep." "We think of Jesus as the Vine, and we are the branches." And everybody—drumroll, please. Now, I was about eight in 1970, as this last statement was said by a bishop—not a bad guy mind you: a very, very kind man. But being kind doesn't mean that you have any idea what you're spewing. So then he announced the final "truth" in his trilogy: "And last, we think of Jesus as the Bridegroom and the Christian Church as his Bride." Choke, cough, cough, choke. There went my candied sweet potatoes, regurgitated with the sour.

"Excuse me, sir." Through sips of water and a driving force within, I found my voice and looked at this very religious man and said, "Excuse me, but who did you say Jesus married?" And the bishop looked somewhat bewilderedly at my father, and my father jumped into the conversation and answered . . . I must say not so much as *patronizingly*, but with that glazed "I know my Jesus personally" kind of look. He answered, "We see Jesus as the Bridegroom married to the Church," both he and the bishop shaking their heads together in reverence. Oh, jeez. I said, "But who was Jesus' Bride?" And my father answered, "We believe the Christian Church is his Bride." "Well, what about Mary Magdalene?" The church leader looked a little uncomfortable, and I knew I was pushing it—but I couldn't stop. He and my father went into some speech about Mary Magdalene being a sinful woman, a woman of ill repute that got saved and blessed by our Lord and Savior Jesus Christ. Then she faded into the background as if she were just one of Jesus' many followers.

What they were saying kind of reminded me of a picture I had seen of young women fainting over male rock stars. And, freeze frame. Take that picture. In that moment, I realized that my Mary had been minimalized by The Patriarchy. I realized that I knew that she truly was the Lost Bride. They were working just way too hard to convince me otherwise. This is before Margaret Starbird's book on the lost legacy of Mary Magdalene and before she published *The Goddess in the Gospels*. This is before Elaine Pagels's revelatory translation of biblical texts, texts that were discovered in the twentieth century and unveil much about the Magdalene. This is before Timothy Freke and Peter Gandy's *Jesus and the Lost Goddess: The Secret Teachings of the Original Christians*. This is before Laurence Gardner's involved research exposing the suppression of ancient concepts in books such as *Bloodline of the Holy Grail: The Hidden Lineage of Jesus*. And the list goes on.

Whatever I realized on that brutal Sunday back in 1970, I also realized that I was in a small minority that believed that the Magdalene was a sacred and important piece to the emancipation of Christian women. I had been born a feminist, but that day I knew I had to take the next leap. I know now that my avatar all along has been closer to Lisa Simpson than anyone else. Once I understood that, I had to make a huge leap as I had the taste in my mouth of regurgitated, soured candied sweet potatoes. I understood that the Magdalene was very much still in exile—even as women were burning their bras from coast to coast, I burned an idea into my head . . .

What is the sacred prostitute? What is the sensual spirit? The women's mysteries are ancient and precede the Magdalene by many years. She was someone who walked the walk and integrated her teachings into her Being. Once there were schools for these teachings at which young girls would become apprentices, then initiates, and train, eventually becoming what we would call today medicine women. The information they were gathering was suppressed to the point at which the teachings had almost to be passed down encoded, or those women would be tortured and murdered in many circles. Even during the time of the Magdalene there were disciples who appeared to be against her, the Feminine, and her beliefs. I don't only serve the Magdalene. I serve an idea. The idea of the resurrected Feminine. In different cultures it will carry with it different names. The Secret Book of John, which was also discovered in Nag Hammadi, discusses hidden mysteries in the Christian myth. In the Christian myth the resurrected Feminine is called Sophia for Wisdom, and the Feminine counterpart to Sophia is called Achamoth for Consciousness. The way I understand it, many of Jesus' core teachings, which were uncovered in many of the scriptures found at Nag Hammadi, are really about reuniting the aspects of the Feminine—Wisdom and Consciousness, Sophia and Achamoth—together at the "Cross of Light."

In traditional Christianity the false split gave us two characters: the Virgin Mary and the Magdalene. Of course, within the psyche they must be joined, not polarized for a Christian woman to feel whole. The Virgin Mary has been stripped of her sexuality but has retained her spirituality; the Magdalene has been stripped of her spirituality but has retained her sexuality. Each must have her wholeness. I call this "marrying the two Marys."

There are so many people who come to my shows with this division in them. It seems that you can't be thought of as a Divine Mother type and have the respect of those around you if you're also the sacred prostitute. We divide and conquer on the deepest of levels, by cutting off our own spiritual Being from our own physical Being. Talk about painful. I lived it myself at one point. To have sex, I had to take on a character, because I couldn't be the me that I know and look at in the mirror and express all the different things I wanted to. Basically I didn't know how to "*do* what I just did under the covers" and then turn around and pick up my glasses and books and go to the library as the same person. I am both of those creatures; they are one person; but it was proving difficult to gather all those pieces and have them live together as one integrated Being. And, of course, I see it in the world all the time—the men go to the mistress and then to the wife. And the wife gets resentful because she is not allowed to experience or express that overtly sexual side of herself, and then the mistress gets vindictive because she doesn't get Christmas or Easter.

The piano is the bridge that resolves these elements. Music has an alchemical quality. And there's more than one voice on the piano. You have two hands. One can be playing a celestial melody while the other is doing quite the opposite. The joining of the profane and the sacred, or the passionate and the compassionate, happens right there on the keyboard. It reconciles a bond severed a long time ago. There's so much shame around passion's innate hunger, which sometimes can be deemed profane, but music can access its reality: that which has been sacred but has been severed.

That is what the sacred prostitutes understood. Termed the Hierodulae, these priestesses of the love goddess—whether you are calling her Inanna or Ashera or whomever—these sacred women knew how to transmute the sexually profane. Do I know how they did this? No. But I was taught that these sacred prostitutes could not have transmuted anything if they had "taken on" or become the sexual projection of the male whose company they were sharing. That would mean that they had gnosis of how to balance the sacred and the profane. They had an understanding of the sexuality that lives in the unconscious, which if not pruned and nurtured will take over a person's garden and choke all growth. Wasteland. Game over. Next player.

Sometimes, it seems, we're all looking for something outside ourselves because there's been this rejection of a piece of our consciousness. Mistakes can be made when taking on this division. A lot of people will say that they channel the Magdalene, but then they take the sacred into the realm of the profane and leave it there. I was taught that when you're working with archetypes you have to remember that you are connecting with an essence much older than yourself, whose character you must respect. We are not those creatures. We each have a pattern inside. You can see when Aphrodite is working through certain people. It's an aphrodisiac simply when they walk into the room. You smell it in them. And it's not something they learn. This is core, this is within. And you can't dissect it or examine a blood sample. But if you're using this stuff and you don't integrate its lessons and transform yourself the way the original myths described, it can become quite a destructive situation. Passion's hunger can become addictive and abusive. That was something that took me many years to learn.

If you walk down that road, then you must define the role of the sacred prostitute. You're walking into an arena where women do not take on the projected image the men have of them during sex. Whoever the man wants to think this woman is, that is not at all who the sacred prostitute is for one second. They know who they are. And they have integrated this and owned this concept in their bodies, without even a mortgage to pay. They own it. They had to do the work to achieve this ownership.

I know that today there are women who have taken on the title of sacred prostitute and are trying to walk that path. But what we're talking about occurred at a time when these women weren't called prostitutes: they were the Hierodulae, or the Sacred Women. Their role was revered, and they trained their whole lives. They were initiated.

There have been many other performers brought up by very religious parents, and then when they are able to own this essence and put it into their music, the sensual-sexual thing that they were not allowed to acknowledge and partake of in real life actually materializes in the music. If anybody knew you were consciously partaking of this sensual-sexual thing, you'd be ostracized. You would be thought of as sinful. Elvis went through something like this, if you think about it. Trace the roots of American popular culture, and the story is there.

ANN: *The confrontation that changed Amos's life replayed the clash that produced rock and roll in the first place. A tussle with authority was involved, as well as a toss in the imaginary hay.*

TORI:

When I was five—I remember it well—my missionary grandmother, Addie Allen Amos (Grandma Amos again), wrote me a letter that said,

"Until you learn to love Jesus, there will be no Christmas under the tree for you." She was studying me. She had marked me somehow. I think I'd said that I found Jesus cute. It was completely natural for a young girl to see a picture of a boy, even if he was a little older, and think he was cute—to me that was healthy. But she and the Church knocked all the health out of it.

She would have been throwing that stone at the Magdalene, there's no question. And there have been women like this through the centuries. They have been queens, or wives of the vicars, or figures in the Inquisition, or pilgrims. They were the "good" women of the community. As I said before, she was the most revered woman in the community, my grandmother.

The hierarchy of the Church as a whole, and my father, still chose not to see the division between Mary Magdalene and Mother Mary as a paradigm inflicted on Christian women. And my grandmother believed that you could never integrate these two. The Magdalene was the whore, and if there was anything in her granddaughters that smelled of that, we were gone. We were being seduced by the Dark Side. My "extended Christian family" perpetuated this idea of a Satan that can come within and take you over unless you walk their particular Christian path, their way. They let me know that you can literally be possessed. In the spiritual sense, not little men with horns . . . but I believed their God was the sinister one. Don't worry, I'll get to him in a minute.

ANN: *The piano and her songs carried Tori through childhood and into adolescence. The instrument became her vessel as she entered Peabody Conservatory and began playing in church and other public settings. Yet it also continued to transport her into the dominion of her own fantasies and longings, a place where she had ever more to hide.*

TORI:

I remember being quite young, back in Baltimore, before I was eight, in the bedroom I shared with my sister. She wasn't there. It was afternoon, because the light was coming in, and I had this afghan made of wool. And I remember lying underneath it and squeezing my legs and pretending Jesus was there. I didn't know how you had sex, but I felt this feeling at the base of the spine and inside. In the soft place. I was just squeezing, like you do, and feeling him. And it was Jesus; I was thinking of the picture they had downstairs. That's around the time my grandmother said I needed to learn to love Jesus—I just rolled my eyes at her and said, "Grandma, you have no idea."

Around that time I started to listen to Led Zeppelin, focusing mostly on Robert Plant. I would listen to the records and kind of study him. I wanted to figure out why so many Christian fathers were intimidated by him. I remember this very well; the powerful men in the Church didn't want Led Zeppelin records in the house. My father would come home from board meetings and say, "This Zeppelin thing is just a thorn in everybody's side." The girls were moving their hips in a way that was just primal, and it was something that couldn't be controlled or contained—they couldn't stop themselves. See, Robert Plant tapped into something there. The whole band was a part of this, but there was something about Robert that lifted it into a different category. Because he was part of, and continues on some level to be part of, the belief system I was trying to uncover for myself, that marriage of the sacred and the profane.

I was around fifteen when I really learned how badly what I was doing could be perceived in other's eyes. My sister came back from medical school to visit one time, and I tried to get to a place where I could talk about masturbating. And she said to me, "You've got to stop this now. Stop talking about it, and stop doing it." This is how we were brought up. My hand was going to fall off, according to her. It's right back to that shame place, because there was no initiation, no rites to aid the passage into sexuality and make it sacred. Anything you did was profane, even if it felt romantic. Everything went into the music then, after that conversation. I didn't stop masturbating, of course, but I knew I wasn't supposed to do it and that I shouldn't talk about it. We go back to hiding it in my sonic paintings.

I've had a laying-on of hands to try to rid evil from me. I was in confirmation class; my father was there. It was an extremely powerful experience. Not intimidating, but almost as if there were salvation there. In confirmation class everybody had to go through a process of kneeling at the altar, and all I remember was, at a certain point they said something to the effect of "Do you have a desire you need to confess?" and I said, "I desire to masturbate." And the hands went on and they said, "Satan will leave you now." At that point I realized that it wasn't accepted in my inner Christian circle. And you know what I also realized, though I couldn't act on it right away? I didn't need to stop masturbating; I had to change my inner circle.

Masturbation was so, so, so not publicly talked about when I was a teenager. Now, the Internet has changed things in a good way and a bad way; at least kids can find out about such things, even if they're in Bumfuck. Misinformation and exploitation can be spread, but so can people's experience. There are women talking about masturbation now. The sacred, the profane, the balance. I was never exposed to any of that in a way that said it was okay. It's definitely in the songs and will continue to be in the songs.

When I looked back and realized my first crush had been on Jesus, that alone gave me a clue to the type of relationship I wanted in real life: a relationship in which a woman is treated like an equal partner. A relationship in which a woman is respected. From the Gospel of Thomas, also known as the Secret Sayings of Jesus (another one of the manuscripts discovered at Nag Hammadi), I quote from the translation by Dr. Marvin W. Meyer from his book *The Secret Teachings of Jesus: Four Gnostic Gospels.* I'll set the scene for you first. At the end of the Gospel, Jesus is answering questions from the disciples and from Mary Magdalene, and the final question is an inquiry about when the Kingdom will come. And "Peter said to them, 'Let Mary leave us, because women are not worthy of life.' Jesus said, 'Behold, I shall guide her as to make her male so that she too may become a living spirit like you men. For every woman who makes herself male will enter the Kingdom of Heaven.' " Hang on a minute, all you feminists: wait for the translation. In Dr. Meyer's notes he explains, "Here Jesus' response to Peter, though shocking to modern sensitivities, is intended to be a statement of liberation. The female principle is saved when all that is earthly (that is, allied with an earth Mother) is transformed into what is heavenly (that is, allied with the heavenly Father), thus all people on the earth, whether women or men, require such a transformation."

That Jesus stood up to Peter and elevated Mary Magdalene to the male disciples' status made me think, *No wonder Mary dug this guy.* Once, a while ago, I had a kind of waking dream that became a conversation while I was playing the piano. A conversation with Mary Magdalene, who, like a jazz musician, just sat in and started jamming with me. I looked at her with a guilty conscience and said, "You know, Mary Magdalene, I didn't mean to have a crush on your man." And because I didn't hear a response from her, I kept rambling. "You know, maybe it was more like James Taylor. I mean, in 1971 Jesus and James could kind of pass for brothers, and didn't Jesus have a brother named James?" And all of a sudden I heard this throaty, sexy laugh. And in my day-tripper dream world

Mary Magdalene said to me, "Don't you see, you're looking for a guy that treats women a certain way—a guy who wants a complete partnership with a woman." And then she was gone.

SONG CANVAS: "The power of orange knickers"

I started to think about the word *terrorist.* It's a word you hear several times a day now. I started to think about what being a terrorist can mean in different situations. I wanted to explore the realm of personal invasion. Now this would be an invasion by someone you know personally, not a stranger. We all know about strangers being filled with hatred—strangers who lash out against a government or an ideal. As a result, this stranger kills innocent people, tragically, people you may know personally. But when there is an intimacy between two people and one person starts to feel invaded by the other person, that is personalized terrorism. As we all know, the battleground between two lovers, or two friends, or two coworkers can be vicious. Painful. Heartbreaking. And bloody. I started to think about the weapons that might be used in this kind of battle, and as I kept digging for an answer, I stumbled into the Realm of Assonance. I started to think, *Okay, what is the paradox of terrorist?* And Assonance, that beautiful creature, came to my aid and whispered, "Kiss." And sure enough, we have all felt invaded by a lingering kiss, for good or ill. But I had to find terrorism not just in a relationship of a couple—representing two divided Beings—but within one Being. After all, isn't that the ultimate discovery, the ultimate pain—division within the self, the soul from the body, the mind from the heart, wisdom from consciousness, the addiction from the cure, the two Marys . . . divided?

The lyrics started to come to me quickly . . .

The Power of Orange Knickers, under my petty coat. The power of listening to what, you don't want me to know. Can somebody tell me now, who is this terrorist? Those girls that smile kindly, then rip your life to pieces. Can somebody tell me now, am I alone with this—this little pill in my hand and with this secret kiss. Am I alone in this?

ANN: *At the conservatory, the safe space her family had chosen for her, Tori gained sight and sound of the reconciliation the Church denied.*

CONVERSATION BETWEEN TORI AND ANN:

The funny thing was, my father saw music as the thing that was going to save me from sexuality. It was my protector from possible disaster, because I was at home practicing, not hanging around after school getting stoned or getting pregnant. And right under his nose I was discovering the free space of music. I would watch the guitarists, these men with their axes; it was seductive, and they were one with their instruments. And nothing came in between them and their desire. It's kind of the hard-core version of Brooke Shields saying "Nothing comes between me and my Calvins," as she did in the famously racy 1980 advertisement for Calvin Klein jeans. My dad, hypothetically speaking, could pull me out of, you know, a car if I was kissing some boy. If he wanted to, he could physically pull me out. But here were these musicians, right in the place where I was supposed to be, and they were conjoined with their instruments. You could not divide them. And you couldn't invade them, either, unlike the way the Church and its ideas had invaded my consciousness.

I still didn't give up the Church. You have to remember, my father was my manager after I left the conservatory. I was playing in gay bars, but he was steering my career. I'm still going to services every Sunday at age twenty-one. I felt at the time, I think, that I could overcome the contradictions. I had never believed that degradation was the path of the Magdalene. I didn't care what the interpreters of the Bible said. And the more I researched it, the more I discovered what was right. At the same time, I was looking for what Robert Plant was tapping into. This sensuality without the subservience. But really, in my life, I was still experiencing the division between the sacred and the profane. I was not experiencing the transformation of the profane into the sacred. Not yet.

Finally, a month or so after my twenty-first birthday, I moved to L.A. Partly, I was trying to get away from my father's control. At a certain point, the curfews he was imposing, the protectiveness, it was just over-bearing—considering I worked six nights a week, bringing home my own bacon. At the time we were having too many disagreements. Whom he wanted me to date and whom I wanted to date . . . it was just all falling apart then. And I knew that I had to become a woman.

In L.A., ironically enough, I lived behind the Methodist church on Highland and Franklin. But I started running around with all sorts of people and getting exposed to all sorts of ways of thinking. This period was a huge turning point for me because I decided what I was going after, even if I didn't know how to go after it yet. I was around other people who'd come from kind of the same place I had, escaping their upbringing, so everybody was always searching. I was exposed to other cultures and began to see how different people worshiped and how different people looked at the joining of two people. Yet I was still having personal relationships in which I had to take on a role. And this lasted for a long time. Until I was broken down enough on such a level that something in me rose up to the powers that be and just said, "No. I don't need you to see me as an honorable woman, or as an object of desire; I don't need to pay respect to your Gods."

During those years in Hollywood, what worked was the rock chick type or the folk poet. So much of the music business is about men desiring you.

I mean, there weren't a lot of ugly women getting signed. Maybe in some way I decided, *This is what the industry seems to want, and everything that I'm doing isn't working.* When I would turn in the tapes of me at the piano to various producers or A&R men, the responses would be, "This is not happening. Nobody wants this. The piano girl thing is dead." To you who are reading this right now, that statement, "The piano girl thing is dead," seems ridiculous in light of what is occurring right now in music. And it was a ridiculous, unfounded assertion. But it was implemented by the Record Company Cheeses, and it did its damage.

It took a while to recover and reintegrate. By the time I finally got to make *Little Earthquakes,* I made a conscious decision not to be objectified here. My material had to be about the content, not the powder-puff compact. They couldn't come between me and my piano. So in a way, no matter what people wrote about how I was onstage at the time, I think I desexualized myself. I was trying to find out who this person was who played the piano. There was a return to the girl I had been at five, who had her own beliefs when she stood up to her grandmother. When she stood up to the patriarchy of the Christian Church. At this time in my life there was a reclaiming of a person. A person whom I had locked out of the proceedings at a certain point.

I wrote a song during the recording of *Little Earthquakes* that never got released, and one of the lines was "Boy masturbating down the hall in the dark"—that's how it starts. I can't remember much more, but I remember the next verse:

I have 50 hearts, they're all in 50 different drawers
When you come calling I always put the purple one on
If I dumped all 50 out on the living room floor
would you say clean up the mess before I get home?

It was just one of those moments of seeing fifty different girls inside myself. There's a girl who goes and does business. There's a girl who attends church. There's a girl who has sex, too. She knows her trade. There were so many girls, I couldn't keep track of the keys to the hotel . . . And the men I was dating at the time may or may not have seen these divisions. Here I was, declaring myself a steward of the Magdalene, uniting the two Marys, and yet in my life I was the complete opposite. This was the paradox.

SONG CANVAS: "God"

With *Little Earthquakes* I started to face down the split between the Marys, both personally and in the larger sense. I continued to explore it during the *Under the Pink* phase. I think taking on the role of Ms. God, or God's lover in the song I wrote called "God" (from *Under the Pink*) was a big step for me personally in reuniting the two Marys within my Being. I began to realize that I needed the voices of both Marys to hold an anchor for the Ms. God archetype I was to embody in order to sing this song. I'll ask myself the question that other people have asked me over the years: "Define which God, Tori. Which God is the God in the song 'God'? Do you mean God, God?" And my answer is "It depends on who you think God, God is." In *Beyond Belief: The Secret Gospel of Thomas*, Elaine Pagels makes the "God behind God" concept of certain early Christians quite clear by quoting from different texts found in Nag Hammadi. Referring to the Apocryphon, the Secret Book of John, Pagels writes, "The Secret Book tells a story intended to show that although the creator-god pictured in Genesis is *himself* only an anthropomorphic image of the divine Source that brought forth the universe, many people mistake this deficient image for God. This story tells how the creator-god himself, being unaware of the 'blessed one, the Mother-Father, the blessed and compassionate One' above, boasted that he was the only God ('I'm a jealous God; there is none other besides me'). Intent on maintaining sole power, he tried to control his human creatures by forbidding them to eat the fruit of the tree of knowledge."

Here I need to refer again to Dr. Meyer's *The Secret Teachings of Jesus* from the Gospel, the Secret Book of John. The one we know as Jesus the Savior is teaching his disciple John:

> Now Sophia, who is the Wisdom of Afterthought and who represents an eternal realm, conceived of a thought. She had this idea and this invisible Spirit of Knowledge also reflected upon it. She wanted to give birth to a being like herself . . . rather, something came out of her that was imperfect and different in appearance from her, for she had produced it without her lover. It did not look like its Mother and had a different shape . . . she threw it away from her, outside that realm, so that none of the Immortals would see it. For she had produced it ignorantly. She surrounded it with a bright cloud and put a throne in the middle of it except for the Holy Spirit, who is called the Mother of the Living. She named her child Yaldaboath. Yaldaboath is the first Ruler who took great power from his Mother . . . this gloomy Ruler has three names: the first name is Yaldaboath, the second is Saklas. The third is Samael. He is wicked because of the mindlessness that is within him when he said, "I am God and there is no other God besides me." The Lord continued speaking to John . . . "The arrogant one took power from his Mother, he was ignorant, for he thought that no other power existed except for his Mother. He saw the throng of angels he had created and exalted himself over them."

In *The Gnostic Gospels*, Elaine Pagels writes, "According to the *Hypostasis of the Archons*, discovered at Nag Hammadi, both the mother and her daughter objected when 'he became arrogant, saying, "It is I who am God, and there is no other apart from me." . . . And a voice came forth from above the realm of absolute power, saying, "You are wrong, Samael" (which means "god of the blind"). And he said, "If any other thing exists before me, let it appear to me!" And immediately, Sophia ("Wisdom") stretched forth her finger, and introduced light into matter, and she followed it down into the region of Chaos. . . . And he again said to his offspring, "It is I who am the God of All." And Life, the daughter of Wisdom, cried out; she said to him, "You are wrong Saklas!" ' "

So to answer the question, this is the God to whom I refer in the song "God." I am not referring to Jesus' Divine Father termed the "holy Parent, the completely perfect Forethought, the image of the Invisible One, that is, the Father of everything, through him everything came into being, the first Humanity," again from Meyers. In this translation Jesus frequently refers to himself as "the Child of Humanity."

CONVERSATION BETWEEN TORI AND ANN:

At that time my life as a woman seemed settled. I was involved with my producing partner, Eric Rosse. We thought we were a lifelong thing. We were looking at buying a house in the Taos area of New Mexico. But the truth is, we were more collaborators than man and wife. We were really dear friends. There was a deep respect and pairing, but I wasn't his girlfriend at heart. I wasn't his squeeze.

After making *Under the Pink*, we were just worn out. We broke up during the tour. The whole crew knew about the breakup and saw other men sort of coming in and out of my life. There was certainly gossip. Mark, my future husband (who kept his distance), was around; he was the engineer on this tour. He just kept to the sidelines, observing, occasionally bringing me a cup of tea. I had a crush on him from the first day I saw him, but this was months and months before we got together. And I was busy chasing baby demons.

The *Under the Pink* tour was long, and the compartmentalization within me had gotten worse and worse. The fragmentation process had worked perfectly. It can be very functional. I think that's why a lot of women have affairs, why they lead other lives. It all has to come out some way unless you find a way to say, *No, I'm one person, I let my hair down, I have a good time with my friends, I put my hair back up, but either way I'm the same person—I just have different sides.*

Shapes with different sides . . . The hexagon. The honeycomb, a structure of hexagonal cells constructed from beeswax. While writing the songs for *The Beekeeper,* my latest album, I've been walking through many different types of gardens. The songs were trying to show me that they formed a shape and were independent but connected to each other, no different from the structure of hexagonal cells that make up the beehive.

Margaret Starbird, author of *The Woman with the Alabaster Jar: Mary Magdalen and the Holy Grail* and *The Goddess in the Gospels,* has been inspirational to many daughters of the Christian Church, myself included. She is also "a faithful daughter of the Roman Catholic Church" and years ago set out to prove that the idea of Jesus' being married to Mary Magdalene was a heresy she had to clarify. This educated Christian woman has shaken one of the pillars of the Christian patriarchy. In her words, "It is my conviction that Christianity and its inception included the celebration of the hieros gamos, the 'sacred marriage' of opposites, a model incarnate in the archetypal Bridegroom and his bride—Jesus Christ and the woman called Magdalene." In her latest book, *Magdalene's Lost Legacy*, she writes about the symbol of sacred marriage: ✡. "Jewish rabbinical tradition teaches that the Ark of the Covenant kept in the Holy of Holies of Solomon's Temple on Mount Zion in Jerusalem contained, in addition to the tablets on which the Ten Commandments were inscribed, a 'man and a woman locked in intimacy in the form of a hexagram'—the intimate union of the opposites."

The beehive, formed of hexagons, was foundational for the visual piece of *The Beekeeper*. Once it was clear that we were working within the structure that was made of six sides, I began to subdivide the album into six segments. A large subtext of *The Beekeeper* is the garden, though our version of "the Garden of Original Sin" metamorphoses into "the Garden of Original Sin-suality." Our garden is made up of "the archetypal symbols for male and female, the V (chalice) and the Λ (blade)" (as mentioned by Starbird in her book, *Magdalene's Lost Legacy*). She goes on to say, "This feminine association of bees was known and honored in ancient times: priestesses of the goddess Artemis were called *melissae*, and Demeter was called 'the pure Mother Bee.' In Hebrew the name of Deborah, one of the great Old Testament heroines, means 'queen bee.' "

Our sonic garden for *The Beekeeper* is made up of Desert Garden, Rock Garden, The Orchard, The Greenhouse, Elixirs and Herbs, and Roses and Thorns. This is where the story of original Sin-suality between male and female takes place.

SONG CANVAS: "Marys of the sea"

There is a chorus here, clearly. Funny, but this one was inspired by an old folktale that I was reading the other day, the tale of Mélusine. I'm just beginning to write the verse lyrics and chorus. The music I've been haunted by while developing the verse for this is a piano riff that I found for less than—oh, I don't know—less than a minute on the tape I was listening to while on the rowing machine. I haven't committed to any final melody to go with this verse. I've got about seventeen that I sing in the shower, and none of them has won "Ms. World" as the melody for "Marys of the Sea" yet. But I'm haunted by this piano riff, knowing that it has to join up seamlessly with the chorus. The verse piano riff is a musical motif that keeps circling itself, conjuring the picture of a ring, an image that happens to work with our story.

While I was researching this I found out that the early Christians were into ring dancing around Jesus' time, before the Council Creeds of

Mary Magdalene

Nicaea (A.D. 325) and Constantinople (A.D. 381) were imposed on Christianity. This compelled me to dig for information wherever I could. I found a folktale based on the power of the ring myth, which had me chasing the Ring Lord myth (the one on which Tolkien based *The Lord of the Rings*). Historically there is a Ring Lord culture, harkening back to ancient Sumerian and Scythian times. In ancient Sumeria (pronounced Shumeria) in the Mesopotamian region, the Anunnaki gods and goddesses from approximately 4000 B.C. were implementing the ring as part of the municipal government. I wanted to chase down a historical story that originated with Tiamat, the Dragon Queen, and I found one. The story of Mélusine, whose tale (and eventually *tail*) finds her carrying the three rings, ends up in modern-day France. She is of a tradition that echoes back to the sacred feminine. The story seems to date from A.D. 733, which shows us that the ring dance had been able to sustain itself for thousands of years. It seems to have occurred in ancient Sumeria possibly originating in Scythia, which stretched from the Black Sea region over the Carpathian Mountains, known to us as the Balkans.

The philosophy of the ring culture seemed to spread from Scythia to Mesopotamia to Egypt to Europe to what is now known as Ireland and Great Britain, where the ring represented eternity, wholeness, and unity. Many goddesses have been featured through ancient history with the symbols of the ring and the rule, the rule symbolizing a just universal law and the ring symbolizing sovereignty. Some historians think it is possible that Jesus danced the ring, that he partook in the dance as an ancient sacred ceremony. St. Augustine of Hippo, according to ancient texts, wrote about a ring dance ascribed to Jesus and the apostles. This would mean that the Magdalene probably danced the ring as well and might have brought the rings' symbolic wisdom to their inner circle herself.

As I'm pulling in different possibilities to try and crack the code of this song, I sketch everything on the canvas. There will be many canvases for "Marys of the Sea"—*Les Saintes Maries de la Mer*. Because the Magdalene went to France in A.D. 44 and died in what is now called Saint Baume in A.D. 63 in Aix-en-Provence, she is remembered as the Mistress of the Waters. I've chosen to incorporate the phrase in French, because it has existed in this form for hundreds and hundreds of years as the story has been passed down and is with us today.

I'm trying to include different sides to the Magdalene myth in "Marys of the Sea." Naturally this includes Mary Magdalene as part of the *hieros gamos*, sacred marriage, but also included as a subtext is the sexist attitude toward women held by the disciple Peter and the apostle Paul, fathers to the theology of the Roman Catholic Church. This sexist sentiment was echoed by men hailing from the early orthodox Christian tradition, one of whom was Bishop Irenaeus (who could be a dead ringer for my religious grandmother if you ignore their sex difference). Bishop Irenaeus was not a fan of what we call the Gnostic Gospels, and neither was another religious man called Tertullian. From Elaine Pagels and *The Gnostic Gospels:* "Tertullian directed another attack against 'that viper'—a woman teacher who led a congregation in North Africa. He himself agreed with what he called the 'precepts of ecclesiastical discipline concerning women,' which specified: 'It is not permitted for a woman to speak in the church, nor is it permitted for her to teach, nor to baptize, nor to offer [the eucharist], nor to claim for herself a share in any *masculine* function—not to mention any priestly office.' "

"Marys of the Sea" was also inspired by *The Gospel of Mary Magdalene* translated from the Coptic with commentary by Jean-Yves Leloup. This Gospel sheds a lot of light on the inner relationship of the disciples. Peter's envy of Mary Magdalene is obvious when, in this Gospel, Mary is recounting what Jesus (the Teacher) had taught her in private. When she was finished, after Andrew (Peter's brother) expressed that he did not believe the Teacher had spoken these ideas, ". . . And Peter added: 'How is it possible that the Teacher talked in this manner, with a woman, about secrets of which we ourselves are ignorant? Must we change our customs, and listen to this woman? Did he really choose her, and prefer her to us?' "

After Jean-Yves Leloup's explanation of this quote, which expanded my perception of this, the Gospel continues, "Then Mary wept, and answered him: 'My brother Peter, what can you be thinking? Do you believe that this is just my own imagination, that I invented this vision? Or do you believe that I would lie about our Teacher?' "

In that moment it becomes crystal clear that this is a woman who just cannot win. She cannot win in history, as she has been relegated to her position as prostitute. She cannot win with her contemporaries, many of whom are disciples, because they are filled with jealousy over her intimacy with Yeshua or Jesus (the Teacher).

I have chosen to highlight Jesus and Mary Magdalene's intimacy in the song "Marys of the Sea." I was partially inspired to do this by a quote from the Gospel of Philip (59:9), which I quote here from Jean-Yves Leloup's introduction in *The Gospel of Mary Magdalene:* "With regard to the unique and particular nature of his relationship with Mary Magdalene, the Gospel of Philip insists, for example, that Mary is the special companion of Jesus (*koinonos*) . . . 'The Lord loved Mary more than all the disciples, and often used to kiss her on the mouth. When the others saw how he loved Mary, they said, "Why do you love her more than you love us?" The Savior answered in this way: "How can it be that I do not love you as much as I love her?" ' "

Also referenced in this song are the scarlet women, the sacred women—the Hierodulau. The Black Madonna has been attributed to the Magdalene by many. From *Bloodline of the Holy Grail* by Laurence Gardner:

The Black Madonna has her tradition in Queen Isis and her roots in the pre-patriarchal Lilith. She thus represents the strength and equality of womanhood—a proud, forthright and commanding figure, as against the strictly subordinate image of the conventional White Madonna as seen in Church representations of Jesus' mother. It was said that both Isis and Lilith knew the secret name of God (a secret held also by Mary Magdalene, "the woman who knew the all"). The Black Madonna is thus also representative of the Magdalene who, according to the Alexandrian doctrine, "transmitted the true secret of Jesus." In fact, the long-standing Magdalene cult was closely associated with Black Madonna locations. She is black because Wisdom (Sophia) is black, having existed in the darkness of Chaos before the Creation. To the Gnostics of Simon Zelotes, Wisdom was the Holy Spirit—the great and immortal Sophia who brought forth the First Father, Yaldaboath, from the depths.

Hundreds of years after the historical *Les Saintes Maries de la Mer* occurred, apparently because the Magdalene traveled with two other Marys as well, we discover the historical Mélusine who brings her rings to France from the old Pictish lands of Caledonia (in the far north of Britain, which was later incorporated into what we now know as Scotland). In the end, Mélusine will likely end up evolving into an entirely different song and "Marys of the Sea" will remain her own. An amicable split will eventually occur—as cells in the body would do—creating an offshoot of the original bloodline.

ANN: *Change can come slowly or hit like a hurricane. Entering her thirties, Amos kept on her journey toward integration. As her renown grew, each recording showed evidence of the next step on this hard path. The leap came with* Boys for Pele, *a head-to-head encounter with the dismembered feminine. The claustrophobic, clear sound of that album reflects the moment when Amos stood at the lip of her own volcano and made a sacrifice of her illusions. Stepping out of the realm of metaphor, Amos suffered a real initiation. Through it she met the Hawaiian goddess of fire, who became her album's namesake. She also met a male essence that she'd been chasing, and avoiding, for years: the Dark Prince, the other muse for the fiery efforts of this period.*

CONVERSATION BETWEEN TORI AND ANN:

During *Pele* I really started to explore the Dark Prince archetype. It's one that a lot of men have been able to explore, from Jim Morrison on down to Trent Reznor, and I felt it was calling me. With my religious upbringing I felt I really needed to discover that. It was different from the Magdalene essence. I'd been studying her for a long time, and she was a muse. But I needed to access the Dark Prince in myself, instead of pulling in men who had access to it. But that was yet to come.

I was courting demon lovers at the time, but I didn't know who the real Demon Lover was. I knew I needed to initiate myself. So I went to Hawaii by myself and began that quest. I worked with a woman, a shaman, who was reputed to know how to take you on a spiritual journey by uncovering things you were avoiding in your view of yourself. While I was in Hawaii, locals were talking about the goddess Pele in a way that I had heard of, but so distantly; it wasn't something that was in my framework like the Greek goddesses or the Norse or the Celts. Eventually I began to see, not a malevolence, but—through Pele, Kali, and Sekhmet, a few of the dark goddesses—I was really beginning to discover anger. I didn't know how to contain it yet.

So an apprenticeship began. This woman had done a lot of work with medicine men in South America and Central America, and because she was of the Feminine I felt comfortable with her. We spent a lot of time diving into archetypes. I began to have a relationship with the Dark Prince; I allowed his archetype to seed in me.

When I use this term, *the Dark Prince*, this is my definition of a male essence that is able to shed light in darkness. Darkness, in this context, is referring to that which is hidden. Access to the Dark Goddesses and the Dark Prince had been strictly forbidden as a "daughter of the Christian Church." The idea formed in me that somehow Satan would be there, waiting, exposing any of us young women—sort of like the Gestapo—to the hierarchy of the Christian Patriarchal Church. There were times when I began to think, with strange humor, that Satan secretly worked as an undercover agent for the authoritative side of the Christian Church. I could almost feel the hidden cameras on me, sort of like a Christian moral majority Big Brother, watching when I or any other woman would pick up controversial works by people such as Carl Jung. Works that began to dissect the unconscious. The shadow. The darkness. Thereby making archetypes accessible and tangible. Archetypes as a Forethought and an Afterthought, heralding us as imprisoned Christian women to break the Apostolic chains that were like anchors on our clitoris.

So when I use the term *Prince of Darkness* I see his essence more in cahoots with a doctor of the unconscious—Dr. Carl Jung. *Satanic*, however, is something I started to find very much ingrained in our day-to-day world. Now, obviously, when I say that, clearly there are different levels of satanic—the horrific acts that we hear about, whether on TV or through personal experiences. In a more subtle way I found it more sinister in a "business as usual" manner. The key for me here was the idea of hypocrisy, the definition of which I take from *Collins English Dictionary:* "the practice of professing standards, belief, etc., contrary to one's real character or actual behavior." I found this subtle form of the satanic in the forms of friendships. I found it among the crew. I found it within people with whom I worked in the music business. I found it within myself. The hell-shattering moment was when I realized that satanic hypocrisy was not out there somewhere, out there with the terrorists in the world . . . but that hell was in the inner circle. But so was heaven. The teacher tried to ingrain this in me: "You cannot control the fates, but you can control how you as Tori are going to respond to them."

Ayuhuasca is a root from the Amazon that tribal people would take in ceremony. It's an eighteen-hour journey, and it invades the psyche. You're aware, you're awake, but everything you store in the unconscious starts to get unleashed. It's very parable-oriented; things are in parables, and you have to be able to read them.

It can burn you up in some ways if you're not ready to look at certain parts of your subconscious, and, especially if you view your life as a situation in which everybody else has done everything to you, it's not going to be a good journey for you. You will start to see how you've also been manipulative. Nobody is blameless. If you take this substance, you will see that there's not a "Get Out of Jail Free" card; there's nobody you can call. You're on that trip and no shot can bring you out. And I've been with people on the journey; in groups I've done it . . . there was one girl who was trying to bite her own arm off. Because you can go that far down. You want to devour yourself because of what you've been up to. It's always a shock to see your own reflection.

I fasted and prepared myself for ceremony, and I knew that I was on my knees. I was at a place where I couldn't extort somebody else's essence and energy like an emotional vampire. There had been people who wanted to have power over me in some way, or be voyeurs of my life. I had to stop blaming them and realize that I really wanted to merge with this essence. But we're back to the idea of merging the sacred and the profane.

A lot of people around me at that time were turned on by cheap come-ons, drawn to thinking that the Dark Prince was somebody who would handcuff you and give you the orgasm of your life. Well, he

pele, the Hawaiian fire goddess

doesn't need to handcuff you. It's boring. Go handcuff yourself. I'm not talking about Satan, either; people have projections on Satan, as we've talked about, and I have my own, too.

The revelation to me was, I was at that place on my path where, instead of the darkness being outside, it was inside. I needed to acknowledge what it could do. I would always say, *Well, everything will work out in the end.* But if you're not able to acknowledge that some people are fundamentally greedy, you will be surprised that, when push comes to shove, even people that you care about may not choose the moral code. I needed to see that there were people, including myself, who could have good traits *and* traits that would enslave another person. So I went into ceremony and met the Dark Prince.

When I went on this trip I had a sexual/spiritual experience with a creature named Lucifer. The word *Lucifer* is from Latin, meaning "light-bearer," also defined as the planet Venus in its appearance as the morning star. The other Being I had an experience with was called Davide. He seemed like a blond angel figure. Light and dark. So to me they represented Dionysus and Apollo—that's the best way to put it. In my Being I was merging, and I remember him saying to me, "The seed is being planted, a really important seed. You will be pregnant, but with yourself, with a part of yourself. You need to give birth to a part of yourself that has been cut out." *Circumcised,* I think was their word. A part of my soul had been circumcised. And they really made love to my woman in a way that I had never, ever—I mean, you want to talk about being loved out of my own purgatory . . .

They said to me that I had to find the male within myself who is this demon lover. He has to love my woman. So I asked the Dark Prince, "What are you made up of?" He said, "You have to stop chasing baby demons. A lot of people think darkness is making somebody emotionally defecate on themselves. That's baby demon stuff." He said, "Let's get to a place where you can call these guys teachers, and I say that with a small t. But the lessons can be huge. These baby demons can be wonderful in some ways. Wonderful in some ways, highly conscious in some ways, but until they've done their work on their shadow, they are more concerned with the power of seduction and the control over another Being than anything else." He said, "The baby demons are obvious because there's nothing that they're hiding. They're not even trying to hide. They don't even dance with profanity, they don't respect profanity's power over them; therefore, they drown in it, unknowingly. Pulling down with them everyone who is attached to them. And in the end, honestly, women are there solely so that these baby demons can put another female scalp on their belt." "Ouch," I said as I crossed my legs. "You asked," is what I heard back.

He said, "The tricky thing is when you have people who really do good things for humanity and to free the soul, but then in other ways will hook you. And you feel that it's a betrayal because you didn't think that this was possible in them. And until you've really, really done the work on yourself and you're able to catch yourself, when you're fishing for heart bait, this will keep happening." I began slowly to see how I would come across people who do wonderful acts for humanity, whether they were involved in making music or in social causes that were great for the world, but then would come home and shame their girlfriend.

Boys for Pele ended up being about those people, and that spirit in myself. We all have the capacity to act in a way that could invade another being. And until you're willing to see this in yourself, you think that you're above it. *Pele* was about not being above that. Before then, I could not see how I was a part of that, because I was on the victims' team. I had to look at how members of Victims Anonymous could wear badges on their sleeves and hold everybody hostage to their victimization. So it's coming to understand that essence, really. And it's in songs like "Blood Roses" and "Professional Widow."

I did have to listen to the Dark Prince when he said, "Stop playing with the baby demons. Baby demons are men in training on their path who will defecate on women in any way." If you're drawn to that, as I was during that time, you need to look at what in your own male aspect is fucking your woman up the ass with her head smashed into the pillow. That's stuff to make you throw up. And you have to take responsibility. I wanted baby demons because I desired what they could access. But once it got down to it and I would be in a room alone with one of them, I would kind of go, "Do I really desire this guy?" And my inner chick would say, "He's a turnoff; I mean, his hands smell like onions—and he's not an Italian chef." These were guys who became friends but first drew me in because I found in them something I needed to see in myself.

That's what the Dark Prince told me. "You need to spend time. Your male needs to spend time with your woman, take her shopping." I did that. I spent a little bit of time before I got into another heavy relationship, which was Mark after that.

ANN: *The romance with Mark Hawley led Amos into a new kind of fairy tale—not the ravishment of the princess by the beast, but the less obviously dramatic story of the unassuming sweetheart who waits in the wings until his belle is*

ready for ordinary happiness. Hawley offered Amos respect and artistic partner-
ship; as the main engineer on Boys for Pele, *he created a pristine space in which*
she could articulate the rage the Dark Prince and the dark goddesses demanded.
Over the years, they have forged a creative partnership and a model for contem-
porary marriage—equal parts passion and humor, exhilaration and amicability.
Their relationship has allowed Amos to turn back to her project of integrating
the sacred feminine and profane in her music with a new sense of poise, to turn
outward, beyond confession, with a better understanding of how these patterns
affect all women.

CONVERSATION BETWEEN TORI AND ANN:

I hadn't had a date with him; he had just been on the sidelines, sort of
watching me do all these shenanigans. We didn't have much interaction
beyond hello, good morning. I had a crush on him for ages, though. I had
sexual feelings for him from the beginning. I wasn't thinking about having a conversation with him. I wasn't thinking about making music. I was
thinking about a walk in the rain and getting caught. I was thinking about
an affair.

JOHN WITHERSPOON:

It sounds really patronizing, but I gave her permission to pursue him toward the end of the Pink tour. She implied she kind of liked him, and I
was like, "Look, he's a really good sound guy and we're in the middle of
a tour. The last thing we want now is something going wrong because you
two got together and you fall out and then he leaves, and Marcel the monitor engineer will go with him because he's his best mate and . . ." I said,
"Can you just like hang on a little bit?" But she couldn't.

It was actually very well planned, their getting together. It had to be,
because nobody else really needed to know except them, and me, and Joel,

her bodyguard. So it was a case of trying to get them together but keep it private. It was a day off, I think, in South Bend, Indiana. And they kind of arranged that they were going to go out for a walk. It was funny, 'cause Joel and I had to sort of patrol around. Mark and Tori came down into the lobby and I was in the little gift shop, and I saw Joel hiding behind a newspaper and I had to go out an emergency exit. We were just trying to give them a bit of privacy.

CONVERSATION BETWEEN TORI AND ANN:

Eventually Mark and I did become friends and started sort of confiding in each other. And I remember, one time, he said, "Tell me why it is that women invariably pull the same kind of men to them? The one that will taste them, eat them, swallow them, and then spit them out." In this British accent, I'll never forget it. It's embedded in my mind. That's when I knew this was it. He went on: "Spit them out, leave them at the side of the road, drive away, back up, kick the door open and say, 'You want to go for another ride?' " And I sat there and thought, *There are knights in this world. This is the prince.*

ANDY SOLOMON:

It was a surprise to me. I came around the corner one day—I think we were in New Haven, Connecticut—and I literally, like, came around a drape onstage and I ran into them and they were hugging. I was like, "What's wrong? You guys okay?" I thought they were comforting each other because somebody had died or something.

A few people knew before I did, but that was when I found out. Later, we would have talks on the bus and I'd say to Mark, who'd been my friend for a long time, "Look. This is not such a good idea, you know. If you're bad in bed your career could be over." He'd be like, "Don't worry, don't worry. Everything's going to be fine." And I was wrong, you know. And I'm happy to be wrong.

CONVERSATION BETWEEN TORI AND ANN:

I really feel like my husband is my boyfriend. I am having an affair with my husband, and sometimes plates fly. There's no question. This is someone who is tenacious and has his own way of looking at things. I mean, he wanted to get married, but only if we lived in England. To be his wife required serious change for me. And there are serious boundaries. It is about monogamy with him. That's just it. I think marriage takes more perseverance sometimes than any other endeavor. But this suits my skirt just fine, primarily because I've always been reticent about the concept of "Happily Ever After." The garden will have weeds and pests that may damage crops; it may even have pestilence to contend with once in a while. But with the right combination of elements, including bees and butterflies, the garden will pollinate and become a garden—not an emotional wasteland but a place of sensuality and balance. So it may need a good beekeeper; all complex gardens do.

ANN: *Having found her human partner, Amos is free to refine the expression of sexuality within her art. She continues to make this task the focus of her work, both onstage and in the studio.*

CONVERSATION BETWEEN TORI AND ANN:

In the beginning I knew that the Magdalene was my teacher. But I couldn't get the information and I didn't know the walk. I didn't know how to do it. So you're casting your lines of questions into what seems a silent, visionless sea, and you know you're stupid because the sea can't be visionless. You're looking for signs all the time . . . but what do they look like? So there you go again, casting your line, looking for little signs. But do you need X-ray vision to even see them? Well, first of all, I had to redefine the clichéd term *freedom for women.* I've heard women who do X-rated movies say that they're liberated. That's their right. In a way, it's no different from the way I was approaching sexuality at the beginning of my career. But when a woman is being defecated on emotionally or physically, then we are up to our necks in the Profane, with Sacred nowhere near that casting call. The whole sensuality is gone. It's the brutality of power at its cruelest. We've missed what it's supposed to be about, which is the ecstasy, the coming together. Sex becomes about one person being the subject of somebody else's power, which so often is what Religion is about, too. I've never quite figured out if Sex is in Religion's harem or if Religion is in Sex's harem.

I've asked myself, *Is there a way to reach orgasm and keep your spirituality intact?* To me that is the orgasm of all orgasms, which is what I think I'm experiencing in performance. Not literally, but in an artistic sense. And what you ultimately want is to experience this when you join with your man or your physical counterpart.

We are penalized if we are able to hump energetically like the men. It pisses people off because we don't need them in that case. And it makes people nervous as hell.

SONG CANVAS: "LUST"

I had to bring performance to the sacred for myself. That doesn't mean that there isn't a lot of sensuality and sexuality involved, or that you don't get passionate. There is a primal thing that goes on when it's hot, as they say. There's this magnetic quality. It's like you're having an emotional affair with thousands of people, if you look at it like that. It's funny—we do these little meet and greets sometimes before a show, and I'll hear people say, "She's a really lovely lady" backstage before I go on, after they've just met me. But they're quite surprised that lovely ladies can go do what I do onstage.

If we can just for five seconds get past Bodily Functions 101, get past that first step of masturbation and into a higher level of eroticism, maybe I can explain it. I think we have to walk into another culture for a minute. Let's talk about the Kundalini being activated. At the base of the spine, the idea of the snake is coiled. And that's what a song like "Lust," which I wrote after marrying Mark, was really tapping into. The idea of rolling and unrolling, coiling and merging—energy moving through the underworld to the real world. Under flesh into the heart, then taking it back to the real world.

Similarly the song "Sweet the Sting," on *The Beekeeper*, makes my hips sway. This to me is a musical example of the marriage of the sacred and the profane.

CONVERSATION BETWEEN TORI AND ANN:

I've realized that my childhood instincts were right. Take Robert Plant, for example. When I met him, I talked with him about what I thought about him when I was a girl. He told me he had been into the white magic thing, as they say. We've joked about how he so famously called himself a Golden God—I said, no, you were the Golden Goddess . . .

My whole goal has been to penetrate the patriarchy from the day I was five. Sometimes what you have to do is inspire young men so that they don't want to become a part of the abusive side of all that. We all have to reapproach the question *What is a powerful male, a powerful female? How are those roles abused?* If you go after that core, you don't have to worry about who is part of the peace movement, who is part of Earth First, who is part of Amnesty International. That will take care of itself. But, if you've got 15,000 kids chanting, "Die, bitch, die" at a concert, you may have just lost the battle. They are not going to vote for a female president in that state of mind. So you have to come back to the question *What is political? What is social?* But if you go for the core, then you will automatically invite both of them to come in and be characters in this play. Sometimes I have found that just to be able to permeate the rigid power stance you come up against in a confrontation, the key is not to try to match their venom but instead to crawl inside their psyche. I want to be right back there in that pituitary and crawl in like a snake.

SONG CANVAS: "I'm Not in Love"

I covered the 10cc song "I'm Not in Love" on *Strange Little Girls.* Neil Gaiman, who worked closely on the project with me, and I developed this character who was very much based on the film *Betty Blue* and certain women that have come to my shows—this element of the dominatrix. I did research on dominatrix behavior because I have met a few and I got along with them, but of course I wasn't at the end of their whip and would never be. It just wouldn't occur. We would have tea, preferably Japanese.

I called Neil about this one gal I met, because he does a lot of research on his characters. As I was going to let this character embody me, I needed to understand all that I was taking on board. My Poppa always taught me that if I were going to shape-shift and let these essences inhabit me, then I really needed to prepare myself and understand the psyche I was going to be taking on. He always insisted on this in order to protect my personal essence before I took on another character's essence.

So Neil went through the character's different aspects, asking me questions. *Betty Blue* was one element; that film really had an impact on me, and so she was there somewhat representing the way in which my character was damaged as a female. That's one thing. Another aspect of this character is that she provides a service. A very important one. And I needed to be able to take on board, as a consenting adult, what that service was.

If we go back into the mythic, as long as there is domination of the feminine, we must have dominatrices to correct that imbalance. You know, I'm told that certain old-school men in the music industry require dominatrices to rebalance them so they can be ruthless in their work and immune to the pain they are inflicting. They're doing their penance, these entertainment industry cheeses who then subjugate their artists.

CONVERSATION BETWEEN TORI AND ANN:

I investigated a similar character in "Amber Waves," on *Scarlet's Walk.* The Magdalene and America are really good synonyms, because they've both been pimped out, though they always resurface. I'm talking about the land of America now, not the government. She appeared to me as a fading porn star. That character is based on an acquaintance of mine who had turned her life over to a man; I was watching her demise. In part it comes from a film, too—in *Boogie Nights,* the Julianne Moore character's name is Amber Waves. But in the end, she's another version of the Magdalene. That's why the song is sexy and not just sad. She retains her dignity in her soul by asking the question "Are the Northern Lights drowning or are they just waving?"

ANN: *Whatever form Amos's music takes next, it will, in some way, still serve and reveal the Magdalene. Fervent afternoons in her childhood bedroom, patent leather nights in L.A., the revelations of Hawaii—these are all part of the seedbed. There, too, plays Natashya, always a presence now, the embodiment of a new generation of girls forced to cross the divides forged by history. For her daughter and all young innocents, Amos hopes to offer a bridge.*

CONVERSATION BETWEEN TORI AND ANN:

Today I feel as if I walk a line of Mommy and the Sacred Prostitute. It's funny—because of where we live, Tash is going to a Christian school. She comes home with ideas about God. She said to me just the other day, "Mummy, do you believe in God?" And my instinct was to ask her, "Do you mean the God behind God?" And you know what I did? I said to myself, "Jeez, T, back off, she's only three and a half. This is your point of view, not necessarily hers." She says she wants to pray. So when I see that what Tash really wants to do is to just hold hands and say grace, "Let's go, I say, let's bless everything." And we do. She prays for absolutely everybody—dogs, children, mermaids, God, Mrs. God—literally everybody. We're also weaving in dear Mother Earth; she prays to her as well. She understands Baby Jesus and she understands there's God, but she understands there's a Mother, which hopefully for her will be the two Marys united. Since the two Marys have never been subjugated or divided within Tash's Being, then it makes sense that the two Marys were born married in Tash's little world. Mother Earth is sovereign. Mother Earth has awakened her daughters.

TORI:

Back in the conference room at Doubleday Books . . .

The door opens and my publishers walk into the conference room where I've been waiting, flanked by their twelve disciples who will be covering everything from publicity, marketing, and sales of the book. We all sit down, with Chelsea and Johnny on either side of me, creating the effect of a Honey Baked Ham on rye sandwich, hold the cheese.

My publisher looks at me and says, "We've read the Magdalene chapter, and whatever you and Ann are doing, keep doing it."

I breathed a sigh of relief, because if they hadn't liked it, sure, I may have lots of songs up my sleeve, but I don't have any other books. This is all I know.

Then he added, "Just keep going. Don't even think about it."

I responded, "That's it?"

They smiled and said, "That is what most authors would love to hear after having turned in their first chapter."

I said, "You don't mind the cursing or the profanity? Because we've just had to edit the DVD of any and all profanity, or else they were going to slap a big 'Parental Advisory' on it."

He said, "This is literature, Tori. Curse as much as you want. And by the way, the Magdalene's been very good to us. We've got no problems with the Magdalene."

And as I looked around at all *The Da Vinci Code* paraphernalia surrounding me, I glanced up at my publishers and asked, "So then why aren't you guys aggressively seeking to publish the Gospel of Mary Magdalene?"

They looked at me as if I were speaking an alien language and said, "What are you talking about?"

"I'm talking about the Gospel of Mary Magdalene."

With shock they responded, "As in the Matthew, Mark, Luke, and John Gospels?"

I said, "That is exactly what I'm talking about—a real Gospel, from her perspective."

"Do you mean it was written by her?" they asked.

"Well, no one can prove who wrote Matthew, Mark, Luke, and John, or any of the Gospels. But yes, there is a Gospel attributed to the Magdalene."

"Well, when did this happen? Why didn't we hear anything about it?"

"It was discovered in 1895."

My publisher looked over at one of his twelve disciples and said, "Get on the phone with the religion department."

I thought to myself about how people were shouting from the rooftops about Mel Gibson's *The Passion*, that people were buying *The Da Vinci Code* in droves, and yet the words attributed to this woman, Mary Magdalene, are still being kept under wraps almost two thousand years later. Her light hidden under a bushel. The question that I have to ask myself, and the question I have to ask you is . . . *Why?* Maybe this truly is The Greatest Story Never Told.

saraswati: the art
of composition

DOUGHNUT.

ANN: *A lost river flows from the Himalayan peaks of India to the Arabian Sea. Some people believe the Saraswati has been buried for four thousand years, while others claim it never actually existed. What everyone knows is that this mysterious watercourse shares its name with the deity that governs another elusive stream—the force of creativity itself. The goddess Saraswati is the consort of Brahma, lord of creation; she is Vak, the guardian of speech; she nourishes all who make music, write poems, and love to learn. She is usually depicted riding a swan, the symbol of pure knowledge, while in her four arms she holds the implements of inspiration: meditation beads, a book, and a veena, the sacred seven-stringed lute, the tone of which resembles the human voice.*

Throughout her mythology, Saraswati stands for the unstoppable, yet often seemingly untraceable, flow of the mind at play. She guides her faithful to embrace the form their inspiration takes. Legends abound of her ability to nourish eloquence, restore memory, and help bring hopes to fruition. The Mahabharata call her "the mother of the Vedas," the source of India's foundational sacred texts. She can be impetuous, even cruel, as in the legend of when Brahma settled an argument between her and Buddhi, god of the mind, in favor of the latter, and she condemned her consort to never again being able to hear his own name said in prayer. She can also be warmly generous, as when she nourished one sage in a land stricken by drought so he could preserve his land's history, or restored the damaged memory of another so he could recite the Vedas and find peace. The Jain sect named her the Remover of Infatuations, the patron saint of getting serious about what you really love. Some archetypal beings represent our cravings for power, erotic connection, or material success. Saraswati stands for respect. Only by learning to respect herself and earn the respect of others can the dreamer become the doer.

Like the Saraswati River, running now on imaginary shores, the sources of creativity can often be frustratingly obscure. Many artists experience a productive rush early in their careers but lack the skill and discipline to sustain the quality of their output. True creativity, not just the shapeless splatter of expression, demands structure, attentiveness, and time. The artists who sustain themselves are those who overcome their addiction to the thrill of emotion and ego, define a larger vision, and keep working.

Over a lifetime of learning to compose, Tori Amos has perfected her own methods for transforming raw creative material into art. Her process takes her from preliminary, inspirational wanderings throughout the world and within her well-stocked library to the calm space of her workroom and then into the recording studio, where she leads her small crew of collaborators in realizing her compositions. Each song that Amos generates becomes its own environment, sustaining elements of myth and legend, of her musical forebears and her own innovations, of autobiography and fiction, wildness and precision. Asked the secrets of her trade, she shares not merely a handful of tips but a spirit of adventure, the exhilarating sensation of diving in.

SONG CANVAS: "Garlands"

I've been by the sea on and off for a few weeks now. The girls are coming in on Jet Skis. The songs seem to know where to find me. Writing a work through the changing of the seasons—autumn, winter, spring, summer—has an impact on the work. If you figure in the tastes and the aromas that go along with the changes, the seasonings—the herbs growing in the garden, which then make their way into Dunc's kitchen; the burning of fires that happens in autumn; or just the budding of spring . . . all of that is woven into a song's tapestry. "Washington Square" or "Garlands" (I'm still wavering on the title: clearly you will know as you read this which one I chose in the end) was written when we were frozen in—sorta like when it's too dangerous to drive because of icy roads here in the west country of England. I started this song in the autumn, when we were in Boston doing a big radio show in October 2003, and then I couldn't find its foundation until we were iced in down in Cornwall. I bundled up and took a walk with my boots on, bundled up in Husband's ever-ready big bomber jacket, until I wandered back around, not to the house, but the barn, smelling fires on the way, making a beeline for the Böse. Isabella was waiting there for me in a shaft of light by the piano and she said, "Write me in a song. I want access to this dimension." I said, "Talk with me awhile." I just started playing something random so as to not lose the moment. Then she said, "You're still hurting." I asked her, "To what are you referring?" She said, "I was there that day." I asked, "What day?" "That day when you walked through Washington Square and I saw a tear you were hiding, and I held up a candle to guide you." I looked at this glorious vision of light, and I giggled softly. "Well, Isabella, we know which song you are in, then, don't we?" She held me a moment and then danced back into the shaft of light from which she had come. I finished "Washington Square" (or "Garlands") that day.

The word *garlands* had been married to this melody since its inception, had wanted to be used but had eluded me for months, mainly because I associated it with the ancient custom of wreaths and flowers for weddings, funerals, and celebrations as old as Beltane and May Day. Then that day after Isabella sparked my . . . I guess you call it my sixth sense—she had turned up the volume on that one—I started to have a funny feeling that my definition of garlands was the reason that I couldn't weave this tapestry together. I sat down on this old couch that supposedly came from Russia in the nineteenth century; I've had it recovered at least three times because of coffee stains and baby dribble, but it's my thinking spot, and it's my dolphin couch because of the two brass dolphins on either side. I have it in a sagelike material, which reminds me of New Mexico, that plateau covered with white sage right by the Sangre de Cristo Mountains. I looked at the color of the wall, which I had painted to remind me of those New Mexican skies, this creamy tangerine, or as Tash would say, vanilla Satsuma pudding color.

It drew me to pick up a book that would have drawings in it. I had just that week opened a box of art books that I had gotten on my travels. Many were still in their plastic wrappings on the floor. One caught my eye, and there it was. A book of Chagall lithographs. These garlands of lithographs—bundles bursting in color—are what the lovers in the story use to chronicle their love affair. Our lovers meet in Washington Square and go uptown to see the Chagall exhibition. As they walk in and out of these pictures, we get a vision of their love for each other, some of the beliefs that they're wrestling with, and a dark force in their relationship that seems to be

penelope, wife of odysseus, the hero of homer's *odyssey*

coming between them, whether it's his father or her professor at art school who seems to be wanting to control the path her talent takes, a little too possessive in Isabella's opinion. I decided to notate the lyrics in this CD booklet so that Chagall's painting titles were italicized and that way people could go and reference the lithographs visually, which also influenced the phrasing of the music.

CONVERSATION BETWEEN TORI AND ANN:

I am a songwriter twenty-four hours a day. I'm not a performer twenty-four hours a day. I'm not a wife twenty-four hours a day. Even Mommy—to be honest, when I'm on that stage and channeling, Mommy's taking a break. But the writer in me is always present.

As a songwriter, I'm gathering clues and possibilities all the time, whether I see a piano that day or not. I've tried to explain to people how I collect these dispatches, because I think anybody can do what I'm talking about. Once I do plug in, I might get only one line and two bar phrases of the melody. I always have elements of songs around that may never ever get recorded. As far back as *Little Earthquakes,* I began to realize that I needed to have a library of notes, phrases, words, things that might prove useful at any given time. Within a few months' time I'll gather hundreds of those fragments. Half won't be used. And then the craft comes in, the part that is about painting a world. You want listeners to smell the lavender, to feel the point of those knitting needles in a handbag of the granny who happens to harbor a loyalty to Madame Defarge. You want the listener to know the wood's burning in the stove when they walk into the song with me. Music is about all of your senses, not just hearing.

I think of the structure of any particular song as a house. The bathroom is the bathroom, and you have to understand the shape of the bathroom and its needs. The kitchen's the kitchen. Sometimes you want the chorus to be the kitchen in a song. Sometimes you want the chorus to be the shower, very cleansing. Sometimes it's the bedroom. Or sometimes the chorus is that shower, but instead it's about being naked and soap and it's sexy—or it's not sexy at all, but an eradication of someone or something. It could even be akin to "I've gotta wash that God right outta my hair," depending on what sticky archetypes have been prodding through the night. The point is, even in terms of the emotion expressed, the shape matters before the story does. Without the structure, there's nowhere for the story to live.

Peter Gabriel taught me, when I worked with him a bit in the early 1990s, that attention to structure is what you have to develop if you're going to be a composer/songwriter generating effective work throughout your life. He said to me in 1995, "Look around you—you have these engineers. You could build a studio, a workshop. Tori, you never know: your workshop studio may be the only way you can keep your art from being tampered with if you are at war with your label but they still want product." (Little did I know that he was reading my tea leaves, forewarning me of an ominous battle that was yet to ensue, but we're not there in the story yet.) Everybody's got one good record in them if they're half decent. But then once you've done that, you've used the best of your picks. That's your style. People know your style after the first time and then you have to develop skill as a songwriter. Do I write a lot? Yeah, I write a lot. I write hundreds of songs for an album. Fifteen or twenty get chosen. I have hundreds I've forgotten now. I have at least 150 that are complete but just didn't quite work.

There are times when I'm doing lots and lots of research, and I'll start gathering words and phrases from various sources—books, conversations, visual art. I'll start pulling my references out, and I have no idea which ones will prove useful. I'll just start jotting down ideas. I can do that for hours, but a lot of it is a load of crap. I can play piano for myself for hours. It's nonsense, most of it. It's like doodling or doing a puzzle. Exercising. And I just enjoy playing sometimes. But that's not composition. Within a few hours, maybe a rhythm pattern will arise, and I'll write it down in my script, or usually I have a little tape recorder and just put my ideas into that. Then I'll listen to that tape when I'm driving. And I'll go, "Oh, okay, stop the tape, rewind—now that is not a load of crap." I'll jot it down in some kind of musical handwriting so I don't forget it and notate where to reference this catchy motif. That's how I found "a sorta fairytale." "On my way up north, up on the Ventura"—I had that on tape, and then I went into a whole other load of crap. But when I heard that line months later, when I was pulling songs together for *Scarlet's Walk*, I thought, *I know that line.* I knew it was potentially a good song because foundationally I was working with marble, not linoleum. I like linoleum, but you have to be a little bit more selective, because linoleum can be a completely bad idea in a lot of structures, whereas marble, if it's good-quality marble, is always useful somewhere, even if only as the kitchen worktop.

It still took me months to develop "fairytale's" musical theme, because it was such an involved theme and I had to build it around a traditional fairy-tale form, to make it a modern rendition of what is known as a folk-tale. Matt and I recorded it a few times to get it right. Polly Anthony, who was president of Epic at the time, had an instant flirtation with the song, so when it came time to pick a single she was adamant that it be the one for America. My first single for *Scarlet's Walk* was being released in early September 2002, and she felt the nation could use a dose of whimsy, as there would be many heavy hearts still working through the grief from September 11. She called Mark and Marcel, asking them to pull together an edit from the almost five-minute-and-fifty-second "fairytale" to a four-minute version without losing too much of the story line and its sentiment. Tricky, but they did it.

TORI:

Tapes upon tapes upon tapes of ideas sit on the Bösendorfer. I find that this part of the songwriting process takes the most discipline. Playing every day at the piano or the Hammond or whatever keyboard is fun, I get whipped into a frenzy of playing, and of course I tape most of it when I'm in composing mode. I tape it on my little crap tape recorder (the boys are trying to get me to go digital). Anyway, at some stage I have to sit down and listen to the hours and hours of jamming on tapes to find the nectar, the sweet—jeez . . . it can be painful. I have art canvas books set aside, in which I record the building and development of the motif. A motif is a recurring melody. Sometimes I'll have more than a hundred different motifs going—a motif can last anywhere from a single bar to maybe a six-teen-bar phrase.

Now what happens, do you think, if you keep your tapes in order? Then you can see how a motif develops. I, on the other hand—*D'oh* (that was my Homer Simpson who just showed up for a minute)—clearly don't keep my tapes in order. So wherever I start, I start, but thank God I'm into drawing these silly little maps, sorta like a Yellow Pages, of where the song motifs live. Yes, I make twice the amount of work for myself because I don't keep my tapes in order, but eventually I memorize where every-thing is. If you do it in order, however, like a clever person would, you can observe how the original motif will change in the hours and hours of tape. Instead of spending days trying to find a sliver of a bass line that's God-knows-where amid fifteen tapes . . . yikes. While you are writing many songs, writing many motifs, naturally some keep coming back, refusing to be forgotten. Sometimes they will change in a way that isn't good for the motif—it weakens it. So you go back to the part of the tape where it came together, and this may be for only ten seconds. I transcribe this onto a canvas, catalog it, and keep mining. I call this mining for songs.

But hey, I never wanted to be Snow White, more like Glinda the Good Witch mining ancient stones with Grumpy. The motifs begin to have many variations as the weeks go by, but the most powerful ones tend to keep creeping up. There are those treasures that happen only once, only for a moment, and if I lose that tape it's gone forever, because I can't remember thirty seconds of music I played hours and hours ago. I've spoken about when the songs come and the euphoria of that, but the truth is, if I don't go through this painstaking cataloging process, then these pieces of music are just ideas that never become tangible. It will all sort of fade into a hallucination experience that becomes like an ecstasy trip unexplainable to everyone, even yourself. So, I will spend two hours a day just notating what is on the tapes, weaving them together, tracking them down. You see, as I get further into the developing of the song, sometimes I choose the original seed idea and sometimes I find that the motif has improved a few stages in. This might take weeks to decipher, but if you as the songwriter keep a mental file of all of the song Beings, even if you have to associate these new creatures with key words that make them more tangible, you will be able to track those songs down. Track them like a lioness tracks dinner for the whole pride. This is what I call hunting for song frequency.

MARK HAWLEY:

I think it's quite easy for Tori to come up with little melodies and little bits of music. As with a lot of musicians, the hard work is in finishing ideas. Eventually a song reaches a certain stage and comes out and it's beautiful.

But beforehand, whether it's one line of a lyric or a middle-eight section, that's what she works on for hours and hours.

Certain songs, like "Marianne" from *Boys for Pele,* were written, performed, and recorded spontaneously. How long is that song, five minutes? That was how long it took her to write it. She went into the church, played it, wrote the lyrics, and recorded it on the spot. When that stuff happens—well, you know I don't believe in magic, but that's it. That's when somebody *out there* is telling her how to play a song. I would never believe it unless I'd seen it. I've seen that happen maybe five or six times. But I've also seen the hard work, when she's had a song idea and it takes years. She started a song called "Lady Jane" in 1994 and she hasn't finished it yet. She's still working on it.

TORI:

I'm recording today once Hayley, Tash's beloved nanny, who is our resident Mary Poppins, takes her on her playdate. Strangely I'm not recording the first piece for the new album but for the rare B-side portion of the Live DVD *Welcome to Sunny Florida.* Because the Live DVD package will be released soon after Mother's Day in the United States, the song "Ruby through the Looking-Glass," which I started writing for *Scarlet's Walk,* has signaled to me that her time has come to enter into the mass consciousness. Ruby is in utero, hearing her mother trying to protect her in the womb while her mother is clearly in a fight. Not only is the mother having to defend herself, but by addressing certain things that were done to her as a child, she makes a decision. She at all costs makes a vow to Ruby to be aware as a mother, and promises her a different way of communicating, instead of fighting. It will be almost two years since I began writing "Ruby" . . .

Do I think songs have a time line? Can a song's meaning and the response by a listener change because of when it's presented? Well, obviously. "I can't see New York" was perceived and will always be related to the September 11 plane crashes, even though it was written in May 2001. When "I can't see New York" walked into the room, slid into the wood through the strings, claiming the keys, which in turn played me, I did not choose to project actual events onto the song creature herself; otherwise I would probably have superimposed my perception of the TWA800 disaster of 1996. Sometimes you have to order your own pictures to leave your mind, knowing that they are a tainting influence on the translation—talk about being lost in translation. This is a focus, a skill, a meditation of sorts, to keep a clean slate, to keep Tori Ellen's opinions out of the way when a song walks in full force, almost completely intact—this is definitely about taking dictation. These songs happen rarely for me, hearing one pretty much as a finished song for the first time, and hearing it very much how the public will hear it for the first time in a completed form. Only when I was walking down Fifth Avenue on the afternoon of September 11 did I understand—in song language—the subtexts and energy of death and loss from the point of view of a plane victim. As the song played over in my head, I kept walking toward the burning.

CONVERSATION BETWEEN TORI AND ANN:

There isn't just one kind of song that I write. One side of me loves atmospheric British music, like the Cocteau Twins and Talk Talk, and then there is a side that loves story songs—Springsteen's "Born to Run" and "Thunder Road." Other times I'll incorporate a burlesque or vaudevillian quality. There's a tradition of pop songwriters who do that—Lennon and McCartney did it quite a bit in songs like "Martha My Dear." It's supposed to be a release; sometimes you need that humor. In my songs—"Leather,"

"Wednesday," "Mr. Zebra"—there's a sinister force moving within the song, just as there was in burlesque. But they can definitely have a giggle, those Girls.

What I know I'm not is a "write me a hit at the drop of a hat" type of songwriter. I don't think I could contrive a song that the world would embrace just because it targets a certain demographic. To me one of the best classic pop writers is Carole King. Her songs go beyond the usual limits; they're not the kind you hear one week on the radio and then a year later it's out of there. A part of me wishes I could write like Carole King, but it's not my orientation. I think that my deepest desire would be to dive behind the masks people wear every day and find out who they really are, and then write about it. Now I realize that if I dived behind some masks, certain masks, let's say the Clear Channel mask, then I might just strike a chord, thereby lowering the drawbridge into the castle that is radioland . . . or, the drawbridge would stay up and the arrows would come flying from the top of the tower. It's a crapshoot, but I adore rolling emotional dice.

JON EVANS:

The classical influence in Tori's music comes through in her harmonic choices and articulation. Her voicings are very classical. They're not jazz voicings with tight internal work-ins. It's very grand. But it works; it's really beautiful and it's kind of majestic in its own way.

Coming from a jazz background, I was used to improvising, and I have formal training, too, so I get the classical aspects of Tori's work. But I soon realized Tori doesn't write standard songs in any genre or tradition. She begins with her voice; there are meters and bars thrown in that complement her vocal lines. She might leave space to put in three extra words, so then that measure has an extra beat and a half, and that's just life, you know? Even her singles, like "Spark" from *Choirgirl,* have a ton of time changes.

The first thing I ever did with Tori live was play "Spark" on the David Letterman show. That song just has its own logic. It's hard to get the rhyme and reason of it until you play it a bunch of times, and I just remember I was playing at that taping and looking over at Matt and saying, "What's going on?" It just was funny. You get used to the oddities in her music—you might be sailing along in a time signature, and then all of a sudden there's just an extra beat, or it might switch from one time signature to another without warning. Then some songs are just straight ahead the entire time, or you might have one that's kind of a waltz.

I think her writing style has evolved this way because of how she records; she's always recorded her songs alone first and then brought in other musicians once they're basically formed. It's only since she got together with Matt that the drums and piano parts have evolved at the same time. Before, if she wanted to add extra elements, she would just do it and her band would deal with it later. Her structures emerged organically, almost spontaneously.

There's more time on this new record, *The Beekeeper.* We're all here together and we've been spending a lot of time trying to give every song its own personality. Oftentimes when we are tracking, Matt and I will do something that will support Tori's getting her performance down. Something that she feels very comfortable singing and playing over. Then we'll go back and do something very different afterward. Matt will build a drum track that is completely different from what he did when we were tracking. I'll do something that goes along with that, so things kind of develop in that way. But every song is so different, and since we basically have a full day to do each track, some of them end up completely different from where they started.

CONVERSATION BETWEEN TORI AND ANN:

Melodies can come at any time. If I'm driving, for example, I might come up with something, and if I don't have a notebook I'll just jot it down in a paperback novel or whatever I happen to be carrying. I scribble on the back of whatever I can. It used to be bills, but that led to a whole set of other problems, so now it's whatever I can get my hands on. I've developed my own form of writing music, because I never did well in music school as far as theory. I had to take Theory IV twice. Mark did really, really well in theory, so he can advise me on those matters, and in the studio Jon charts things out for everybody. I can't do that. I have my own way of understanding rhythm and remembering the melodies I'm working in. I guess you could say that a notation has developed over the years so that I can write my music out and remember it, but it's definitely not a traditional musical form. Verses are setups; choruses are payoffs. They need to be. Music and words often come together when a song Being initially shows herself to me. I don't always get the full story. But usually a thought comes with the melody, or perhaps just the sound of a word that begins to give me clues as to who and what this creature is.

I work within music and not poetry because in my form the two elements work together. I'm shifting and shaping words as I vocalize, too. Sometimes I don't see it until after it's written. I'll look back and see the pattern of a melody, and what the words are doing; sometimes the melody is doing the complete opposite of what the words are doing, and it creates a contrapuntal line. It gives the story another subtext. You could have a dark lyric with a jaunty tune; the lyrics might not rhyme, but the music might, in a sense. Humor usually comes from the music. That's true in "Yes, Anastasia" and "Mohammad My Friend."

It's a mistake when critics focus on lyrics alone. Without vocalizing, a songwriter would just be a poet. But we're different. Most lyrics read terribly on the page. They can be poetic, but a dress can be poetic, a kiss, whatever. When poets try to write songs, that's also usually a mistake. And musicians who think they can publish books of poetry should, for the most part, think again. Some can cross the line and live in both worlds—Leonard Cohen, for instance. His performance of his own compositions has always been its own art form. I imagine that as a songwriter he had a tear in his eye when he first heard the rendition of his "Hallelujah" by Jeff Buckley. Even if you are known as a performer of your own compositions, when someone else puts their heart and soul into a song that you wrote, your mountain has just got to move and you've got to say, "Amen, brotha'."

TORI:

I sit at the piano. We're in preproduction for the new work. *The Beekeeper*. On tour it would be showtime. 8:50 p.m. I start to play, but as I go into my zone, I don't see the four barnlike walls of the studio painted a shade of Tuscan Madras—I'm on a stage somewhere. Anywhere. It doesn't matter. I'm amped. Body and soul, I am experiencing an otherworldly "tune-up." My tape recorder is on; I'm playing one of the new songs as I would live, and something new is being played by my hands. A whole new section, a melody, marches out of my mouth over my lips. I feel a bass line, a kick pattern in my hips. I am meeting a piece of this song creature that I never knew existed. Because they change when played live, I've been trying to find the songs in the future and then bring them back in that particular form so that then I can decide which of the song's different forms work better on tape.

ANN: *Just as Saraswati manifests with instrument in hand, so Amos cannot separate the act of songwriting from playing piano and singing. Her voice de-*

*fines the often unconventional shapes of her melodies and time signatures,
while her beloved Bösendorfer guides her into new rhythmic patterns and harmonic combinations. With each album, Amos has challenged herself as a
player and a singer, and in doing so has pushed open the boundaries of her song
structures.*

TORI:

> The songs are structures in themselves. Once I'm able to find my way into
> one of them—and that might be only a four-bar phrase—that does not
> mean that I have access to this song creature. Imagine that you have been
> able to let yourself into this fascinating architectural space but you're in
> only one room and you do not know how to get to the other rooms because
> as of now there are no doorways. It becomes like a sonic puzzle. Sometimes
> it takes months for me to find my way around a song, because I have to find
> harmonic code, but once I do the song seems to let me into another room.
> This doorway has been put in place by the song itself. The structures al-
> ready exist. I'm just interpreting them. Now, can I trick the songs by writ-
> ing them and imprinting them with any architecture I want? No, but I can
> trick myself. The songs, though, will never resonate the way they were in-
> tended to unless I work with them to crack their codes. It's sorta like . . .
> you can say you love this person—everyone wants you to love them and
> make them your partner, because it's what makes sense to everybody else—
> but you know somewhere inside whether you truly love them, or whether
> you are pretending to feel something and you call it love. Because you kind
> of have a special feeling for this person, but honestly, it's all becoming a bit
> of a headache . . . and it would make everybody happy if you just loved
> this person. Does Venus know you're not really in love? Of course, and so
> do you. This is what songwriting requires—the ability to listen to the heart
> of the song.

Sometimes as I'm hunting for songs I get very still and realize that in "real life" I may feel hunted as well. "Parasol" came out of this feeling. The words and music are done, the arrangement is very close. I keep seeing the painting that reached out to me a few weeks ago from an art book and pulled me in through its page into the picture itself. *Seated Woman with a Parasol* became my protector and still is my protector during times of heightened confrontation—whether that draining, devouring energy is from an outside source or an inside force. *Parasol* is my friend and I trust her.

I remember seeing the songs as paintings when I was little. The only place people could not get to me was in the songs. These were my sonic paintings, where I would notate truthful events and save them and store them by threading them into the symbology, into chords, the melodies, and the rhythm, the breathing—and it seemed that even my gum-chewing had a backbeat. There was no way that they could extract me (whoever they were). Sometimes I couldn't even extract myself.

The painting *Seated Woman with a Parasol* by Georges-Pierre Seurat is a study on his painting *La Grande Jatte*. I found myself staring at the seated woman with a parasol in yet another painting by Seurat entitled *A Sunday on La Grande Jatte* (*detail: woman and child*).

CONVERSATION BETWEEN TORI AND ANN:

Each album I've made represents a period in my vocal development. In *Earthquakes,* if you listen to the singing, there is a consistency, mainly because I was continually having to find my inner voice. *Venus* is very consistent—to me, there's a real beauty throughout the album with that vocal. By then I could move into anger and out of it instead of experiencing it as an uncontainable emotion. On *Pele* I'm almost, you know, burning up. Whereas now, if I wanted to represent a woman in flames, I would detach myself, study it, make the needed shifts, and move the hands on my clock so that I could step into anger without being burned up.

Pele is really where I think the voice unleashed. And sometimes in a way that wasn't contained. Once I found it, I could move on to temperance. At different times, you write different music for your voice and for you as a player, but you also write music that you can emotionally contain. Your soul—your psyche—what makes your inner world a wasteland or fertile or both, is the deciding factor in what will make up your song garden. With *Choirgirl*, after the *Pele* thing, I wasn't in a bloodletting place. I had lived that. There's a lot more containment—I was tracking with musicians who were really skilled, and I needed to be spot on. With *Pele* I was also in a church, so you can imagine what was going on there—talk about an exorcism, praise Jesus. It was about time. This girl was finding her Kundalini and letting it come forth right at the altar of the church where they would have their sacred communion. I was able to have sacred communion, finally, with the Feminine in the place where she had been circumcised. That's one reason for the haunting background vocal in "Caught a Light Sneeze," "Inanna Inanna Inanna bring your sons"; it was such a resurrection for she who is Mrs. God, right there in the church. With *Choirgirl*, and later with *Venus*, I was home. There was time to let the wife, the lover, the friend, catch up with the part of my woman who was living in these song realms. If your human woman doesn't catch up with what's happening in the song world, then you can't imprint this knowledge and thread it into your living tapestry.

Working on *Strange Little Girls*, I found new qualities within my voice. To sing "New Age" like that—there's a lot of power in that chorus.

To hit the tone I wanted, I needed to come more from the chest. Sometimes I will use that, but I don't always need to; there are many, many ways. For "New Age" I just wanted a certain tone, and I began to explore and realize how power and tone can be used together. So I'd been playing with that a lot, and you can hear that on *Strange Little Girls*, particularly because in those songs you can clearly see the different characters. That album was so much for me about being a singer and knowing how you use your voice. I did use my voice to step into different parts. I was able to do that because I had done *Pele* and strengthened my vocal instrument. I could never have sung all these various ways in 1992. No way. I didn't have the experience. I had never sung with a band. In 1998, I sang with a band in front of 15,000 people in Madison Square Garden on a steroid shot, with a concussion. Having done that, you don't sing the same anymore. You have to go out there and get your vocal sea legs.

This is why I've told people, "You have to tour." No matter what happens in the world, as a musician, as a singer, you really, really need to do that if you want to keep changing. Because there's a physical change that will happen to you as a singer just because you've done it, and it expands your possibilities as a songwriter. Use it or lose it. That's one reason I do tour a lot.

Singing, songwriting, and the piano are inseparable for me. I need to play the piano just to be who I am. I don't mean I need to play for people. I enjoy that, but it's a different experience. When I'm playing in our studio I'm not thinking about all the things I think about when I'm performing; I'm not thinking about what I need to take on board in order to project what it is I'm seeing in my head. I don't have to pose in front of the song. I don't have to communicate it just then—it's communicating itself to me and I'm trying to translate it.

I play the piano every day, with very few exceptions. When my piano is gone from me, there is just something missing. There are periods when it's not around, when it's flying or on the boat. It takes three weeks to get it from New York to England. A long time. An instrument is a friend, and some friends come and go. But if you had to tell me that I could achieve world peace by never playing the piano again—I'd have to think about whether I'd be willing to do it. It's that serious.

In fact, I rarely sing without playing the piano. If I do separate them, I sing and play differently. I'm not saying that there aren't certain songs for which it's better for me to separate them when recording. I did an over-dub vocal on "Cornflake Girl" because I was playing so hard that you could hear my breathing on the tape, and it was too labored. On some songs I will track the vocals separately because I find that I need to stand up to get the control and the tone I want from my voice. I'll try these songs at the piano first, and if I can't get my body in the right position to get the tone I need, then I'll compromise.

I did spend one period of my life without my own piano. It was when I was first trying to make my career fly, in Los Angeles in the 1980s. I didn't see a lot of other piano players, especially women, doing it at the time. Everybody was saying that the girl-and-her-piano thing is dead. I kind of had a funeral for it with *Y Kant Tori Read*. We all know how that effort went.

I was laid low at that point, wondering, *How did I end up here, from the conservatory to this place?* I had a friend who was a little bit older, Cindy Marble; she'd been in L.A. for years trying to make it with her band, Rugburns. I was talking on the phone with her, lamenting my life. She said, "You know, when you sit and play the piano and sing, some-thing is real about that. That's when I sit and listen. Everything else just doesn't feel—honest." She had a piano. I went over to her house that night and she lit some candles and asked me to just sit there and play. She was having a smoke, I didn't smoke any because it would harm my voice, but I was hypnotized by the aroma. I just played for her for a while, a couple hours. I got a piano within two weeks. I rented one. I couldn't afford to buy one.

I was living behind the Methodist church on Highland and Franklin in Hollywood. I was thinking a lot about ethics and morality. And I began to realize that I had betrayed my instrument, the thing that had always been my conscience. I listened to the corporate side of the music industry, and it took me as low as I could go. From child prodigy to being called a bimbo in *Billboard*? You don't get lower than that. I vowed never to abandon the piano again.

In Cornwall, the piano room is my workshop. Mark's building me another piano room so that if this one is being used for some other purpose during the recording process, I'll have another place to play. The piano is at the center; it's always at the center for me.

I married somebody who understands the relationship I have with the piano. That's key. Mark knows when to leave us alone—I think he'd like to be left alone most of the time anyway. But he really does understand it. He's observed that when I have time to go to the piano and do as I've always done, so many things pass through me that even he doesn't hear, because that's just part of my process. Even if I don't write every day, I'm playing to express myself; that's my time, and, along with being Natashya's mommy, it makes life worth living.

ANN: *The image of Amos alone with her piano is romantic but not complete when it comes to her songwriting. She taps into many springs to feed her imagination—texts she has long loved or ones she only recently discovered during hours of prowling bookstores and museum shops around the world; tales she learned at her mother's knee; and others that came to her from the mouths of the wise women and men whom she has sought out during her adulthood; conversa-*

tions within her esteemed circle of friends and fellow players. Music, classical and contemporary, stirs her, too, though she is careful to guard the taps on those fonts. As the connections that figure into Amos's cosmology spark and multiply, she becomes absorbed in the energetic current and loses all sense of time and place until a new work is born.

TORI:

The song appears as light filament once I've cracked it. As long as I've been doing this, which is more than thirty-five years, I've never seen a duplicated song structure. I've never seen the same light creature in my life. Obviously similar chord progressions follow similar light patterns, but try to imagine the best kaleidoscope ever—after the initial excitement, you start to focus on each element's stunning original detail. For instance, the sound of the words with the sound of the chord progression combined with the rhythm manifests itself in a unique expression of the architecture of color-and-light. Some are dark. But their beauty astounds me. They are pure form, and when I'm able to travel through them I feel as I've never felt otherwise. My cells change; I feel as if I'm walking through a different dimension, and yet I haven't left my piano bench. It's quite humbling. Sometimes I don't feel I've translated them correctly. I listen to other songwriters and think they have translated their Sonic Light Being more concisely, so I study them and try to gain the tools to become a better interpreter of light into sound. Because this lives in a dimension where there are no real estate agents of light—at least not yet, thank God—I know it seems intangible to some people. But the sonic world can be visited. I started visiting this world when I was three, listening to a piece by Béla Bartók; I visited a configuration that day that wasn't on this earth. My toes were curled up in worn Methodist carpet, and I knew I wanted to take more journeys like this. It was euphoric. It is euphoric.

CONVERSATION BETWEEN TORI AND ANN:

For years I've gathered various books, sources. When I was little it might have been Tolkien, and so I would have just four books around me. I couldn't afford many books at the time, so I'd have what I had. Maybe I'd tear out ten or twenty pictures from magazines because I couldn't afford art books. I would check out library books and try to keep them as long as I could, but I couldn't jot my notes in them. For any particular song, I can't tell you the books that were on the floor, the photographs on the floor. I don't let anybody keep a record of that. Those are the secret ingredients.

Some sources are continual and obvious. I use myth; I use fairy tales. Fairy tales can be quite harrowing, especially if you go back and read them in their earlier editions. Information is hidden in these tales—they deal with incest, violence, rape. They also deal with cause and effect. And a very difficult truth, which is that stories don't always end the way they should.

Sometimes I like the word *folktale* rather than *fairy tale* because *fairy tale* has become a pejorative. That's shifting now. With *Harry Potter*, you have a whole generation so immersed in magic that kids believe they can go to wizard school. There's a whole new crowd. But people still get confused, because they haven't gone back to the original. Take leprechauns. People think of them as red-headed fellows chewing on corncob pipes. But I've lived in Ireland, and it was made clear to me that the Irish hold the Tuatha Dé Danann and their myths as sacred as any religious texts. These ancient stories are so deeply rooted in their fabric as a culture that Brigid—the goddess of music, inspiration and poetry—was adopted by the Christians and was made St. Brigid in 450 A.D. Here in Cornwall, Tintagel, King Arthur's birthplace, according to the locals, is just down the road, and it's a ruin of a massive, great castle. So it's a real thing, though historically I think it's more related to the story of Tristan and

Isolde, not Arthur. What I notice is that when I'm in a place where these things have occurred, as when I spent time in France and began to understand the Black Madonna myth, I get such a better sense of them. Then I can go back and do the reading. Getting a read on Native American stuff over here is just impossible—that's why *Scarlet's Walk* came out of time spent touring the States.

As for being influenced by more contemporary sources, especially other pop songs, it's tricky. When I'm in heavy writing mode I usually keep my ears pretty clear, so I don't listen to too much music from the outside world. Dunc is always playing something in the kitchen, but other than that I try to stay away from it because I don't want to unconsciously weave a melody in that I might have heard on the radio, or off the iPod. Sometimes I'll describe a new song Being to Mark, Marcel, Matt, and Jon by referring to the vibe of another record. This is a reference point for me, a jumping-off point. It's necessary to keep checking that you're not subconsciously weaving someone else's song Being into yours. It's no different from superimposing certain qualities of your daughter's friend onto your kid. Yes, the two girls might have some things in common, but they each need to be treated as a unique entity. You can't borrow qualities from another child and give them to your own. You can, however, be inspired by how another child is taught or even disciplined by their parents and borrow this tactic, but then you might have to redesign it for it to apply to your kid. No different with songwriting: you might be inspired by the way the rhythm and melody fit like a hand in a glove, so you might borrow this tactic, but then you need to apply it to your song Being, which has a different makeup, because all songs are unique or should be. Let's remember something here—there are only twelve notes, so sometimes you have to be careful that you don't borrow too much, because according to copyright law, if you borrow too many notes in a row in a melody line, then the judge will think you've borrowed a bit too much. Sometimes I'll have Mark listen to a song, too, and he can tell me if he hears someone else too much in it. I am meticulous about it. It's not something you want to be doing.

I flirt with other people's songs sometimes. Even if I hear it only one time, there can be a flirtation going on, where I say, "I can do this, but I'm going to approach it in another way." A couple of bands inspired my riff on "Precious Things." But my song is so different from theirs. You can't necessarily make the connection.

I was taught very strictly at the Peabody to be extremely careful about borrowing. This is a difficult subject because it can be such a gray area for all creators. That's probably why I want to talk about it. I adore shades of gray, and I find that there are so many shades of gray within the spectrum itself. As more and more songs are getting created, more things are sounding similar, because unless you have compositional theory deeply ingrained in your brain, it's hard to write new combinations of notes. Naturally, I get exasperated with Elton John and Bernie Taupin simply because they wrote many of the great songs that just might have come to visit me if Elton and Bernie had been abducted by aliens. On the other hand, studying their song structures was sort of like being an architect apprenticing to one of the great songwriting teams of the twentieth century. Elton knows the doors we had to break down, and the preconceptions people have had because we play these big classical-looking whales called pianos instead of a hot little sexy strap-on Gibson. But let's face it. I think it's much harder to be me than Elton (giggle), because after all, I'm having to come in twenty years after he and Bernie wrote a lot of the good stuff . . .

Recently, because of sampling, some of the new composers need to be careful about knowing when they are taking too much from an original piece as opposed to what is considered to be acceptable. When I say accept-able, I think we all have recognized a similar melody from an older song in a newer song—even some of the notes may be the same in short se-quences. But c'mon, guys—not half of the song note for note . . . There are going to be similarities in songs, because, like I said, there are only twelve notes. It's truly overwhelming when you think that we have all this music coming from only twelve notes.

I think it's a cheap shot to take too much from the public domain, be-cause those guys were those guys and their work should be treated with respect. I've heard some showtune writers directly lift Mozart's melodies. I'm talking note for note, people, not just a hint of a famous theme. Unfortunately, some get away with it, and I don't think that's right. I think you need to hear his operas in their original form, because I do think they get bastardized. It's different if someone's using a little motif and turning it around—of course you're going to do that. But when it's almost a direct rip-off of a whole song, not just a phrase, that's just bad.

CHELSEA LAIRD:

She's constantly doing research. The passageway between the outside world and what's inside her, processing things creatively, is constantly open and working. She's open to being inspired by anything. Having spent every day with her for this past year on tour, I now see very clearly that she takes in the "how and what" of a situation very differently from the way I do. For example, we'll be sitting at whatever coffee shop we might find ourselves in that day—doing research, working on an upcoming proj-ect, building the set list—and the next thing I know the woman sitting next to us has become a song. That woman—maybe the way she wore her scarf—has inspired a whole story inside Tori's mind about where she came from and how she found herself here. Of course, that story will be woven together somehow with another story that Tori may have read the day before in the paper from the last city we were in. And those elements will be woven together with a hint of the lavender left in her dressing room two nights earlier. That song may never be recorded, it may just be something fun to play around with during sound check, but it's just one example of Tori the storyteller, weaving her web. Of course, then there is me, half noticing this woman in the café.

Not to say that it's always like that: a lot of times it's all about research. She'll write lyrics down here and there. On whatever is available. On tour she'll leave them with me to keep track of and when the time is right we'll break them out and do some research. Finding, ironically, that they all seem to tie together in some kind of interesting way. The common thread becomes an amazing foundation for a song.

Of all the questions that Tori gets asked, the one that crops up most often from budding songwriters is "How do you continue to write so many songs?" Even the Peabody Conservatory, where she studied piano as a child, continues to ask her to come speak to their students on the subject of song composition. I'll look at her and say, "How can you even begin to formulate an explanation for that one? I live with you and I still don't get it."

TORI:

You're asleep or you're awake or a bit of both—it doesn't matter. You're always composing . . . in the shower, watching a special on the global development of football (soccer), listening to the farmers herding the cattle through the mud, falling out with a friend, getting a call from someone whose lover committed suicide with a chicken, staring forever and a day out of those windows on the train to London, in Selfridges as the cashiers talk about what almost happened the night before . . . If you are a composer in your soul, you are constantly gathering details for characters that could be an extension of yourself, which all become seeds to plant in your song garden. If you are a composer in your soul, you chase frequency, sound, melody, rhythm, chords, the word, and if you're lucky, once in a while they chase you. This is musical shem-an-na (the ancient word for the ultimate food, for the Light-body or Ka). Even before what we read in the Old Testament, in the Bible, about this magical food they call manna—coming seemingly down from heaven—the ancient Sumerians, more than a thousand years prior to the biblical reference, were partaking in their own version of what is shem-an-na. So here we have this musical shem-an-na, traveling from God knows how far, unlocking portholes to bring Divine Essence. Miraculously, we as composers get to cocreate with these sound compounds that can activate us spiritually as well as physically. Because tone is so vital in this kind of form, the tone of the word combined with the tone of the note, combined with the tone of the chords—all this creates a sonic alchemical marriage. How long does this alchemical marriage last in song time? Maybe it lasts two seconds, maybe it's half of a bar at the most sometimes, this alchemical joining. But don't you see, everything in the piece is designed to set up this two-second, five-second, ten-second, whatever it is, magical moment. It's all about how you fill space. It's similar to making love: setup, payoff, basking. I believe this occurrence lives on in your body. You can access this any time—as you do with pictures that live on because you've filed them to be saved in you, a human computer.

Before I go into how I see the songs, let's begin with the idea of a discipline. You have to spend a couple hours every day building up an arsenal of ideas. I call it a song palette. As a composer, you have to bring in different materials to inspire you. It could be books of photographs, books of wood carving, different web sites you go to; it could be a TV show you've gotten hooked on—something that sparks some story in your head. Whatever these things are that stimulate you, you don't devour them like a locust devours and leaves nothing in its wake. You do bring it into your metaphorical paint box—whether you're writing it down, highlighting words, developing character traits: your metaphorical palette can exist in your notebook with chalks and pens or on a computer. But you are keeping a book of this, a record of this, without it being either a book or a record necessarily. This way, over weeks and weeks and weeks, you will have sifted through the information that you've pulled in, and you've extracted the honey. You've extracted where it comes together and fertilizes. You may have one-liners that are random, on their own. You may have one word on its own. You may have a melody that you've written down, that you sang in the shower, and it's only four notes, but it's included in the paint box. This is being a collector of ideas. Great composers are collectors of ideas first. They are able to unite different ideas that might not work on their own but together are complete, a pollination of ideas. This alone was the budding idea that led to my latest project being called *The Beekeeper*. Then, as with dominoes, the beekeeper concept precipitated a myriad of other related concepts that all deal with the male and the female, the union, birth and death, and the art of relationships stripped to its foundation.

This is what the album is about: the different kinds of relationships, healthy and unhealthy, that exist in this woman—let's call her Tori—that exist in Tori's world. So the composing process is everyday. I am composing every day. Do I write a song every day? Of course not. There is a lot of researching. It's a good thing I'm curious, because sometimes I just research how a soccer player kicks a ball and the impact it has on his foot. I haven't used this yet, but I might. This is part of my process. My telling you this doesn't mean that you within your soul are a composer, but if you are, telling you this might light a fire under your bottom so that your palette keeps rotating, no different from the earth, and you keep it topped up, from chalks to charcoals to watercolors. This is my blueprint as a composer. This is how my process works.

The pollination trail has always lured me in. A friend of mine who's a garden architect dropped a book by the beach house. A few weeks later she asked me about it, which reminded me that I even had the book, and thereby I read it and then misplaced it for several years again, until . . . Chelsea found it on one of my bookshelves a few months ago, which got me thinking about beekeeping again. Yes, Meg, I'm going to get you your book back. Sorry for the four-year delay. Meg, fondly called Megnolia, designed the exotic garden with me in Florida which has been completely destroyed by Hurricanes Frances and Jeanne.

MARCEL VAN LIMBEEK:

The nice thing about working with Tori is that all the records sound different. To achieve that you need different elements. She's always done piano; it's always something she's come back to at the end of the day. She's incorporated other keyboards—the harpsichord, the Wurlitzer—and now it's time for the organ. It seems like a logical place to go. It's still an organic sound, not a cheesy synth sound. There are proper organs set up with a Leslie tone cabinet. I actually like it better than any of the previous keyboards she's tried. The piano is a percussive instrument and the organ is more of a sustained sound, so she can hold the notes longer. As long as she can physically hold the notes down (because there is no sustain pedal, unlike on the piano), the organ's sound will actually change while she's kicking that Leslie pedal in and out. It's funny watching her change shoes to play the organ. Recording "Not David Bowie" (a song on the latest record that is a nod to the great man himself but a slag to the bad guys), she had one foot on that Leslie pedal and the other foot on a guitar effects pedal that was maneuvering the sound of the Clav (a Clavinet D6, which Tori affectionately calls the "Stevie Wonder keyboard"). There are no guitars on "Not David Bowie." I suspect that Tori probably wanted people to realize what these organs can really do. Until Mac Aladdin finishes guitars for the album it's hard to know if he'll be adding to this track as he is on most of the others. And with her swapping between keyboards as she does, I think the B3 and the Clav are a great marriage. It excites me because it's a new sound, another instrument. It's as if she's playing with a different musician, only it's herself.

TORI:

The piano has organs. One just came over the Atlantic Ocean from a Gaelic Christian church somewhere in North Michigan. Another one of the piano's organs came from a source here in the west country of England. One of my close musical mentors, John Philip Shenale, has been pushing me to marry my piano with these booty-shaking organs. And I did. A spruced-up and restored clavichord is being flown in this week from a restoring doctor in California. *Wood made of Woman.* This is a subtext for this new album, compositionally and as a thesis. Therefore, the living organism of this Wood Woman needs organs that serve an imperative function if the piano herself is to make this musical transmutation. Or if we're pushing a thought, it being Sunday when I'm writing this, the piano herself has made her transubstantiation—if my father, the Rev. Dr., were inquiring. Yes, Dad, very simply, She Is Risen. Our Lady of the Wood.

SONG CANVAS: "sweet the sting" and "sleeps with butterflies"

Yesterday I spent hours on "Sweet the Sting"; from playing the piano riff over and over to listening to it on my crap tape recorder, to making changes and incorporating them. The story started evolving soon after the B3 Hammond organ, whom I have named "Big Momma," was delivered. Every time I entered the room in the morning to begin my practice time, Big Momma would be humming. Yes, of course her power had been left on, but I'm talking about the kind of humming you detect in a girlfriend after she's had a romantic evening. Turns out Big Momma has a boyfriend. Another organ, specifically another B3 organ. This romance led me to the story of two B3 players, one female, the other male, whose erotic dance revolves around each impressing the other by how well they play their own organ.

I've been researching and listing words that I like the sound and look of for the pollination stakes competition. There is a list of hundreds, so to give my mind a break, I had a wander down the back field to the vegetable garden and the greenhouse. I just hung out there, deciding with Husband where to plant the lavender—anytime there is sun about in England you can't take it for granted, you must bake in it, making yourself the sacrifice, if necessary—just to maybe make it last all day. So, since it was one of those glorious English summer days in the middle of spring, I played hooky from playing piano and flirted with the sun. On my way back from the field, with flower choices in my head, Husband headed off for the Arsenal game and I headed for the picnic table where my gardening book was. I passed the studio with the huge barn doors of the big recording room painted in Madras, a Tuscan Peach, which I had open all morning while I was practicing. Then Bam. There it was . . . After all these months, I looked at Böse, she looked at me, and I went right up, turned the tape recorder on, and Bam . . . the chorus to "Sleeps with Butterflies" was spilling over the keys and I knew she was complete. So after weeks of trying to write my idea of a chorus, the real chorus stepped right up and said, "T, honey, you just take this down and I'll be off to enjoy some flirting with the sun myself."

Did the day effect this? Did the weather? Sure. If I were in another space, then something as simple as a bird's song changes things. Having started a song at one place in the world, say in Bumfuck on the road, then finishing it on a winter's day—with that soft muted Cornish light putting the M in Moody, bringing with it its own references, senses, and perfumes . . . All of these elements get included in that ever-rotating palette.

ANN: *Streams become rivers by merging as they move oceanward. Amos can tap into strong creative currents on her own, but as she has matured she has increasingly sought power in the insights of carefully chosen partners. Entering the recording studio with complete compositions, she opens up her work to the influence of the players and engineers whom she considers her soul's companions.*

CONVERSATION BETWEEN TORI AND ANN:

In my music, bass and guitar are often the male characters. They personify the male or provide underscoring for that element. Sometimes I have to choose which instrument represents what. If there are a couple of male characters, if there's a father in there and if there's a lover, or if there's a female who's in there too, and it's a triangle, the way the instruments interact represents that. The musicians I collaborate with have to be able to hold all that and develop it.

The song structures are in place when I bring the musicians in. I bring Matt in first, or Matt and Jon. I sit and sing a new song to them, and I'm always very shy. And they're counting the bars. I listen to the playback and perform it once more, just to make sure I got it right and they're not notating the wrong version because I was nervous. Then I leave while Mark plays different parts and they notate it. Once it's notated and the sheets are down, then we can go track it. They always have to have a map to go tracking.

I myself never use a score. Never did. For some reason it slows me down and I get trapped in it. I can't get the notation and I find it very confining. I spend too much time sitting there trying to figure it out. And I have quite a good memory. Everyone banks on the fact that I've memorized the song. I've recorded it in my head. I do forget lyrics all the time—everybody who comes to the shows will tell you that—but I rarely forget the music. Sometimes there's a chord change or a voicing, or a left-hand thing that I'll need to record on my little tape recorder, certain details, and the musicians are used to me taking a minute to pull it out.

I invite the players I choose into a collaborative process when it comes to recording. Once the songs are written, then they come and help arrange and develop their parts. Just as they respect me as the songwriter, I respect them as the creative forces behind their parts.

I couldn't imagine somebody calling me in and telling me exactly what to play, and I don't do that with the guys. Why would I be calling in these particular players if I did that? Anyone would do. Artists or producers who dictate their musicians' parts aren't utilizing them well. Matt will come up with something you never thought of, because you're not a drummer and this is his *life*. But telling Matt absolutely anything that can help give him a clearer picture of the world in which you are trying to frame the song is going to give him immediate jumping-off points. As far as Jon goes, what's easy about working with him is that it's hard for him to get confused when it comes to chord voicings, mainly because he's a bad mamma jamma. So that makes it smooth sailing most of the time.

Many people think they're musicians when they're not. Some producers think they know what's best because they're wannabe players. But when you're pulling in players of the caliber of Matt and Jon to tell them precisely what to do, you won't get the best out of these players and it shows where your ego is. I might give them a line on the piano and say, "Let's work around this motif," and sometimes even with the guitar players I'll say, "Can we work around this line?" and "We need our guitar melody to be contrapuntal," or "How can we do this so that somehow you are emphasizing a parallel sixth in the B section?"—I'll do that with them. But to say, "Play exactly like this," when I'm not a guitar player? How offensive.

JON EVANS:

The first time that I felt I really got to explore was when we were recording *To Venus and Back*. I really felt I could do anything. Some songs contain all these sounds I made on bass, and you wouldn't know it, just weird little sounds and tones that I got to experiment with. Tori always wanted me to do whatever I wanted, and if there was a really strange sound that was fine. She didn't want me to "play bass" in the traditional sense, just to feel free. So every song on *Venus* has something particular to it.

Matt had some electronic drums during those sessions and Tori had a bunch of different keyboards that she programmed, doing a lot of loops. Each of us encouraged the others to come up with some other sound that would add to the mix.

MATT CHAMBERLAIN:

The way Tori writes her music allows me to do things that I like to do. When most people write a song, it'll be verse, chorus, verse, chorus, bridge, verse, chorus. The basic song structure. What are you going to do to that? You just play through it. But with her it's so open because she's not laying down anything specific rhythmically. You can do whatever you want, you can play percussion, electronics—it's crazy. It's great. To me it seems like improvisational songwriting. She'll have a topic or something in her head that she wants to convey and she'll just put it to music. For example, I think it was on *To Venus and Back* where she said a particular song was about being on an ice planet. She wanted me to play that kind of drum part. So I came up with what I thought was an icy sound.

Every song of Tori's is so different. Some want to be churchy or gospel-flavored, requiring a funky drum kit sound, and then some songs are more electronic in nature and require sound creation as opposed to just plain drums. A lot of her songs are tribal, tom-heavy, and I use bongos and sticks. She doesn't reference things literally in her music, so you can get away with doing things that would sound too literal if applied to another writer's work. I can play bongos and congas on a Tori track and she's not going to sound like Miami Sound Machine. Whatever song it is, I try to do something that seems interesting from a drummer's point of view. That works with her. It doesn't work with any of the other artists I've worked with. I don't know why.

With each record I experiment; even if it doesn't work, it's safe for me to stick my neck out and see what happens. With *Scarlet's Walk*, the first thing I told Tori was "Okay, there are two things I want to do on this record. If you guys agree with me, great—if you don't, then we'll work it out. The first one is, I don't want to use any electronic drums or drum loops. I want to play everything in real time." And the second one was more of a technical thing; I wanted both the bass drumheads to be on the bass drum. Usually drummers take the front head off and stick a microphone inside, and the drums end up sounding really modular, rather than the complete kit making a unified impact. I wanted the sound to be really hyperacoustic, a great recording of drums in a room. Just a really great, timeless drum sound that in twenty years you can listen to and go, "Cool, I'm glad we didn't use the technology that was hip at the time." She had written all these great songs and I really just wanted to stay out of the way. So she agreed, and we got that sound.

On other occasions, I've taken the opposite approach. For *Choirgirl* we tried all kinds of crazy stuff; I brought out some Native American drums and I would just play some grooves into the computer and we'd find little bits and chop them up and make drum loops out of them, and then we'd layer things on top, maybe put some live acoustic drums in on the choruses. And then on *Venus* we ran electronic drums into the guitar amps and miked those amps, so all the electronic drums you hear are completely intertwined with the guitar. In general, I'll just say, "Tori, let me try this," and I'll disappear for a while and then bring what I've discovered to her and Mark and say, "Check it out, what do you think?" And I'm so lucky because usually she's like, "Yeah, let's do it."

The new record is actually a lot of everything we've done so far. A little *Venus* and *Choirgirl* and *Scarlet* combined. Electronics, a bunch of percussion, a bunch of acoustics. She was saying the title was *The Beekeeper,* so keeping that pollination factor in mind I could go anywhere. It's just combinations of things—acoustic drums with electronics or electronics with percussion or a B3 with her Granny, her Hammond chord organ. A combination of instruments we haven't gotten into specifically. There is one song, the title track, "The Beekeeper," it's all electronic drums pretty much, until the end bit, when we shift to acoustic. We haven't really done that kind of combining since *Choirgirl,* where it can change that drastically—organs, electronics, drums. There is a lot of stuff going on. A lot of cross-pollination kinds of things. Most of the stuff as far as the drum kits go isn't traditional, either. I'll piece things together and end up with a hip-hop-style drum kit. Smaller drums instead of the big rock drums we use for a more acoustic sound. So now these drums are really small and focused and the sound is more focused.

There is definitely a sound to this record. More focused and stripped down. It's organic yet electronic, a lot of different things. Songs like "Hootchie Woman" and "Sweet the Sting" are total percussion, full-on Afro-Cuban. But it's definitely different from the last album. Less Americana and more pulling in all sorts of sounds. It's everything we've all learned, all at once. Marcel and Mark, Tori, Jon and I. Everything everybody has ever learned about making a record together is all being laid out on the table for everyone else to grab from, different influences. Everyone has a big enough vocabulary now because we've worked together so many times. Someone can say, "I want to do this." I'll want to go electronic. She'll want to go with the organ. Jon will grab his stand-up bass. Put some percussion on it. Everyone just goes, "Cool, we know how to do that, let's go."

TORI:

You cocreate with an infinite source . . .

There are songs coming right now that are exciting to me as a player because they are a bit different for me. I've increased my rhythmic ability since working with Matt and Jon for hundreds of hours. When I got the organs, the B3 (Big Momma), the A100, and the Granny, I would just spend time finding my way around them—jamming on them, developing my own kind of relationship with the organ itself. Then I began to be able to interpret these creatures differently from how I would have three years ago. But these particular song creatures didn't come to me three years ago. And I have to ask myself if that is because I didn't have the ability, as an organ player, to interpret them. With "Witness" coming in, and

"Ireland"—they reveal a side of my playing that some people won't be as familiar with. But I don't think that it will surprise Matt and Jon at all, because after all these years, I've been put through their Booty Camp. Funnily enough, I had Booty Camp T-shirts made up for them in January 1998.

When these song Beings first started coming in, I would look at them and say, "Hey, I'm glad you crashed my party, but are you sure you don't want to be traveling over to hang with the seventies funk band, Rufus?" But the message I keep getting is "Our time is now, and you'd better deliver us. Because we are ready. And we will groove your world, Miss T."

I believe that the songs choose you, but you have to be willing to develop and stretch as a player, or your repertoire is only going to be of a certain type.

MARK HAWLEY:

Tori has learned to leave more space in her music. And she likes the results. This comes from Marcel and me saying to her, "Yeah, it's great to have a loud vocal, and we want to have a loud vocal, but there's got to be room for a loud vocal." And if there's less stuff in the mix, so that everything really counts, then it makes for a much more spacious arrangement, and you know every element will be heard well. It's not that she just took our word for it; she sees the results in the mixes. So when she goes back to writing again, she's clever enough to be able to incorporate that.

JOHN WITHERSPOON:

Tori learned how to be a producer making *Boys for Pele*. There were certain people around her who were saying, "You can't produce your own record, you've got to do it traditionally, you have to go to the studio, you can't do it in a church, you can't do it in a house. Go and do it the normal way." In the course of making that record I certainly learned something, and she did as well, which was that the traditional way of making records involved big kickbacks from the labels to the suppliers they worked with, and half your money went nowhere, as far as you could tell. That's when we took over all of the finances. Basically we said, "Just give us the money and we'll make a record." And that's what we've done ever since, on every record. We pay the bills and the musicians and just do it ourselves.

MARK HAWLEY:

I think we spend a lot of money making a record, but we put it into the record. We live very well, but the point is that record labels will blow a lot more making one video than we do making a whole album. And you're lucky if that video gets played ten times on MTV. But the people who are telling you how much the budget is are the same people directly involved in marketing. Videos, photo shoots—they want to spend money on what they're doing. We spend it on the music.

CHELSEA LAIRD:

In the studio, Mark and Tori have a relationship that's like any working re-lationship. And like any working relationship there are occasional fights. A producer is telling her engineer, "No, this is the way I want it," and natu-rally he'll respond saying, "Well, I think you're wrong." But there is no hes-itation. She's not thinking, *I have to go to bed with this man tonight—do I really want to piss him off?* It's all for the art in the studio. They'll fight it out and work it out. But at the end of the day we all have dinner together, no matter what. It's a big round table; Duncan cooks and we all eat to-gether. Whether it's the band, the mastering engineer, Jon Astley, Marcel, Adam Spry—our resident tech, Helen Gilbert—the Martian accountant, or whoever happens to be working at the studio that day, we all have dinner together every night, and by then whatever's happened in that day has been left there. In a sense it's another cleansing ritual.

MARCEL VAN LIMBEEK:

Mark and Tori are my best working friends. Their relationship isn't a factor when we are working. Of course, it's Tori's product and she's the boss. The way it works within our triangle is that none of us can live with either of the others being unhappy with any piece of the project. I can't stand it when Tori doesn't like something and she can't stand it when something is bugging me. The way it works is that we always have to agree. It's Tori's record and she'll always have her end say, but she always listens to Mark and me. She won't let anything slide by knowing that I don't like it or Mark doesn't like it. The fact that they are married doesn't come into it. It's good. It's something I'm very proud of.

CONVERSATION BETWEEN TORI AND ANN:

During my career, I've learned from making mistakes on both ends of the spectrum. I've not been present as far as what's happening in the studio, with terrible results, and I've been too pushy, too. I've learned to be a little more democratic without abandoning my authority. You have to be able to delegate the details, so that you can keep your focus on the architect's plans.

The one tricky thing I've learned from being a producer is how to be able to walk in and out, keep my ears fresh so that I could pick up on things. That's the best thing a producer can do in a mix room: come in, come out, come in, come out. And you have to find ways to keep your mind rejuvenated. If you stay in the room all the time, you're in the exact same space as the engineers. You always need an outside force to be coming in and out of that mix room. We decided, the three of us, that that would be me. Because I'm not an engineer, it would be silly. Some producers are engineers, so then they have to have another person who walks in and out. It is really vital that somebody has that role. Because then that person's able to say, "Well, you know, the drums are a little bright." Or "The EQ isn't right on this—we'll need to go after a different effect." Things jump out at you because you haven't gotten used to them—you're not dulled to them. It's a lot like being an editor.

ANN: *What kind of tale does a song tell? On one level, it tells of its own making, capturing the thrill of that first inspirational rush, the more difficult progression of choices that gives it structure, and the give-and-take of its blossoming forth from a single artist's vision during collaborative performance. One thing is for sure: though they have authors, songs do not tell stories that belong to one person. Songs, those puzzle boxes of memory, longing, and bliss, speak beyond their makers' intonation, breathe beyond their realities. They could not possibly stop at only one story.*

CONVERSATION BETWEEN TORI AND ANN:

The story world is always running parallel with my world. I've allowed myself to be okay with taking hikes into that world and then coming back. Tash will go with me into story world, which is great. Sometimes Mark will say, "Okay, guys, I'll see you back in our reality in a few minutes." It's wonderful to have a little friend who will go with me. She's very much about, well, let's play school, or let's take on this character, take on that character. The latest permutation of this is her playing Mommy and me playing Baby. It's gotten to the point where Husband will say, "Excuse me, Baby, I need to talk to my wife a moment." Tash will say, "Go ahead, Husband." Then Husband will say, "No child, my real wife." But the great thing about this is that I hear Tash rehash phrases that Mark and I have said to her. So when she's playing Mommy I get a sense of how what I say is heard by her and the effect it has on her developing tapestry. We learn from our role-playing.

So much of what you do in songwriting is role-playing. That's how you develop your different characters within the song. It's not as if the stories merge to a point where you think they are your life, but you do let them in through the front door and the back door, and it's okay that sometimes certain characters stay for dinner.

The songs give me the ability to live a thousand lives. That's why people keep trying to connect real life with our songs. They ask, "Did this really happen to you?" Well, all of it did, on some level. And none of it did, on another. Meaning, not exactly as I write it. Because I wouldn't be a writer then. I'd just be keeping a diary. And also, I'm cocreating with a song, with its soul—talk about a soul song . . .

In a way that's the most misunderstood thing about my work: where and even whether I am in the songs. I don't think anybody really and truly knows what character I am in a given composition. They can presume, but even Husband doesn't know. Somebody said to me the other day, "Don't you need something to happen in your life to be able to write about?" I said, "Are you nuts? Have you just missed the whole boat of what I do?" You think this is about me, and I've made you think that, but you don't know which "me" I am within my work. I may not be the benevolent character in every scenario. Sometimes I'm exploring sides that I see in somebody else. It strikes a chord in me and I play it out in the song world.

SONG CANVAS: "cars and guitars"

One morning not long ago, I was driving into town in Cornwall, and a scenario occurred to me that involved a woman who just keeps driving.

She gets up in the morning, has to go to work, has to get the kids ready for school, has to deal with the in-laws, the husband, everybody's needs. She becomes completely depleted, and hormonal—God knows what's happening that day. So she just says, "I can't do this anymore" (sound familiar?) and keeps on driving. She doesn't pick that kid up from school—she makes a call and says, "I need you to pick him up, take care of him until I get home." Then maybe she just walks out of her life. She doesn't necessarily kill herself, but just decides, "I can't do this anymore." Now, this story probably happens every day. It's not me—I didn't keep driving. But I want to explore that. I think it's hard for the audience to accept that an artist they love, who is one of the good guys, as they see it, would even explore one of these archetypes—in the case of this story, Kali, goddess of destruction, is at play here—and that can be scary. Certain archetypes are scary because they bring up specific qualities within us that maybe we have buried deep, deep down. And sometimes these qualities erupt, and this is where Pele comes in, and she can be quite a 50-Percent-Off-Your-Personality-Clearance-Sale type of teacher. But I can hang around for that.

CONVERSATION BETWEEN TORI AND ANN:

I'm usually in my songs somewhere because I can understand the subject matter only if I've had some kind of experience that helps me get it. But the work transcends my own experience. I've tried to explain this to people. I'll say so many times after telling a story to someone, "It's not necessarily about my own experience but someone else's, and yet I've had a similar experience that brings up the same reaction that this someone might have had. How many of you have had the experience I've explored in any given song? How many of you haven't experienced that exact set of circumstances that occur in the song, but you still have an emotional response to that song, because it has triggered something you can't explain?"

Sometimes I'll be in a public place, eavesdropping on another table. The way the person I'm listening to tells her story is putting her friend in Snoozeland. This would especially happen when I was playing piano in lounges. It's not as if the elements of the story aren't crackin', but there is just no framework to allow the listener to dive into this story painting. I'd just see someone, blah blah blah blah, and I'd be playing and listening and remaking the story in my own head. Because such people don't know how to weave a tale, unlike Scheherazade. They can't bring you into it, or push you away from it, which could make you want to be let into the story—sometimes that's a tactic, too. Another tactic is, you just leave everybody on the outside. Don't open that museum door, let them stand outside the Louvre going crazy because they can't get in. There's an exhibition in there, and they can kind of catch a glimpse of it, but they're irritated because they want to see more and yet still they won't leave. Why? Because they are tantalized. I've written songs like that.

Then there are occasions when you have to mask your characters. You can't reveal who a person is in a song, even to that very person. I have songs, I must be honest, that to this day people don't know are about them. They'll say, "God, that character is really awful. I would never want to meet them." And it *is* them. But I won't give it away. Because once you blow your source, you're blown forever. No one would want to be around me. Plus, I might not agree that the character is awful. Certain archetypes will push it, and, let's face it, sometimes changes are painful at first.

Since I was three, I've been writing songs and changing certain elements so nobody could find out whom I was actually writing about. I started writing about the church and what was going on and who was diddling whom, the chat you get in choir. I wrote about the puritanical witch-burner old prunes that were holier than thou. The Freak, whose daughter was in the choir, masquerading an upstanding-citizen image, all the while drooling behind his hymnal every time we sang the word "virgin." My friend Connie and I would be like, "Here it comes, here it comes," and, *bingo*, Freako's drool just misses the hymnal. I began to learn very early that there were a lot of shenanigans going on. And it did really shock me, and my mother's the type of lady who would not discuss that kind of stuff. She would not be drawn in.

But even as a kid, I knew that I was a composer and that I had to put this information somewhere in order to keep a record of the truth, because ninety percent of what was really going on got turned around and swept under the carpet. Soon certain events just faded, like paint does on walls; consequently you can't remember why you have such a bee in your bonnet about certain things that get brought up in conversation. So I decided to avoid being a loose cannon. My only choice was to put what I saw into the music. When you're a kid you can't just leave the house and move away—well, for me that wasn't an option, mainly because I adored my mother. But sometimes I felt as if "those who are they" and their need to control were trying to infuse me with their belief system and their opinions so that I would cease to be a heretic. Knowing that I couldn't do anything about my surroundings and everyone's beliefs around me, that as far as Christianity goes there was one Book, and one Book only—there was no place to run, there was no place to hide from being inundated by what I considered to be not the whole truth. But I had no proof. To survive Christian boot camp for twenty years, and I don't mean Gnostic Christian, I had to create sonic paintings that I could step into just so I could nurture my own beliefs while surrounded by the Puritanical Christian Army's "Gospel of *Forward March*" and "Holy Communion of the *Inverted Rope Descent.*"

The people I love, and even those who just happen to be around a lot, unquestionably make it into the work. They're like ghosts. They walk through songs; they come in and out of doors. But I've always said that the songs have their own lovers, and birthplaces, and beliefs. Maybe I did feel something with Mark on the second verse or the seventeenth bar, or something he says will show up in a song that's actually about women arguing with each other. There are moments of Mark in songs. He's part of "Lust," obviously. But that's also about a story of Jesus and the Magdalene being lovers. Lovers throughout time. I think all of us carry the Lover. That's true of many archetypes. How could I possibly own any of them?

chapter four

demeter: the journey into motherhood

TORI AND DAUGHTER NATASHYA IN A DRESSING ROOM BACKSTAGE

ANN: *Few stories that mark the long scroll of myth are as moving as that of Demeter and her daughter Persephone. The virgin's kidnapping and forced marriage to Hades, the god of the underworld, is traumatic enough on its own, but the tale's truly woeful figure is Demeter, the mother whose grief is so great at the sudden loss of her child that it plunges the entire earth into barrenness. Hers is a fate of wandering and rage, of a pain so great that it destroys everything around it, and—when the males who run the show grant Persephone the right to return for only part of each year—of a maternal fulfillment forever tinged by loss. This story, which probably originated in a simple need to explain the turn of the seasons, exposes such basic qualities of the soul—the fear of death that can never be fully mitigated by the acceptance of life's cycles and the unsettling, indeed sometimes perilous magnitude of maternal love—that it became the basis for the Eleusinian mysteries, the central religious rites of ancient Greece.*

Demeter's spirit continually resurfaces in the modern world. Motherhood, always an affair that pulls open the heart, has become complicated by women's changing sense of themselves and their place. Some, having put off pregnancy in favor of self-fulfillment, endure years of struggle to conceive. Once children do come, mothers must fathom how to give them everything possible without losing their own identities in the process. The work of motherhood remains obscured by ideas of what should come naturally to women, its joys trivialized by sentimental renderings.

Tori Amos came to motherhood on a hard and treacherous road. Before giving birth to her daughter, Natashya, she had to face her own physical limitations, the duplicity that can surface within the "fertility industry," and the disconnect between the hard-driving entertainment world and the more cyclical demands of starting a family. Natashya has brought Amos a sense of peace, but also made her fiercer than ever. Growing into motherhood has given Amos new ways to think about music, love, loyalty, and her own heritage. Now, along with other women artists of her generation, she is working to create a new balance between the "public" dominion of work and creative expression and the "private" enclave of child rearing. Acknowledging the unified nature of these efforts without being willing to compromise either, she offers a very personal perspective on the feminine coming to terms with itself.

CONVERSATIONS BETWEEN TORI AND ANN:

My mother taught me about sovereignty, a sense of your own authority. She was the most educated person in our family. She wanted to be a college teacher. On one level I think it's unfortunate that she didn't continue with her career once she had her kids, but what she did get from the world she brought back to me. She showed me how to create my own realm, a realm of the word, without owning any terrain myself. For women like us, who are working, her example still inspires: we go out and own what we own, but when we come back to our children and tell them our stories, we teach them how to possess themselves, however they choose to later take on the world.

I remember being five and hearing about the women burning their bras. I remember this movement. And I remember my mother watching from the sidelines, quiet, as the minister's wife who'd given up her literary career. She had missed that generation. Unless she was willing to give up everything, she couldn't find a place within feminism. It would have been too much to ask her to abandon her life. At the end of the day she really loved my father and her family more than she wanted a career. Yet as the years went on I could see in her a burning, a desire that could not be fulfilled as long as she held the mother role the way women had to at that time.

As a minister's wife, my mother did do something similar to what I do as an artist. When she met somebody walking through that receiving line in church, she would portray what that person wanted to see. This had nothing to do with who Mary Ellen Copeland was. She read a lot of literature and began to become other pieces, reflecting back what that particular person needed to see in a minister's wife.

The conflict I sensed in my mother was one reason I was willing to go on the artistic and spiritual search that became my life for so long. I got drawn in as a really young child, Tash's age, when I was starting to spend all my time on the piano. There was something brewing in me, drawing me to the Magdalene, never the Mother Mary, which is unfortunate. I became more drawn to the mother aspect later.

Waiting to have children is a risk, as I discovered, but there are good reasons to do it. Medical science is trying to catch up with the changes that the feminist movement helped make for us. Our bodies haven't quite caught up yet to help us achieve that. Mentally and responsibility-wise, many of us aren't ready to be mothers and put somebody else first at twenty-five, because in our society we're taught to find out who we are first. I know a lot of twenty-five-year-olds who are not ready to put another Being first. Talk to Chelsea. When she's here with Natashya and me, sometimes she'll just say, "I can't believe how much a child needs." And I say, "Chels, I can't believe how selfish we can be." But we're just in different places right now.

ANN: *Amos was finally ready to enter motherhood in her early thirties. She felt strong in her music, and her soul connection with Mark Hawley had begun. Like so many female high achievers, she thought she would accomplish this next goal as confidently as she had so many others. She soon discovered that the goddess guide who walks you through life's passages might not be the one you'd hoped you'd meet.*

CONVERSATION BETWEEN TORI AND ANN:

Not long before my first miscarriage in 1996, I had my chart done by mythic astrologer Wendy Ashley. I'd had my chart done many times, but I was beginning to figure out who the charlatans were versus the credible people, and this woman is at the top of her field. It's not like you're dialing 1-800-PSYCHIC; this woman studied mythology under Joseph Campbell. I was beginning to see myth in my life.

I didn't want my myth, the one the charts revealed to me. This was when I was making *Pele*, Mark and I were together, and I thought I might be pregnant. I had this first reading and was given the Rhiannon myth. Rhiannon was a Welsh queen who lost her child under horrible circumstances: he was kidnapped and her subjects accused her of not only killing him but also eating him alive. She was then forced to serve penance within the court for seven years, until her son finally returned.

I didn't want to know about that. Are you kidding? Who wants to hear that? I was not even concerned about the other meanings of Rhiannon in popular culture, the fairy thing, the fact that Stevie Nicks had claimed her in a song—I simply did not want to hear that I could even possibly lose a child. I was sitting there, saying, *Wait a minute, where's Dionysus, where's Sekhmet? I can't believe this.* It was a bitter pill to swallow.

Really, at first, I couldn't take it. I said, *That's not going to happen to me.* And of course it didn't happen just once—it happened three times. But I think I was missing the importance of the archetype. What mattered wasn't that Rhiannon lost Pryderi, her son, or even that she was accused of destroying him. What I needed to notice was her willingness to serve, for seven years, when people had accused her. It's a story of survival with dignity, and concentration on work rather than on your own ego. During this time, when I was having so much trouble carrying a child, and also going into dark places in my music with *Pele* and

Choirgirl, I really needed to have Rhiannon's guiding spirit to help me make it through.

SONG CANVAS: "pandora's aquarium"

Because I have a lot of songs in my life that come with archetypes intrinsic to their own myths, I feel as if I've been able to try on many different archetypes. So much so that it feels like a Pandora's box of archetypes sometimes. But not all of them figure in to my personal myths. Of course, they do when I step into the jeans of a song and take on that archetype in performance, whether in the studio or onstage. But I had to separate archetypes that I play with and that, yes, may affect me but are not foundational in my personal myth. Just as I had to accept Rhiannon as one of the pieces that make up my core person, I also had to realize that I am more aligned with Demeter than with Aphrodite, or even Persephone, who seemed like an archetype that I could claim. Even though there is a violation and a rape involved in my life, that story isn't my core. For example, Persephone is Beenie's myth. (Beenie is Nancy Shanks, one of my closest friends. We've developed the habit of calling each other "Beenie," stemming from the expression "Do you know what I mean, bean?") Beenie has been not only a best friend, but at times the nurturing force in our friendship. At other times, I've been the nurturer. Beenie was molested by her father from the age of two through the age of seven, a nightmare that recalls the rape of Persephone and the betrayal by Persephone's father, Zeus, and her entire life has been devoted to healing the deepest, most invasive unseeable scar that one can ever have. She has truly made a journey through the depths—the madness of bipolar anxiety disorder, which now is still a day-to-day struggle. But by making her wound her wise wound, she has transmuted her multiple rapes and betrayals into a fabric that is a piece in the rich tapestry of

Persephone, Queen of the Underworld. Beenie is no longer only the ravished, victimized Kore (Greek for "maiden"). Together Demeter and Persephone are maiden, mother, and crone.

TORI:

According to *Goddess: Myths of the Female Divine* by David Leeming and Jake Page, Demeter "had become the Grain Goddess of the fertility mysteries celebrated and practiced at Eleusis. Her daughter had become the menarcheal Grain or Corn Maiden seed of life . . . Demeter was the giver of the fruit of the earth. She was the sacred Womb Mother of all . . . With her always, and within, was her daughter, as a seed is encased in the moist flesh of the peach. Demeter's law, her nine mysteries, were well known in the land, and it flourished. With the coming of Zeus

pandora

and his legions to Olympus, Demeter and her daughter, Persephone, came to be seen as two—mother and daughter, separate but inseparable." Beenie has lived to radiate and teach with grace, love, and clarity the sacredness of a parent-child bond and the horrific effects for child and parent when it has been penetrated. To see how incest can shred and divide a Being is the scariest thing I've witnessed in my life. "Bells for Her," "Cornflake Girl," and "Carbon" have been inspired by Beenie.

Because of the work that she had done to heal her complicated and painful path, she was able to recognize what work I needed to do in order to heal the snags in my Being's embroidery. I've had to deal with the devouring since I was very little, the devouring of everything I believe in and the devouring that comes from being a possession. That is different from a rape, when we talk about it archetypally. Going back to my Native American heritage, I'm more connected to the myth of someone pimping the land and not understanding the land has its own sovereignty. Back to my mother, too, her need for sovereignty, and finally to my own journey toward motherhood, which felt so much like the scourge that Demeter endured as the goddess of the seasons, that autumnal loss of life.

I had to surrender to my circumstances. I felt a driving force to become a mother and it took over my life. I didn't achieve it for a few years and I wore it around. Do you know that some journalist came up to me and said the word going around was that I was a drug addict? I said, "What?" He said, "Well, everybody is saying that the mood swings and the depression could only mean one thing," and I said, "Didn't you think about what a miscarriage could do to a woman, and not just one, but three? Did you think that I was pregnant when I did that tour with Alanis—did you think that maybe I could be?"

I had to go get my personal life in gear, and that's what I spent a few years doing. I generated music that reflected that time. And it wasn't necessarily stuff that the masses could ingest, but if you're in that particular place in your life, I think those records are a good place to go. And once I had Natashya, I moved into a more nurturing place. And I surrendered to the fact that I'm not the ingenue anymore. I'm not the desired object. I had to accept Rhiannon, and now I know I am in the Demeter role.

ANN: *As painful as her first miscarriage was, Amos had more to endure in her quest to give birth to a daughter. Soon she ran across a chilling situation that far too many women encounter—an unscrupulous member of the medical profession. As she juggled work, her health, and the demands of her muse, she found herself having to take drastic steps to avoid unexpected peril.*

SONG CANVAS: "Muhammad, My friend"

I was working with the dark goddesses during and after making *Boys for Pele*. Pele herself, and the Sumerian goddess Inanna (also known as Ishtar/Astarte), whose name I cry out singing on the song "Caught a Light Sneeze." Then, naturally, Lilith, niece of Inanna, as well as Demeter, because of the loss of a child with my first miscarriage. I had gone to the underworld to try to claim my daughter back. I went to the edges, the parameters of what I know about consciousness on this plane, to try to make deals with the Christian God, with the Islamic God— a relationship I explore in "Muhammad, My Friend." I was willing to do whatever it took to bring her back, anything, anywhere. I was negotiating. Just saying, *If you will, give me my daughter,* thinking I would get pregnant again and her spirit would come back. Not accepting that she'd moved on and picked another mommy, which is very hard to come to terms with.

CONVERSATION BETWEEN TORI AND ANN:

Then something happened, and it was far more frightening than what I'd gone through before. I'd been invited to collaborate with the composer Patrick Doyle on the soundtrack for the film *Great Expectations*. I really liked his work, and I came up with "Siren" based on his theme. I also liked the film's director, Alfonso Cuarón; although we didn't always agree musically, he was the ultimate charming man. The whole concept for the album was to call in songwriters of a certain level to make the soundtrack a real collaboration. We were completely committed to making it work. But while I was working on this, I started hemorrhaging.

It was a three-week project, and the whole time I was bleeding a lot. Twelve pads a day. I was weak, and trying to not be too grumpy. I'd gone through female things before; you develop a bit of an attitude that this is your lot in life. So I was just pulling it all together, even though I didn't know what was wrong with me. I had already been operated on for endometriosis and a precancerous cervical condition. I was thirty-four at this time.

Eventually I called my sister, who's an internist in the Washington, D.C., area and one of the smartest doctors I know, and she said, "You need to see a doctor. I want you to come back home." I said, "I can't, I'm in the middle of this movie project; we're at Air Studios in London and about to do strings." I was singing with this huge orchestra, and besides my song I was going to do vocalizations for the soundtrack. Day by day I was getting a bit worse, but I was still trying to get up every morning and go. Nobody knew about the bleeding at the time, besides Mark, who was with me.

After finishing the soundtrack I was scheduled to take a trip partly organized by Ahmet Ertegun's office, to go to Romania and Turkey and research vampirism. Ahmet seemed to understand the deep-seated need I had to search out clues that maybe Eastern Europe and Turkey held, to fill the harrowing emptiness that had become my solar plexus, my womb. I had been drained, literally drained. I was researching a lot at the time and trying to understand creation—destruction of creation and the missing pieces in the Genesis creation story that seemed to be found mysteriously in texts that had been hidden for ages. Obviously, blood plays a part in creation and destruction, in birth and in death, in a broken hymen as gift to a lover or a shredded vulva in a rape. My next work was going to be about that subject, ironically enough, the sanctity of creation and destruction. *Choirgirl* did end up having a lot about emotional vampirism in it; it's one of the layers. So is creation and destruction. I know this trip would have taught me a lot. It was a three-week trip. We were going to see the Sufi dancing if we could. I was opening up to the esoteric Islamic traditions.

I really wanted to go on this trip. But after talking to my sister, I decided to act on my health instead of just enduring it. I went to a doctor who was supposedly one of the best. Little did I know, this guy would later be questioned for removing women's body parts. There was a major British television documentary about it. I went to this guy not knowing that he was going to book me that afternoon to take out my fallopian tube. He said I had an ectopic pregnancy. I knew it was wrong when he examined me, shoving this huge thing up me—talk about a piercing, talk about pain. It was just this old medieval kind of instrument he shoved up, and blood gushed everywhere. I knew I had to be in the studio in a couple of hours, singing in front of a seventy-piece orchestra. Johnny was at the studio kind of holding ground for me.

My sister, Dr. Marie Dobyns, had said, "Get me on the line when you're with that doctor. I will be up at four a.m. waiting for your phone call before I go to the hospital to do my rounds." So that morning, after I had tests, this doctor character got my sister on the phone while I was sitting there, and he made some kind of negative comment about a female doctor. She just cut right through that and demanded, "What are Tori's hormone levels?" He told her what they were and said, "She has an ectopic and I want to take her today." My sister didn't say anything to him at that moment, but when he handed me the line, she said, "Baby, you listen to me like you've never listened to me in your life—calmly you are going to have to run for your life . . . he's going to destroy your insides. I don't care what you tell him, but get out of there now and call me as soon as you're outside in your car. I will be waiting right here, and I'd better hear from you in five minutes. I'm calling Johnny to alert him of the danger that you are in since he's just across town in case you need help getting out."

My hands were shaking, which is unusual for a piano player, as I put down the phone. I knew that this was one of the most important performances of my life. I told the doctor I couldn't go in that day but I was ready to come back the next day. I even reserved a room at the hospital for the next few days. The doctor had to check me out so I could go back into the studio. He was expecting me to come back and sleep in the hospital that night; I had a bed. The nurses had given me pain pills; I had them in my back pocket. As I was leaving, he said, "So, Miss Amos, you know I dealt with one of the Beatles before." It was just unbelievable. My heart was palpitating. And I said, "I'm going to go do strings at the studio," and he said, "I know where you'll be and you'd better be back tonight—releasing you is against my better judgment." Obviously he knew I didn't have an ectopic, so he knew it wasn't quote-unquote life and death for me. He was just going to take my fallopian tube and had talked to me about in vitro. He told me not to worry if I lost a fallopian tube, that there was in vitro. And little did I know, he had a huge in vitro practice.

As soon as I got into the waiting car downstairs, the driver said John Witherspoon needed me to call him immediately. I did. Johnny said, "Jesus, T, Mark and I should've been there with you; we had no idea you'd meet the resurgence of Jack the Ripper. Call Marie so that we can figure out the next step." I call my sister and she said, "Sweetheart, you're gonna be okay, just hang in there. I've called Johnny, and we're getting you on a flight tomorrow and you're going to see Dr. Marlow"—he's the surgeon who had done my surgery for the other two conditions, he's the big woman's doctor in Washington, D.C.

So I left the hospital and went to the studio and sang. When I didn't come back, this butcher even called Johnny and threatened to call the airline to stop me from getting on the plane. This is where our strategy really made a difference—you give people information, just not the key information. We threw him off the track by telling him I never fly under my own name. Which isn't true. What is true is that I didn't fly under the name Tori Amos. I flew under my Christian name. And he didn't know to look for that. He didn't know how to track me down.

My sister and my parents met me at the airport, and as soon as I got off the plane they took me right to the hospital. I went in and was diagnosed with a bleeding cyst. Dr. Marlow took care of it. They also felt that something had occurred but didn't work—a pregnancy that didn't attach. So I got a D&C. And I flew back to England. Then I was sick for three months. There was the month of not feeling well, the month of hemorrhaging, and the month of recovery. So that was a big deal. Mark asked me to marry him after this ordeal. It was like, *We're in this for the long haul, and you're okay, and I want to be there.*

Going through this horror, I was completely humbled by what it was to be a human woman. I could be a female icon and channel that and hold that and bring the songs in—really, I felt the songs were iconic. But at this point I realized that if you put yourself at the center you've stopped becoming part of the cocreation. You have to understand that you're a piece of it. To not behave that way is to be like a doctor playing God.

It is amazing that I eventually would be able to carry a child, considering all that had happened, but it wasn't over yet. Dr. Marlow wouldn't let me go on the Turkey trip; he told me I could finish the soundtrack and that's it. That was when Mark was building the place in Cornwall, and I went from D.C. to the Florida beach house. Beenie came with me, and I just walked on the beach every day and wrote for a few hours. I was really disappointed about not being able to go to Romania and do the album research. I said to Husband, who wasn't yet officially Husband, that I really wanted to go and immerse myself in Vlad the Impaler, and he said, "My dear, clearly you've already been impaled!"

ANN: *Humor helped Amos and Hawley bear their losses, but it wasn't always enough. Like Demeter gazing toward the underworld in search of her daughter's vital spirit, Amos, especially, found herself in affinity with a host of lost spirits. They came to her because she could give them a voice, but in the end they surprised her by giving her an even more powerful gift: solace.*

DEMETER, THE GREEK GODDESS OF AGRICULTURE AND FERTILITY, AND HER DAUGHTER, PERSEPHONE

CONVERSATIONS BETWEEN TORI AND ANN:

After the second miscarriage, I made *from the choirgirl hotel.* I took on the subject of my loss directly in those songs. The album clearly came from a place of grief, but also from deciding that instead of fighting the patriarchy and expressing rage and defiance, I had to do something new. That was not what I needed then. Those emotions and insights didn't offer the clues to get me through the game of Myst I was playing at that point.

Then the songs started to come, and they held my hand in such a beautiful way. I felt as if I were surrounded by these women and children that somehow knew what I had faced. The songs that came were all the children that couldn't be with their mothers. They were ghosts. It's okay in literature, in a novel like Toni Morrison's *Beloved,* for example, to talk about ghosts, but the idea that there's a consciousness beyond us that can express itself in a song seems weird to many people. I say, though, how can you not believe that? Especially if you're an artist, it's pretty egocentric not to give credit beyond your own talent and intellect—basically that means claiming that you are the sole source of your own inspiration. I don't accept that. I know that my role as an artist is to provide an opening for voices and stories that go beyond my own small, private existence. I knew this with *Choirgirl* because the songs brought me something I needed that I couldn't provide for myself. These songs were children who had found another plane, or mothers who had gone before who had experienced this loss, and they came to share my grief.

Choirgirl was the antithesis of "Cornflake Girl," because it was a case of women coming together to support each other. These songs were the supportive, nurturing women. We walk into Demeter, not Aphrodite. This was an unbelievable mothering I was getting.

ANN: *Taking the hands of spirits who walked her through darkness, Amos also found new ways to view other archetypes in the feminine pantheon. Her next work,* To Venus and Back, *approached the fabled goddess of love, but Amos's deepest sense of that emotion was changing, and her new songs reflected that.*

CONVERSATION BETWEEN TORI AND ANN:

As the live recordings from the *Choirgirl* tour were being completed at our home studios, and it became clear that I should record some new material as well, I had to figure out what I wanted to emphasize. We were nearing the millennium, and I began to see the earth itself as a mother who was losing her children every day. And so I thought she needed a friend, and a good girlfriend. I felt Venus was really important to the culture at that moment. There was so much Mars—so much aggressiveness, especially in music, with the explosion of hate rap. Though I thought the music was really powerful, I couldn't help but notice the violence that filled so much of it.

Venus has a fierce and competitive side, but there's more to her than that. Many writers have felt that such a beautiful woman was unable to hold a space for other women, and some beauties can't. But we know some who can in the music business. I also felt that this was a real healing time, a shifting time for me. What Venus meant to me was changing. She wasn't just this narcissistic goddess. Some women tap into that, there's no question. But I think they miss the point. In our culture we so often turn these archetypes into someone sentimentally cartoonish, and cliché, narrowing the scope of the goddesses in question—their descent and resurrection and true role in the mythical pantheon.

All of this thinking brought me to the idea of Venus. What is the essence of that idea? Love. How could I capture in music the compassionate place that women can create for one another, which is not based just in sentimentality? Because sometimes you have to be quite ferocious to protect the cubs, whether they are real children or ideas. It goes without saying that powerful women are often called bitches simply for being powerful, when in truth some of them can be the most loving, compassionate ones. The crazy thing is, whenever I hear the word *love*, I think of Billy Crystal as Miracle Max in *The Princess Bride* in the scene where the hero, Westly, is lying on the table near death and Miracle Max says something like "What do you have that's so important to live for?" and Westly whispers, more like grunts, "True love." I hear Miracle Max in my head saying, "To blave" and Westly's friends saying, "He said 'true love'!" And Billy Crystal says, "He did not say 'true love,' he said 'to blave.' " And I think ever since that day I've been searching the planet for To Blave, and once I found it I married it. So it's a wonder that the Goddess of Love could decode the nonsense that had been going on in my brain . . . but I was beyond ready for True Love, to blave.

I was also attracted to the themes I explored on *Venus*, I think, because at that time I was waiting to get exiled. I was still not getting a lot of radio play with the *Choirgirl* material, though more than with *Pele*. I'd seen how record labels treated artists who were past their first moment of popularity. For me, making this music was a garnering of strength using the mythologies of some of these women who nurtured other women. I was learning that there was a different walk than the popular one.

I was opening up to the role of being a port in the storm as opposed to the most desired holiday spot. Then Alanis Morissette called and asked if I would go out with her on tour. And I thought about it a lot. We were going to flip-flop every night, but then we decided that I would go first because the piano would be in place. On that tour there was graciousness on both sides, and that was a real turning point. It was important for me that that occurred. The thought form that "if one woman succeeds in the music business then one must fail" had become nails across my face, and I wanted to purge that idea from the ladies' room at the Grammys. The sisterhood had become shit. It was as if we were all part of some modern harem, competing with each other to go down on that microphone. Go down a storm. As if there were only one microphone. The compassionate Venus had no backstage pass. The patriarchal projected Venus, consumed with the need for adoration and approval, had an Access All Areas.

ANN: *As her understanding of feminine power changed, Amos felt herself growing stronger. This was a blissful time, despite the sorrow that had come before. Married, delighted with her band, writing exciting new material, Amos felt she could accept what life presented. Yet life, in its way, soon pushed her over the precipice again.*

CONVERSATION BETWEEN TORI AND ANN:

On tour with Alanis, I found out I was pregnant. Again. I thought it was going well. I really believed the little one and I were out of the woods, out of harm's way. I was on tour, I was watching myself, I was strict on every level. I'd been taking my vitamins for months. Duncan was with me and I was happy. I'd walked the dark road. I was basking in the sunlight. How foolish of me—the tunnel had just opened its convertible top for a moment. I had no idea that this tunnel was going to lead me to Mordor.

After the tour was finished I continued to travel, doing promotional appearances. I was getting more confident and felt we were blossoming. When I went to France to do promotion for *Venus*, alone with Natalie Caplan, who was my assistant at that time, things started to go wrong. I just told Natalie to get me out of there. I mean, this was a country where I could talk to you about wine, but that's all I could do. What was I going to do? How was I going to talk to the doctors, discuss the 1994 vintage from Château Chasse-Spleen? I just remember lying in bed in Paris and starting to bleed. And I remember that week, the second week in

November, some journalist saying to me something like "How do you feel about marketing your pain?" I was so ill, I was worried, I wasn't feeling well. I was sitting there thinking, *Maybe I'm just having a little bleeding, it happens.* I just remember sitting through those interviews, reaching the end of my rope.

I said to him, "How do you define Baudelaire? How do you define Rimbaud? These are your touchstones—how do you define what they did? At least I'm not marketing someone else's pain." That was a cruel moment.

I remember being there in the heart of Paris, and there was something kind of familiar about it all. That's all I'll say. I wasn't feeling as if I were in a place I didn't know or hadn't felt lost in before. I've always been very drawn to certain things about France. Debussy was one of my first ways in to music. But at this moment, in this life, I was lying there and it was getting worse and worse, and I knew what was happening and Mark wasn't there.

As the realization was dawning on me that I was losing this little life, I called Beenie. She picked up the phone and as soon as I heard her voice I let out a cry so aching that I think even Paris must have shuddered. She knew in that moment what was occurring and she said, "Oh my Beenie Bean, feel me right there with you on the bed; my hand is on your tummy and the angelic Beings are there to receive this life." Mark and I had called her Phoebe, and I think that, rightly or wrongly, this pregnancy had felt the most real somehow. Maybe I should say the healthiest. I had done everything right and in that moment I knew that I would never seek to be a mother again. I knew that as I lay there while the sheets were turning to blood and I was having stabbing pains that racked my body, as I cried like a baby. No. Babies don't cry with this kind of pain. They have different pains, but this was the cry of Demeter, whose daughter had been taken from her.

Now that I know Natashya, I understand why I was grieving so deeply. Something in my makeup, in what holds me together—as crazy as it is sometimes—I knew that there was a presence missing from my life, and I ached for this relationship. No different from the simple truth that you cannot find your loved ones when they have died. Neither can you find a loved one when they haven't been physically born. The aching can be great on both sides, because there is an emptiness. When Kevyn Aucoin died, I felt this emptiness. When my Poppa died, and when my little girl hadn't physically been born, time and time again, I wept from the deepest part of my heart.

I spoke with Beenie, who was able to talk about and be present with me lying in my own blood, and I can see now how she held the archetype of Persephone, Queen of the Underworld, and how I, as a second-string understudy for Demeter, was mothered by Persephone's compassion and knowing. The other line rang in the room at that moment. Natalie had called L.A. to alert certain people to what was occurring. In some ways it happened, it seemed, for a thousand years—that day was a thousand years. That day was November 11, 1999. My first miscarriage was December 23, 1996. My second miscarriage . . . I did not choose to keep a date because it wasn't the same as the first and the third.

I picked up the phone, and the suggestion was to go see a doctor immediately in Paris. They were getting names and told me to take a couple days to recover and then go on to Spain to continue my promotional tour. As if a couple days off was a huge boon, a gift.

In that moment a schism happened between me and the music industry. All my shattered discordant pieces of the different Toris puzzled themselves back together with Phoebe's glue. I now understood that I was a commodity. I was a commodity through the condolences, through the "I'm so sorrys." "I'm so worried about you, but the show must go on." I hung up the phone and for the next two hours I talked to everyone from Dr. Rita Lynn to Mark.

Dr. Rita has been a mentor for me for many years, along with being one of the most respected psychologists in Los Angeles, having been part of the Cedars-Sinai psychiatric ward as well as a private practitioner. She has helped me to string together the fragments of my life. She's called it "beading a necklace." So when I called her and told her that "those who are they" wanted me to see a doctor immediately in Paris, take a couple days off, and continue on to Spain to do promotion for *Venus,* she interceded and said, "That is absolutely and positively what is not going to happen. I will call management, record companies, and whoever I need to call to instruct them on how to be humane." Then she proceeded to lay out, very simply, what I had to do. She said to me, once she had walked me through the next ten hours of my life, "I'm calling Johnny, and we will put this plan into action and he can deal with 'those who are they.' "

After I hung up the phone, Natalie was there within minutes. I said my goodbyes to Beenie and I stared blankly at the carpet, now marked by the remains of my wishes for Phoebe and me in shapes that looked like little rosebuds, not bloodstains. I walked out of that hotel room a changed woman in many ways. So we went on the train and I was bundled up because I was really a stuck pig at this point, bleeding. I know, I know—pigs again. There was just this moment of knowing it was the end of that pregnancy. And this was the hardest loss in the end.

Mark met me at the train station alone. He held me like I've never been held. He wouldn't let go of my hand even as I started to retreat inside myself while we were driving in silence through the streets of London with a driver to the hospital. Dr. Rita knew doctors in London, so she sent us to somebody who would be kind. We went in and, of course, the ultrasound showed it was over. They got us a cup of tea, as the British do, and Mark and I wept together. Then we went through the process with a gentle doctor and a twinkling-eyed Irish anesthesiologist who held my hand, and then Mark and I went back to the hotel that night; it was very late. It was the same hotel where, not too many weeks before, we had been talking about the possibilities. In Paris I had bought these beautiful clothes for a little child. I still have them in a box.

In that moment we canceled everything, naturally. The label said I had to do the Christmas shows because I had "Concertina" coming out as a single and a lot of stations said that they would support it if I would do their Christmas shows. That was just the end. I went to Cornwall with Mark and for two weeks—I can't remember what I did. I sat on the steps most of the time. We mourned. And it was over for me then. I couldn't go through this again.

So we decided that we were going to believe the label and the radio stations, that they would do what they said they were going to do. The blackmail of all this . . . But that's how things work everywhere. And it is looked upon as inappropriate to carry a grudge or feel leveraged if the other side does not play your music. Rather the approach should be to mitigate your way through the innuendos of "if she does this then we can possibly consider doing that."

So we went to do these shows. I was alone at the piano and hadn't been for a while, for two tours. I had just the sound guys and a small crew. And I started to find some strength alone with the piano.

Around this time we went and saw a specialist, Dr. Stillman, to try to figure out where we stood. They came back with good news and bad news. It was the same news: they couldn't give me a reason for these miscarriages. So again, I'd had enough. We decided we were going to try to just live. We got a boat—not anything outrageous but just something fun to putter around in—and we got some movies, and Mark really got into cooking. He's a very good cook. Sea bass with potato latkes, that kind of thing. We had that nurturing thing going on. We had some lovely, lovely, lovely champagne; I'll never forget it. Cristal Rose 1990; it was very hard to get. We decided we were not going to talk about it. We had talked about it and talked about it. And now we were going to try to be people. This was the most disciplined thing I ever did.

One day I went out by myself, lay down on the beach, and turned it all over. I was going through such pain and struggle, and at the same time, through the balancing force of traditional psychotherapy, asking basic questions: What is a powerful woman? What is a fertile woman? I had to redefine these things. I knew I would never understand why I could carry all these songs but not one human life. What a mess.

I had already gone to the edge and tried to negotiate, demanded my child back, asked how much more I could do. I had been through "Spark"—where could I go? I'd grieved and turned the story into art, and I was sitting there with the same situation again. That day on the beach, I went into ceremony. I lay down on the ground my mother had chosen for me; she picked our beach house. I wept and gave tobacco to the land; I burned the sage. It was a private moment for me, saying, *I just can't carry this anymore*, literally.

In the end, I got the answer. And it was through a lot of tears. I laid myself on the earth and the message came to me. The earth said, "Surrender this to me. You've lost a few babies. I lose babies every day. I understand this pain. So trust me. Give this to me." And I almost felt as if the earth and I became blood sisters. She said, "You are a great creator, and maybe your children are not in physical form and that's what it will always be. Can you hold that? How many sonic children do you need? You have hundreds, you need thousands—when will it be enough?" I kind of stood back and she said, "You know, some people who have human children would give anything to have a sonic child." And I realized I was beginning to know who I was. Just beginning.

ANN: *Amos had come to understand the words of the Homeric* Hymn to Demeter: *"We humans endure the gifts the gods give us, even as we are grieving over what has to be." She would soon learn that the gifts that come, though always unexpected, can bring not just sorrow but delight.*

CONVERSATION BETWEEN TORI AND ANN:

We took on a project, to do a song for the *Mission Impossible II* soundtrack. The good thing is, we had something to focus on. Mark and I went back to Cornwall, and that was a lifeline for me because I needed to do something and this was one of my favorite covers of all time: "Carnival," by Luiz Bonfa, from the film *Black Orpheus*. I knew I had one more album to record for Atlantic Records, but I didn't even think about that. It was in the distance.

We went back to Cornwall and the crew started coming in, and Duncan was there. I'll never forget it—the band had arrived, and one night after rehearsal I was serving the wine, Duncan was cooking a welcoming dinner for all of them. I just went into the other room and I called Mark to me and I said, "The fish is bad. There's something wrong." And then I said, "Furthermore, this vintage is bad." And he just looked at me. This was one of my favorite wines. I think it was the Château Pichon Longueville, Comtesse de Lalande, Pauillac, 2ème Cru Classe, 1996. He said, "Let me taste it." And he did, and he said, "It's incredible wine."

I thought I had the stomach flu, which was going around. I couldn't eat or drink anything; I was just not well. I wasn't taking antibiotics. The one thing I was taking was baby aspirin. As far as my cycle went, I hadn't even gotten back to any normal sort of anything. I thought we might see the doctor again and try in six months. Then I was open to trying the fertility drugs, the big, big guns. But the doctor had said not yet. You know, you have to heal.

So I was taking baby aspirin and I was still taking my vitamins because he'd said, "These vitamins aren't going to hurt you. They're good for you and you've just lost so much blood now you just need to do this." So I was just minding my own little business and enjoying the Cristal Rose 1990 with Mark, and then I was so ill. And within two weeks I called my sister and she said she wanted me to go take a pregnancy test. She said to take two. And I couldn't believe the results.

My life began to change radically—that is, I changed my life. Hans Zimmer wanted me to come and do some vocalizing throughout the *Mission Impossible II* score. And I've known Hans for years; I was the girl who did the demo for Maria McKee on the theme for *Days of Thunder*, and he composed the score. I got paid something like $150 to come in and do "Show Me Heaven." So I like Hans, and I would have done it under any other circumstances, but I just had to say no.

Mark and I were back on the merry-go-round again. We went to this doctor to get our ultrasound and it was the scariest moment. He gave us little candies to hold and we sat there, and they did the ultrasound and we saw these legs. These legs jumping up and down. I was eleven weeks pregnant. We just looked at each other and I said, "I'm going to go to the beach house. I'm not going back to work." And that's what I did. I was with a wonderful Jamaican physician for the first few months. However, she married, sold her practice, and moved out of state during my sixth month of pregnancy, and then I was under the care of another physician in the practice. I was deemed a high-risk pregnancy, my age being the least of the factors. I had to have scans every other week due to previous medical surgeries. Because I was a high risk my doctor-sister, Marie, decided that

I needed to see a physician who specialized in high-risk pregnancy. She and Dr. Marlow had found Dr. Bronsky in the D.C. area.

So that is why I settled into Georgetown. Funnily enough, I was about a block from the piano bar Mr. Smith's, where I played at fourteen. Mark had to go back to Cornwall to get some things done, but Duncan felt good about being there, first at the beach with me and then in Georgetown, D.C. We started developing this other way of taking care, which I've maintained ever since. High in protein, high in spinach, getting the vitamins from the food. Of course I took my prenatals, and DHA Omega-3 pills—I'd had a phone consultation with the renowned women's physician Christiane Northrup, author of *Women's Bodies, Women's Wisdom.* She said that taking that form of Omega-3 fatty acid was the most important thing to do for Natashya's brain development. Which I did and I still do.

I became Dr. Bronsky's patient when I was about seven months' pregnant, and it turns out that in my eighth month of pregnancy with Natashya, he had a hunch about the miscarriages. Dr. Bronsky tested me for protein S and protein C deficiency, and it turns out that I did have both deficiencies. The result of this, at that time, was that I needed to have shots in my legs in the morning and at night, which Duncan did for me because I had a hard time stabbing myself in the leg with a needle. I couldn't take the medicine orally because it could hurt Natashya, and I think they were worried that I would get a blood clot in the lung.

DR. MARIE DOBYNS:

Virchow, the father of hematology, identified the three factors responsible for vascular thrombosis, also known as blood clots: vessel injury, alteration in blood flow, and changes in the coagulability of the blood. Pregnancy affects all three factors. Your blood volume increases by a third when you are pregnant, and your body doesn't really know how to handle that without all of the mechanisms that occur between the placenta, the fetus, and the mother. If there is any issue that goes amiss within any of those three components, then the fetus won't develop properly.

The body responds to anything foreign that is going to upset the natural ebb and tide of life. Pregnancy is perceived as a hypercoagulable state. This is not a problem for most women; however, if you have a protein S or protein C deficiency, this upsets the hemostatic balance and the body responds by trying to protect the mother. That is why Tori had several miscarriages. Dr. Robert Stillman had a hunch and put Tori on an aspirin a day, which makes your blood thinner, enabling her to get pregnant. She was supplemented with progesterone suppositories in order to help the development of the fetus.

Tori initially went down to the Florida house and was under the care of Dr. Graham, a wonderful Jamaican physician. However, she retired during the sixth month of Tori's pregnancy. Dr. Marlow and I sent her to a specialist in Washington, D.C., Dr. Bronsky. He ran a series of blood tests, and her deficiency was eventually detected. However, the physicians had to find the exact balance for Tori, because the progesterone hormone can increase the chance of development of a blood clot. Therefore, once she got pregnant she took low molecular heparin shots because the progesterone put her at an increased risk for blood clots in the legs and lungs. The heparin shots kept her blood from getting too thick without interfering with the growth and development of the fetus and the placenta. An aspirin a day affects the clotting mechanism such that one who has protein S or protein C deficiency may get pregnant. However, once Tori was pregnant she had to be given heparin shots to thin her blood. She could not take the medication orally because that would have crossed into the placenta and harmed the fetus.

After the baby was delivered she went back to an aspirin a day, which is an antiplatelet drug that prevents the cells from clotting quickly. She also continued with the heparin shots until her levels balanced out. And because she was nursing Natashya, she couldn't take the oral form of the medication. An aspirin a day will decrease your incidence of stroke; also risk of thromboembolism will be drastically reduced with just an aspirin a day if you have this deficiency. Suffice it to say, miracles do happen and blood is an amazing vehicle.

TORI:

During the pregnancy with Tash, the *Scarlet* seed started coming. During the first half of the pregnancy, while I was at the beach house in Florida, I would play piano for three hours every day. So the songs were developing daily, as was this little girl inside me. I would take walks on the beach, and just play to Tash, who would kick to the rhythm, and read. My various advisers told me I had to change my life—I couldn't take any work, I couldn't handle the stress and carry life. So I didn't. I didn't get involved with being a lioness then, except for carrying this life.

ANN: *On September 5, 2000, Natashya Lórien Hawley left her mother's womb and said hello to the world.*

DUNCAN PICKFORD:

I've known Natashya since she was about an hour old. When Tori was delivering I dropped her and Mark off at the hospital. I was supposed to stay but I couldn't bear to—I was just too nervous! I drove around D.C. in the truck, supposedly just buying some sandwiches and getting some juice, and I spent two hours just going, *Oh my God, Tori's going to be a mother.* I'm going to be an uncle. Finally I went back to the hospital and I ran upstairs thinking she'd be back in the room, and she wasn't there, and I'm like, *What's wrong, what's wrong?* And all of a sudden the elevator doors open and she came through and was wheeled back with this tiny little creature in her arms. I've known this creature ever since. I've seen her grow from this helpless dumb little thing that squalls every time it wants to eat into this amazing creature who thinks, and says what she thinks. She uses phrases, she can demand what she wants, she has moods and tempers and an amazing imagination.

CONVERSATIONS BETWEEN TORI AND ANN:

I thought that I would get a little boy, because I'd already put my little girl to rest. We'd known who she was; we'd named her and said goodbye. But the universe kept telling me I was going to have a little girl. I felt like Natashya's birth was a complete gift that came out of Venus.

At this point, I was communicating with friends online, and people were talking to me about how popular music was getting more violent. I felt I had to respond to Venus's pillaging. Male artists were saying these really malicious things—and I'm not talking about tongue-in-cheek statements, I'm talking about men wanting to rip women's clits out. I needed to answer that. Once I had Natashya, the idea really started to take root. Neil Gaiman came to visit, and we started to talk, and then the plot was hatched with Mark, Neil, and me sitting there. I was nursing Tash, and we came up with the concept for *Strange Little Girls*. And I went through with it; we gave 1000 percent to that project, to redeem Venus, who had given us so much.

DUNCAN PICKFORD:

Tori's always been a bit of a lioness. She's always protected her pride. But it's fivefold since Natashya came along. She's always watching for the dangers, and not just the physical dangers but pitfalls in her career, people wanting to rip her off or do her down or whatever. She's much more on the lookout for all of this. It's not in a negative way. She's always been very clued in on the details of her career, but that's sharpened even more. She lets much less ride. She doesn't simply react to things: she acts.

CONVERSATIONS BETWEEN TORI AND ANN:

Becoming a mom has in some way made me seem a lot more chilled out, because I think my energy is more compassionate and loving than in the old days. But on the other hand, where Natashya's involved, don't underestimate the crocodile when you're walking across the pond. Sometimes people take it for granted that when I'm out and about with Tash, I'm free to be approached. But at that moment, I need to be a mom. If they don't understand that, then they will see another side to me. I've had to be much clearer about the lines in the sand. I'm not okay if people take my mommy time away, because when they've taken my mommy time away they can't give it back to me.

When people don't treat Natashya as if she's a human being, and this can be anyone from a fan to a "friend," that is not acceptable. They think they can call on the Tori Amos thing any time they want. I would never call you at your home when you are not on your work schedule to talk about work. But people feel they can call me anytime and talk about my work.

I've chosen to incorporate Natashya into all aspects of my life, which can be challenging for both of us. She was out on the road from November until September and she had already been out on the road on another tour. She left her school, her life, and her friends. There are consequences to that. Sacrifices were made, and when that is not understood and people take advantage, I have to turn around and say, "I am not a possession, and neither is my family." I also have to discern what areas of my adult life Tash isn't yet ready to witness. She is really curious about the world of performing. Kids are curious about what their parents do. And you know,

LIVE IN HOUSTON ON THE
SCARLET'S WALK TOUR

LIVE IN SAN ANTONIO ON THE
SCARLET'S WALK TOUR

FANS AT THE FRONT OF THE STAGE DURING AN ENCORE

ABOVE: TORI AND HER HUSBAND, MARK HAWLEY. RIGHT: TORI AND NATASHYA HANGING AROUND IN THE DRESSING ROOM

ABOVE: TORI AND NATASHYA
PLAYING AT THE PIANO BEFORE A
SOUND CHECK

TORI SAYING GOODBYE TO THE AUDIENCE AFTER HER SET IN AUSTIN ON THE SCARLET'S WALK TOUR

a lot of parents take their kids to work. Then there are so many toys that evoke performance: there's Barbie, there's her Polly Pockets—you can buy little stages for Polly Pockets—and so she really can't see why she can't do it, too. She doesn't know why she can't go onstage with me.

We let her come out on sound check and play, sometimes, for a minute. At the same time you can't overindulge; it is that fine a line. During the shows themselves, she sees me from the side of the stage, but there are certain songs I feel she's not ready for. She's not ready to hear "Me and a Gun." "Professional Widow"—she's not ready to see Mom do that. And she's not ready to see "Precious Things." I know that and so does she, and that's okay. She loves "fairytale" and "Corncake Girl," as she calls it.

When she's not allowed to watch, it doesn't feel like withholding because we don't treat it like withholding. There are times when she's gone from the side of the stage and I know that she and her nanny are backstage dancing or whatever. She's not seeing what I'm doing. I know if they've got screens backstage in every venue we play; I've sussed it out. I may not know every detail of each venue's operation, but as far as what Tash is exposed to, I'm present in that way, as a mom.

She's wanted to come out onstage a couple times, and I have to kind of battle her about it. She is getting to the age of "I want this, I want to do this!" You have to be able to say, *This is not good for you, it's not right, right now.* You can't tell yourself, *She thinks it's right for her now.* She's three years old. Are you nuts? I just say no, and then try to move on to another conversation. She doesn't understand a lot of the time when I tell her no. She says, "I don't like you, Mummy." I say, "You don't have to like me. I will always love you."

I spent so much time, energy, and pain becoming Natashya's mother that I'm not going to take any aspect of her for granted. Yet having a child hasn't lessened my dedication to my work—if anything, it has grown since the work helped me through so many hard times. What's truly difficult is convincing other people that I can manage it all. You have to set very clear boundaries. And there will be people who do not hear you. You try to give them warnings, and if they do not heed them then they are out of your life. I've spoken with several working moms who didn't get hired for a particular job that they were qualified for simply because of the "working mother" stigma, the implication being that a working mother works less than a single working woman. When I heard that, I pulled back from my life like a camera and tried to see if this was true in my case. I concluded that I put in the same amount of time working as I did back in 1992. I just sleep a lot less . . .

I can see why some women artists just throw their hands up and say they cannot deal with all this confrontation. Those women retreat from their careers, or else they grow distant from their children. Sometimes even Tash will say to me, "Mummy, it's Tash time, stop working now." Any mother who works at home or has their child on the "road" with them will understand exactly Tash's and my predicament, because lines that separate work from home life can be blurred when they occur in the same physical space. But the upside of this is that I get more work done and consequently have a lot more Tash time because I don't spend half of my life traveling to work and working away from home. Sometimes "home" is a bus, sometimes home is a hotel room—now, naturally Tash knows this is not her "home home," but it is a bus home and a hotel home and of course, like anybody, she can get homesick for "home home."

Then sometimes as a mom you can feel guilty, and that really pulls on your energy levels, thereby unfortunately creating the climate for "cross Mommy" to be the creature that takes over your body. Tash will say, "Mummy, you didn't get enough sleep. You're cross Mummy. Don't be cross with Tash. It hurts Tash's feelings." And then of course that's like cold water rushing through your capillaries, and sometimes the only thing that you can think to do is take a minute and call your own "mommy."

Luckily I have a mom who knows exactly what to say when I'm upset because I've hurt my child's feelings and been an all together Miss Grumpy Boots. This kind of love is the archetypal Great Mother that all mothers seem to tap into, some more frequently than others, let's be honest. My physical mother has held this loving archetype, I would say more than many—certainly more than I ever have. And because of this, I have a walking instruction manual, a map, that shows me "what is compassion," how to set boundaries firmly but lovingly, how to say no—my mother taught me the most important lesson when she said, "Tori Ellen, I don't have to agree with you all of the time to love you. I may not like something you say or do, but I still and will always love you. Love does not waver from a mother's perspective. Like, however, is a chameleon that can change as a lizard's colors can, and sometimes we can all be lizards. And I still love you when you're a lizard." And I said to my mother, "Surely not a lounge lizard, Mom." And my mother said, true to form, "You can still be a lounge lizard, sweetheart, and play Radio City. A lounge lizard, a particular lounge lizard I know, made a lot of people happy playing lounge lizard music. Don't belittle that, my darling. Lizards have their place, too."

With my mother's heart condition, which I write about in the song "The Beekeeper," I've had to step into a different role in the family scheme. My sister and I and Cody, my niece, have had to become the female caretakers for the older generation as well as the younger. My sister caretakes from a medical "how to keep somebody's heart still ticking" point of view, whereas I have to be more of an emotional problem-solver than I had to be, say, five years ago. Becoming forty, I think, gives everybody a license to have to deal with the complicated family issues that all big extended families/friends have to deal with. Cody, who is nineteen, holds the role of giving a perspective on the real issues and difficulties that her generation faces. We have a lot of family friends in this generation, and I must consider the effects and consequences of a decision that we make as the responsible adults. Cody helps us to see the ramifications of certain decisions before we make a mistake out of ignorance, not maliciousness. There is no way that you know how to be nineteen in 2004 if you've never been nineteen in 2004, but you do know how to be forty if you are forty in 2004.

So as you can see, you don't have to be a physical mother to hold the mother nurturing space in a friend/family tribe, but the nurturing Demeter archetype must be carried by one or more of the women in a friend/family tribe or the hive will be destroyed and the Beekeeper cannot be the queen. However, some women wouldn't be happy, giving mothers if they didn't work. Other mothers are not happy mothers if they work in the secularized world. Very simply, I would not and could not ever consider giving up music. I would consider not being as active in the music industry, but that day is not today. So if I'm not willing to give up the music, or give up having my relationship as it is with Tash, which is right here present in my heart, then the best thing to do is to "whistle while you work." It just takes a lot of energy. But the team I have in place understands this, and if they don't then they're not part of this team. That's very simple, right down the line. Natashya is a non-negotiable.

SONG CANVAS: "Ribbons undone"

A moment with Tash:

> "Mummy, can I draw a picture?"
>
> "Of course, sweetheart."
>
> "I want to use your colored pencils, though."

"That's fine, let me get them for you."

"That's okay, that's okay, I'll get them."

"I'm going to have a sip of my green tea then."

"Let me pour it for you, Mummy."

"Okay, sweetheart, but the teapot is made of porcelain, so it can break if it gets dropped, so can you use both hands?"

"Porcelain doesn't break if it drops on the couch in the living room."

"Well, if the porcelain teapot drops on the porcelain teacup on the couch, then the teapot and the cup can have a crash, thereby breaking them both."

"Look, this water bottle is not porcelain. This is plastic, Mummy. Watch it drop."

So the water bottle quickly drops to the floor, and luckily I had put the lid on tightly.

"Mummy, look! These colored pencils are flowers and this flag protects mummies but not daddies."

Tash has picked up a British flag that had been bought for the football festivities before, of course, England was out of the quarterfinals of Euro 2004. She starts waving what she calls her wand and says, "I'm the fairy, but not the alien fairy. I'm good to mummies and I have these flowers, look. But the alien fairies like black, so I'm going to give them a black flower."

Then Tash proceeds to pull out a black-colored pencil, which had gotten into my colored-pencil flower arrangement.

"Mummies don't need black flowers."

"Mommies don't mind black flowers."

"No, but the alien fairies really, really, really need black flowers, because it's dark."

"What's dark?"

"Where the aliens come from. They come from where there are twinkles in the sky."

"You were a twinkle in the sky."

"No, that was Natashya. I am the fairy. Here, look. Here's your microphone."

At that announcement I'm surprised, because when she's not Natashya she likes to be this creature she's invented called "Alice Lily Horsey Ribbons," which has woven itself into "Ribbons Undone." I did not use those words in that order, but used and referenced them nonetheless, mainly to capture Tash's spirit.

Tash picks up a little tiny flashlight that Mark uses to see gear at the mixing desk during a live show. I start singing a silly song and Tash says—excuse me, the fairy says, "Sing properly. The show is about ready to start."

So quickly my brain is trying to come up with a proper song at seven-fifteen in the morning, pre-kindergarten. And one of the new songs for the album pops into my head, maybe because it has the word *porcelain* in it. So I proceed to sing the song properly and Tash is doing the lights for the performance.

I finish the song and Tash says, "When I was a twinkle in the sky, I wanted you to marry my daddy. And I told you so, didn't I?"

"I guess you did."

"And you heard me, didn't you?"

"I guess I did."

"You were going to marry another boy, weren't you?"

"I don't know if *marry* is accurate, but I had other boyfriends, yes."

"But your last boyfriend was not my daddy, was it?"

"No, you're right. My last boyfriend was the last boyfriend I ever had, because then I was with your daddy."

"But I did not want your boyfriend to be my daddy."

"Well, my last boyfriend was very nice."

"But he was not my daddy! And I told you that when I was a twinkle in the sky. And I picked Daddy for you, Mummy, because I love you."

At that juncture, the postman is at the door and Tash's daddy has just walked in from working out. The postman says, "You won't be needing that flag, deary. The football team all had to go home because they lost."

The postman and Tash's daddy have a bit of a knowing giggle and the postman says, "We all have to move on, so you won't need that flag, deary."

Tash looks up, waving her flag wand, and looks at the postman and says, "This flag protects mummies, not daddies, from the alien fairies."

And at that moment, it was crystal clear that Tash was the one who obviously had "moved on."

kindest eyes

FOR TORI'S MOM, MARY ELLEN COPELAND AMOS

the Kindest eyes
are waving
from the farthest reach
of the Disembarkment
gate.
a Small hand
that for 75 Octobers
has touched the
Canadian Sunset—colored leaves

of the maple tree
reaching reaching
above the heads
staying till
Time's last moment of breath
Flight BA293
is Boarding
and I'm leaving
the Kindest smile.
the things I said at 15
good god.
is he good?
he's a hussy.
But she put away
the Tomahawk
the Feather
the Sage
for Candleland
and
Liturgy
and Lost
her Native fire
only for a while.
She remembered
as we all will
the call
of the Ancestors,
"2012."
She bathed me

and held me

at my ugliest

at my smelliest

at my meanest at 18

when you think

you have the right

to punish the one

with the Kindest eyes . . .

for the men who couldn't see mine

and I'm racing against time now

the Kindest eyes are smiling—is it too late

to memorize her essence

yes it is

I missed that chance.

the Kindest eyes had said, "My angel, dance,

this is not goodbye,

look in the mirror

to find the Kindest Eyes."

dionysus: bringing the music forth

TORI:

She is Black.

She is White.

She is Sex.

She is Death.

I watch Jimi.

I am 5.

I watch Jim.

I watch the Board of Trustees at the church shake their heads—

"No.

No way.

Not our daughters, nor our sons will be going to see

Jimi, Jim, or Jimmy."

Fathers hurling out Biblical sound bites, from

"in Sin you were born"

to

"Gird your Loins."

I think to myself—

Okay, gentlemen, put those loins on the grill, honeylamb.

Medium rare.

A portion.

A part.

The loin of the Messianic Christ is awakening through these men,

Jimi, Jim, and Jimmy,

to name a few.

I hear the call.

Faint, but the trumpet is blaring.

As voices try and drown out Jimi's axe,

all the while the gnosis of the serpent is stirring his Strat.

Upside down.

Left handed.

The pickup switch in his control.

And the wind cried Mary.

And I heard the cry—

in the halls of the Peabody.

In the practice rooms—

some of the most accomplished players of

She who is Black,

She who is White—

play Liszt, Chopin, and then of course there was always Prokofiev.

I wanted him.

I was seven.

Not to play his piece,

Concerto in C-sharp Minor, something I would study one day,

but I wanted the mind.

The mind that could finger that piece.

But in the rests of *L'Après-midi d'un Faune* by my Spirit Brother,
    Debussy,

and in the time changes and key signatures of my guide, Bartók—

I heard the cry . . .

She is Risen.

She is Black.

She is White.

Good night, sweet Prince.

Good night, Stratocaster.

Good night, Les Paul.

Good night, Telecaster.

Good night, Martin.

Good night, Santa Cruz.

I will study you, I will take you in.

Through my skin to my hands.

Thank you.

I have found her.

She is Risen.

She is Bösendorfer.

ANN: *If any god has a right to call in sick to the rock-and-roll pantheon, Dionysus is the one. This Greek sacrificial figure, whose festivals defined old-fashioned frenzy, is invoked so often in the context of contemporary music that his dancing shoes must be worn right through. The philosopher Friedrich Nietzsche and composers like Richard Strauss conjured his spirit in the service of modern ritual long before kick drums and power chords set the kids on fire, but Dionysus got really busy once the counterculture made rock not just a musical style but a way of life. An idol was needed to embody the strange magic that pulsed through rock performers and fans and led people to transform their appearance, their leisure time, and even sometimes their entire worldview. Dionysus, sexiest of the Western deities, fit the bill. Jim Morrison invoked him by name; many other stars earned comparison to him simply because of their genius for rebellion and the fine art of losing control. Rockers who've never heard of Persephone and Demeter, much less Sekhmet and Saraswati, fancy themselves Dionysus's followers. Yet few really bother to consider what taking on that path really entails.*

Preserving the spirit of Dionysus, the wandering bringer of intoxication, allows those who dare the chance to constantly reimagine ways to break free of rules and even ego itself. The ancient Bacchic rites that honored him may really have involved no more than some wild dancing and gnawing on raw meat, but over the centuries they have come to represent a serious step outside society, where art's ecstatic power, not morality, determines our actions. Dionysus, ideally, frees us from all assumptions, most of all those about sexuality. Yet it seems no coincidence that the most vibrant survivor from the Greek pantheon is male. Androgynous, yes, and propped up by a cult of women, but especially as he survives in rock stars' hearts, Dionysus is a quintessential bad boy, indulging all his impulses and leaving wreckage in his wake.

What would happen if Dionysus got back in touch with his ancient feminine side? This is what Tori Amos explores in her live performances. The scene is still bloody, but this is the blood of the god's perennial rebirth, not his dismemberment. Becoming possessed by the music that has given shape to her songs, Amos does not sacrifice either mastery or understanding. The power of rhythm intertwines with the pull of melody to reshape her. Yet she acts as neither sacrifice nor mere reveler. She becomes oracle, that feminine voice through which the stories of all time take shape.

TORI:

Undulating. The rhythm—the Bösendorfer, into my body. The Kundalini has a snapdragon tonight at the base of my spine. We are playing outside. It's over a hundred degrees. Last night, Navajo women came backstage in Phoenix and smoked their Hozho Natooh with us—this sacred tobacco was lovingly picked by their grandmother. As the Dineh (Navajo) woman from the tobacco clan talked with me, she rolled the sacred tobacco in a husk of corn and began her chant, her prayer. First she spoke of things that were personal to me, then she began her weaving of song in her ancient language. I received this blessing with the feeling that I myself had been retuned (like the pianos) to be played by this land. This particular land that was so much a part of the songs "a sorta fairytale," "Crazy," "your cloud," "Indian Summer," and the historical tragedy of "wampum prayer."

Matt and Jon then came along with Chelsea, Ali, and Dunc to receive their message. When we all gathered in a circle in the end, as she sang in her clan's language, Tash demanded in and came to stand before this medicine woman. I held my breath as the two of them seemed to understand each other completely, one a two-and-a-half-year-old and one a woman chanting in Dineh. As the smoke surrounded Tash, I held my breath but did not interrupt as she began to move her small body in rhythm. It was almost as if a hand held me firmly back. The Dineh woman wrapped the smoke (which I thought looked like seven circles of smoke) quickly around Tash. I thought of the "seed of life" Mandala, which is an ancient shape made up of six circles with the seventh circle having been created out of the interconnectivity of the six. Sacred geometry. I felt Poppa's presence. I then realized that Tash had chosen her own Baptism. It was her soul that did this. She had not been included by me originally, but she herself chose to be included as we sat in the circle holding hands. We surrounded her as she sat enveloped in the Hozho Natooh and the Dineh song. In the song "Ruby through the Looking-Glass," I talk about being "Baptized of fire and every beat in the bar." Well, Tash really has been, but by a loving fire; she was also Baptized through song, through the song of the Dineh's true mother, Changing Woman, creatrix of the Dineh (the people) and the seasons.

That was last night. Tonight we are in the basin of Cochise's Holy Mountain. I feel his presence watching over everything I can see. We are in Tucson. Twenty minutes before showtime, I pass Husband in the hallway backstage. I stare at him. He stares at me. He laughs. I hear an underlying warning in that laugh. And a slight nervousness. "Take care of my wife." "Your wife's fine—she's on a long coffee break." We both know she's far away. He knows I'll let her come back. But not now.

SONG CANVAS: "wampum prayer"

An electrical surge shoots through my body. I'm straddling what is most easily described as a pack of wild horses. Stampeding. I am racing. I am still. I am a vessel and I must "ground" this fast. I kneel. In the dark. Sage burning. I call on the four directions and ask them what essence they are bringing with them. I call it forth and ask them to help me hold this within as well as without. My vessel then begins to expand to where each direction begins to pull me. I see this in my mind's eye. The pianos have been anointed with the oils prepared specifically for tonight's journey. Tonight is centered around the true events of *wampum prayer*—we are in her place of historical occurrence where mostly women and children of Chiricahua and Mescalero Apache were forced to march to Bosque Redondo, near Fort Sumner, and cruelly many were killed in the walk. Soon the Navajo (the Dineh) were rounded up, hunted down, and forced to march what they call today the "Long Walk" to Bosque Redondo (akin to the Cherokees' fateful Trail of Tears, which occurred earlier, in 1838). I hear the chanting of Cochise's holy men and women, singing to heal the screams and cries of the hundred innocent Aravaipa Apache who were massacred not far from where we are playing tonight. I hear the old Apache woman, who woke me more than a year ago in the far reaches of Cornwall, her voice pulling me out of my bed in what is known to all of us as that "dark before dawn," tearfully singing what became "wampum prayer"—which has begun our invocation every night, day in and day out, for the past many, many months. And here we are— here I am—point of place. The real place where the real events occurred. I visualize a chord. A simple chord. This silverish-looking rope extends down from what I imagine as Source through the instruments, through us the players—the keepers of the tone on this particular stage, and down into the earth. This is my definition of being grounded— when you're straddling a pack of wild horses. The drums begin; they pull me to them. The revving of the engines has begun. It is showtime.

ANN: *On any given night, Amos and her companions on and behind the stage must find the balance that allows them to merge within the larger organism of the music. Amos may claim the focus of the crowd, but she cannot play star as much as humble servant. Practicing the Dionysian loss of self as an artistic and spiritual discipline, Amos must resist the cliché of self-indulgence in order to gain access to the older gift of artistic clairvoyance.*

CONVERSATION BETWEEN TORI AND ANN:

When I walk out there and hold these songs, I have to become a living library. I have to become an artist that can contain these stories and these shapes for people to walk into. I can pull these songs in and hold the structure, for example, of the sacred prostitute. I work with this archetype a lot, and she joins me when I perform the live version of "Father Lucifer," which I developed in depth on the *Scarlet's Walk* tour. Once I explained to Matt and Jon what I was trying to achieve, we stripped the song back and created a different rhythm track in order to create the right mood for this gal. When I step into this particular archetype and hold that energy, I have to believe that I can achieve what these scarlet women, these sacred prostitutes, achieved all those years ago, but not as Mark's wife and not as the girl my friends know me as. You have to be clear on this when you are working with archetypes—which piece of them is moving through you, so when you walk offstage you really do kind of need to know what part is them, what part is you, and which part of them you want to take back on the bus with you. And quite honestly, if Husband is on the bus that night, I might just take this gal back with me.

Can you benefit as a person by including a piece of this archetype in your personal Mandala? We all have our own personal Mandala that is made up of many mosaics. I know a woman whose personal Mandala is made up of Goddess and God archetypes that are lovers of animals. I know people whose mosaics are mostly made up of God and Goddess archetypes that are all about strategy. But there is always room in everyone's personal Mandala for at least one or two mosaics dedicated to the sacred prostitute. So she's usually at every show. Because frankly, she makes all the other song girls have a sway in their step. Who doesn't want a sway in their step?

CHELSEA LAIRD:

Sometimes people misinterpret Tori's passion as only sexuality. For her it's claiming her sexuality and merging it with her spirituality. For her the music is the ultimate expression of passion, not necessarily sex. But that's what makes it sexy.

JON EVANS:

Tori has a way of expressing herself that's certainly very sensual. It's all entwined with the songs, and it has a lot to do with the lyrics, too. All of that stuff that she does live, the movement on the piano bench, she does in rehearsals and she did from day one. People think that it's just an act and it's not how she is in normal life, but whenever she performs a song she really does internalize it and externalize it, she just becomes a part of it.

Whether she's performing by herself in the studio or in a rehearsal space or onstage in front of people, you're going to get the same level of intensity. But it's not a stripper vibe. It's more just being in touch with sexuality and not being embarrassed by it. She's not trying to be sexy for men, yet a lot of the music has a groove that's very masculine. She can play really heavy and really hard and really funky and be very male in a lot of ways. At the same time, what she expresses has a very female slant. She's definitely sexual for girls, but in a very masculine way. So it's complicated. There are so many preconceptions of women and sex and what they want and how they feel about it. I think with Tori, if you listen, it's pretty clear; it's just not what those preconceptions suggest.

The way Tori transforms as a performer is not just metaphorical; it's musical. She has the ability to transpose really intricate things into keys immediately, as well as being able to start a song vocally in the right key when she's coming from somewhere very different. A lot of people with perfect pitch have a real problem with that because they can hear a certain thing only in a certain place and it has to be there forever. But Tori is really in tune with where she is harmonically, and songs can change keys all the time. If we're segueing in between songs she can be in one place and go to the lead note of the next song, which could be totally not where she was, and she can tie things together in really amazing ways that really not many people can do. In the pop world, most people don't have a flow like that, an ability to create but still keep a thread going through songs and be able to anticipate where something's going to go harmonically.

TORI:

> I'm in Germany.
>
> It's January 23, 2003.
>
> The people are marching.

Exhilarated that they have joined to march, angry that we may go to war. Angry at the potential destruction. Angry at the leaders who are okay with this. Americans in Germany are being asked some very feet-to-the-fire questions. Flags are burning. If as a performer you are to be in tune with Source, you must realize that Source is not American, Source is not German, Source is not African, Source is not even British. You cannot take on everyone's political beliefs—either side. But you can cut through the smoke screens. You can cut through to the unsaid, the said, the mixed feelings, and walk through the caves behind the Intellect of those in the audience. You as the performer have this unique opportunity to go behind the heart. Behind the heart where a spark has taken root. This root has grown into an internal revolution that resists and questions those who are misusing power.

I play in a short while. The set list tonight has not yet been decided.

I know she is here and she is not alone. She is making her way toward me. She always gives me a moment to adjust to her coming. I breathe, knowing my container must expand. She is hard to hold and balance. One of the trickier ones because she holds the polar opposites. Creation. Destruction.

Welcome to Kali.

Welcome to Hamburg.

CHELSEA LAIRD:

Watching Tori go from "Promotion Tori"—having conversations with journalists, getting done what we have to get done, seeing the fans backstage, in between meeting up with Tash—to "Sound Check Tori" is a process. A daily process. You begin to see a transformation occurring. It's about plugging in. There is a process she must go through. Early mornings are spent exploring set list options, late mornings at radio stations or on the phone with journalists, to early afternoons at meet and greets. By the time she walks out onstage for sound check, none of that matters, none of it exists anymore. It happens quickly; she's got precious few moments to plug in and find the electricity that will hold a stage for the rest of the night.

CONVERSATIONS BETWEEN TORI AND ANN:

Years ago I would lock myself away for a couple of hours before showtime so as to be in a state. A calm frenzy. The state of Fuck Off and We Are One. A state where no one could pull me off my course. This comes in handy when you're doing things like big radio shows and big festival shows. I've done radio shows where I'm exposed to other performers and their process, and what would occur was that these artists would walk out onstage to 20,000 people projecting the same aura (or nonaura, depending on the artist) that works for them in a studio setting. When you're in the studio you are solely in communion with the song without having to consider including an audience. You don't have to commune with an audience or commune with anyone else when you're in the studio. And you know what? That can work. You can make a great record. But when you walk out of that studio the grid changes. This is where it gets tricky. But kinda basic. If you don't want to relate or commune with an audience, stay home. Do the studio thing. Be a Radio Star.

Imagine being this performer: you strut out and within seconds lose your stage to 20,000 people who are ignoring you. Twenty-thousand people who are turning on you because, surely, you can't possibly be this piddly-diddly presence compared to what they felt when you were jumping out of their radio into their car—but, woops. You are. Help. You the performer then might say from the stage, "Come on, can you keep it down?" or "Shhhh" . . . Okay, folks, this is not good. This would be a Yikes—all bad, painful. This is called getting your Radio Star Ass Kicked.

Now let's go backstage again at this radio show, where you see performers already in their zone. It's as if you are watching them walk down that red carpet at the Grammys. They are walking around in their performance selves because that works for them. You have no idea how they do laundry. Sometimes I fantasize backstage about how people do their laundry. Woolite? Mixed-color loads? Do they fold? Do they press? Do they Shout it out? And the thing that kills me—do their whites come out dingy? This you will not know with some performers backstage because they are in their iconic selves and icons don't do laundry. I've walked around in my performance self before, because it's a sure thing. Meaning, it's a huge protection device—like having twenty Trojans in your pocket. I have even stepped into my performance self, strategically, for self-preservation, before I've left the hotel. If there is a lot of paranoia and passive-aggressive mind games on the menu, it is a way to stay in your center and not take on any other performers' hang-ups. Hang-ups and freaked-out psycho issues can leak backstage like fluids at an orgy—a bit graphic, but you get the point. Festivals or radio shows can be the heavyweight championships of *arrogantly detached clusterfucks*. So you are thinking, *I can rise above this,* and your ego may think it can. But if you've been thrown off your center, your ego will run for the ladies' room so fast, and then you'll be thrown onstage so fast, reaching for your John Thomas, needing it to rise, and realizing you don't have dick. You see, you are surrounded by a group of people who have partly made a career by seducing the world into focusing on them, as *the* center, for the thirty minutes they are onstage—or if not on "them" specifically, then on their message . . . me included. Now are you clear enough not to get seduced yourself? Depends on the day.

Now let's go backstage again at this radio show. There is a nod. A smile. A blow-off. It's all going on. Then in catering I find myself talking to some guy who is a dad, and because we both have daughters, we are comparing notes. In that moment he's a dad, in that moment he's a friend. We are people again. Not somebody else's projected whatever. Not even our own projected whatever. I watch him take the stage, and *bam*. The dad has become Apollo. Since we'd spoken, his transformation, which took only about twenty minutes, had taken place. He took his private moment to do whatever it is he does to achieve this synchronicity. It seemed to me that his real self, whom I had met, was walking with his performer self. They know each other and that is always inspiring to watch. I was watching not just an Icon, but a Dad, who can access the performer and transform both into one being. Hard to do. But it can be done.

I don't think that many performers necessarily want to see their audience empowered. I think a lot of performers, no different from priests, need the hierarchy. Modern, celebrity-driven entertainment turns the stage into an altar, and so many celebrities refuse to be removed from those altars once they manage to ascend. They will not be taken down— the Goddess is offended . . . As a storyteller in the old tradition, you held an important place at the circle. Your position was fluid, not necessarily permanent, but it demanded that you respected the others witnessing your performance as much as they respected you.

All storytellers, all troubadours worth their salt knew their myths. To conjure another image . . .

The party invitations have gone out for this reality archetype TV show (without the TV) and told through the eyes of the Bard. I'm hoping that everyone will RSVP. Muhammad, Zeus, Lucifer, Josephine. They are all on the list. As I'm sitting at my piano, in the piano bar somewhere in the galaxy, I look out and see them in the crowd. The Archetypes have all arrived. Josephine fighting for a seat next to Cleopatra. Freyja, surrounded by her cats, hand on her necklace, head thrown back in the air with a throaty giggle, as Aphrodite brings her up to date on her latest sexploits. Pele letting her hair down and chalking her cue, knocking some balls back into the net with Isis. And through all this, like Sam in *Casablanca*, I sit at the piano, never stopping, listening and watching the songs get ready for the show. It's as if I'm an observer of this scene, no different from when I observe an audience at a show, but I'm not sure those in the audience are aware of the Archetypes they carry. We all carry them. These Archetypes are not only embodied by the songs, but they run through all of our lives, just in different amounts. Similar to baking—the ingredients in a cake will be similar from a lemon pound to a chocolate cake. Both have sugar, both have flour: clearly there are similarities here. The difference is the lemon, the chocolate, a few others. In songs, some will share ingredients / archetypes, but then there will be a few twists that make the songs different. Sometimes it's just the measurement of the sugar—how much Aphrodite a song might have.

ANN: *Balancing conscious effort with the need to let the songs overtake and guide her, Amos becomes a paradox: a conscious oracle. Every act of divination requires tools, and Amos's voice as the public knows it arises only in the presence of her beloved Bösendorfer.*

MARK HAWLEY:

Tori hardly ever sings when she's not playing the piano. Her sense of rhythm is so much better when she's playing, it seems. Most people couldn't even manage to play and sing at the same time, but

Isis, the egyptian goddess of fertility

she depends on it. And I think people will be surprised to hear her play the Hammond B3 organ. The last thing you expect visually when you hear it is a small redhead playing this big, fat, soulful organ.

JON EVANS:

She's a really, really strong player. She has a really wide depth of range, just dynamically, and she knows the instrument really well. With some pianists, you feel like if they weren't watching all the time they wouldn't nail it, they're just not very sure. But with Tori, it's as if she's made for the instrument in a certain sort of way. There's some sort of spatial relationship between her brain and her body and the piano—everything's always right there. She rarely makes a mistake, even when she's doing something that's not rehearsed or if she's improvising.

ANN: *For many years, Amos needed only her piano to carry out her enlightening enchantments. Yet a real musician craves two things: companionship and challenge. Amos eventually exhausted the possibilities of solo performance. She had always experimented in the studio and wanted to widen the musical possibilities of her live show. She worked through several approaches before settling on her current setup: a jazz-style trio that rocks like a thunderstorm.*

CONVERSATION BETWEEN TORI AND ANN:

People say that when you're touring you have no time and no space. Actually, I do have space. The stage is my space. With Matt and Jon, it becomes our space, our music space, which is sacred space. Those two are in that sacred space with me. That's when they're free, too. Nobody can call them. If there's an argument going on with friends, family, whomever, they cannot get to those two guys. It's impossible. We're in a sacred space up there. That's why we're so close.

MARK HAWLEY:

I think Tori can, without trying to, make a musician very nervous. A lot of pop musicians play by ear—they don't even read music. Because of her training, Tori's got her theory down. She can tell a musician exactly what notes he played right after he played it, and she can tell him what notes she wants him to play. Jon is very accommodating, but he's also very sure of his abilities. Tori doesn't faze him at all. He's on her level, and there aren't that many people in pop on that level these days.

TORI:

To play with Jon and Matt means chops, chops, chops. Gotta get 'em up . . . Fingering. Practice. Fingering. Left hand. Shake booty. Right hand. Plié. Left hand. Shake booty. Right hand. Start again. Let's face it: artists who dictate their musicians' parts aren't utilizing them well. Especially someone like Matt who has played on so many records. Because I promise you, he will come up with something they can't. This is his life. You don't need to be the sharpest knife in the drawer to figure out that if Matt Chamberlain walks in the room, you don't tell him, hit the snare on two and four. He'll come up with something that they couldn't in a million years think up. Do I honestly think that if you give me a piece of clay I'm going to give you a Rodin? I have no illusions: I am not Camille Claudel. As a musician I have no illusions—I am not a drummer, I am not a bass player. It always puts me in a fit of giggles when an artist tells a musician what to contribute without even hearing what the musician is moved to play. In order for there to be improvisation onstage, you cannot keep such a tight leash on your musicians or they won't be able to be spontaneous. In order to do this, however, you must be able to keep up with them. Which brings me back to chops, chops, chops, practice, practice, practice.

MATT CHAMBERLAIN:

Tori's the only person I'll tour with, unless it's some really bizarre and cool project or my own band. I hate to tour. It's usually a boring drag. With Tori, though . . . she's so strong and musical, it's different. You feel like a better musician after being with the tour.

The way we've been touring lately, it's a traditional trio—piano, bass, and drum. It's not unique in jazz; it's unique in rock or pop. We don't even have a rhythm guitar, so all the melodic information is coming from Tori. I don't really contribute to the melody; I contribute more to the color. I'm like the context and texture person, who helps determine whether a song is going to be earthy, light and ethereal, funky, or rock. Jon gets to do a lot of stuff that a bass player doesn't often get to do— he gets to play chords and other melodies besides just the bass line, because there are a lot of guitar parts he's trying to cover at the same time. The fact that the instrumentation is so limited and you have to make it work makes the experience unique. There's a lot of room for everybody. I don't need to just play a basic backbeat; I can add a few things here and there. The structure forces you to play to fill up the sound. But then, a lot of times it's great just to be really minimal because we can be. There's so much space.

JON EVANS:

I think it's really good for us to be playing without a guitarist. For me there's a lot more to play, and I just like that sparer sound itself. There's more opportunity just to hear everything that's going on. Guitar takes a lot of room, especially Steve Caton, who worked with Tori for many years. He added so much—it was a really big part of the sound. He used a lot of orchestral effects that really filled up the whole sound. It was like a blanket. It was really beautiful, but you take that away and there's a lot more opportunity for subtle colors to come out instead of a big color.

CONVERSATION BETWEEN TORI AND ANN:

The other keyboards bring in another tone, to add dimension to the piano. The piano does a lot of things, but there are things that a Rhodes does, that these old Hammond organs do, that are great. Like a Stevie Wonder influence. And I believe in incorporating that. Even if it's simultaneously one hand on one—the piano—and one hand on the other—the organs—which is kind of my thing. I've been developing that, straddling the piano bench in the middle like a horse and playing on both sides. It's quite challenging, but it also brings the male and female together, because to me the piano represents the feminine and the organs represent the masculine. It is the *hieros gamos* (sacred marriage) of the two that makes me feel as if I'm the link in the middle of this love affair. Like Hermes, sending messages back and forth between two passionate lovers who can only touch each other through a human.

JON EVANS:

She's very much a part of the rhythm section. It's not about bass and drums and then this thing that happens on top. Ultimately she doesn't even need us to be there; she's done it all her life by herself, you know. She has bass lines and she has inner voicings and she has melodies, all on her piano, and they all work in a certain way and they create a rhythm. It's really about making all that happen at the same time.

Tori has a heavy left hand; she knows it, and that's something that we've had to work out since day one. There are some times when she's just pounding away in my zone. That's fine. The piano goes higher and lower than I can. I'll just find a line that's rhythmically contrapuntal, or I might just completely get out of her range and do something totally guitar-oriented, because she's doing a full-on bass line. Or I might do exactly what she's doing, just to reinforce it. There are tons of different options, and there are no rules. She's never saying, "Do this"; it's just more like, "This is what I'm doing, so you figure it out."

MATT CHAMBERLAIN:

Just the drums can really change a song in concert. If she plays a song like "God" live, it's totally different. On *Under the Pink*, "God" has all electronic drums. Live, it can become way funkier, an almost improvisational thing. And she'll work off that. She reacts to the rhythmic choices I make as if it were a jazz gig. I've played with the jazz pianist Brad Mehldau, and he's like that, too. Most jazz musicians are always reacting to the other players. Tori does that, but within a pop song. We'll be playing a song we've played a million times, "Girl" or something like that, and I'll just add an extra little tom thing and she'll do something different on the piano. Or "Cornflake Girl"—the last part is a piano solo, which for her is sort of prearranged, it's all worked out, but I can react to it in whichever way I want. And then she'll change it a little bit, too, in response to me. You can always get a reaction out of her. She'll smile and go, "Yeah!" And do something interesting. I react to her lyrics or her vocal rhythms, too. Her vocals make you do bizarre drum phrasings that you wouldn't normally think of, but somehow it works because it's part of the music.

I just find different things every time we play a song. She likes that, which is great for us. With bandleaders who like to write parts and don't encourage people to improvise, it's a drag, because you want to react to it and you're not allowed. I feel completely satisfied at the end of a gig. I feel I've played some music. I don't feel I'm up there just *bam bam bam*, chopping wood, which is what drummers mostly get to do at pop gigs. It's a satisfying musical experience.

CONVERSATION BETWEEN TORI AND ANN:

Even in live performance the songs are like moving paintings, and I—I as a person and performer that may be changing inside and outside at different times during a performance—cannot change who and what the songs are: they are sovereign. However, there is backstory to a song, there are conversations that the songs have with me from day to day—in that way they are alive. But "Leather" will be "Leather" whether I become an old granny who has become a vegetarian or a celibate carnivore. "Leather" will not change herself for me, and I cannot ask her to and would never. But in live performance—because of, let's say, current circumstances in the world that day, in the city where I'm playing that day, in me that day, in Jon and Matt that day, in the people that will come to the show that day, the perspective of "Leather" can change that day, and that is because how we look at her is constantly changing. For instance, there were these working girls in Vegas who sent me a note (through a person who knew a person who has a sister, yada yada yada). These gals worked as a duo act, and apparently while doing what they do best they would put "Leather" on repeat. This is a part, a piece of "Leather's" exposure to other people that has pulled her into their lives. So when the duo act comes to one of the shows, clearly they will be having a different sensory feeling experience from one had by, say, my mother. The duo act will have pictures in their memory banks that will rise to the surface, no different from my mother, when "Leather" is played.

The difference is only what the pictures are. My mom always tells me, "You know, darlin', I just love the swing of that piana. I used to sell a lot of honky-tonk records back in Carolina." So as you can see, these factors, compounded with how "Leather" is used in the narrative of the show that night, may change my relationship to the song itself and how I feel about her. Because a live show is sonic theater, for a few simple hours in my life or in the life of a person in the audience, we are descending to the underworld. Here, very personal internal feelings about ourselves, other people, and issues can take off their masks and show us where they truly stand. Then, as we ascend into the fifth and final act of the show, we can choose what we want to take back with us: a piece of our underworld self that, frankly, the cheating boyfriend may need to meet, or the boss that doesn't appreciate you, or the terrorizing Bitch at school—or maybe you're the terrorizing Bitch, maybe I am. Some fragments that took their masks off while we were on this underworld journey sometimes walk quietly with me. Only I know that after the show they will be staying with me as my figurative New Renter in my seafront condo, down the street from Pituitary Lane, behind Heart Terrace. Then again, some unmasked Beings that I see during a performance find me once I'm back in my dressing room and receive from me the "Okay you, thank you for the perspective and the vision, but in this century you can't just chop people's heads off and feed them to your cats, and I know these guys are bad guys, and thank you for the vision. So you can haunt me during the show again in Indy."

Songs can be used as an exit door from an ideology that might not be working for the people. Songs can become the getaway car from a relationship, especially if you are in a relationship with a guy who is driving the physical getaway car. Songs can penetrate when hours of talking with a parent only seemed to build up walls. Songs can tear them down in minutes if the parent and the child are willing to listen. Songs can remind you that you don't want to leave this space, although your bags are packed and ready to go. When we think of space, some of us stand outside at night and think of it as this endless outer space. For me, the songs are that space we can walk into. For me, songs are a state, a state of being that can make you see your physical place completely, in a new fresh way—or a state so vast and varied, like the state of New Mexico. The belief that the songs are a space doesn't change. When I walk in it, though, what I choose to hang on the walls and bring into the room can change. But whatever the space, the challenge is to find the root of what and who the song Being is. It might be a lullaby, or a waltz. If I can go back to the song's original form and retain the core of that form, then I can still thoroughly justify the interior decoration, what I call the rearrangements of the song, in whatever the space is.

CHELSEA LAIRD:

When she sings certain songs now, they come from a very different place, and they've evolved into completely new arrangements. "Hey Jupiter," for example. You listen to the version she plays live next to the one that's on the album—the lyrics are the same, but the arrangement is entirely different. I think that's just because that song kind of became something else for her. That's true for basically any song from *Boys for Pele*, because she wrote that album when she was going through a dark time in her life. When she sings those songs now they naturally come from a different place, because her life has evolved on so many levels since she originally sang them. She's retained the integrity of the songs but sings them from a different perspective.

CONVERSATION BETWEEN TORI AND ANN:

Some songs are easier than others to apply to my life now. "China," for example. It doesn't have to be about the same people who inspired it. *I can feel the distance getting close* . . . That situation can be with a girlfriend, or with a different man than the one I wrote it about. With other songs, it's hard for me to connect them to my situation. But the songs aren't overly sympathetic with me about that. They sort of imply, "Look, T, we're not just existing for you to relate us to just your little life. If you can't relate to us on a specific day, then try to see our narrative occurring in someone else's life who is going through what we're talking about."

SONG CANVAS: "winter"

It's always shifting. When I sing "Winter" now, I don't necessarily get the same pictures I did on the last tour or the tour before or the tour before or the tour before. When I was writing that song, I was considering a relationship between a girl and her father, or grandfather. Or any male who held that space. Because as we know, some fathers don't hold that space. My perspective isn't always about a girl and her father. "When you gonna make up your mind? When you gonna love you as much as I do?" There was a moment for me when those lyrics were referencing Kevyn Aucoin. Especially when he died, that was my need. The song allows me the space to have my perception of it as I go through my changes, and yet I still hold the integrity of a girl and her father when that song enters my body in live performance. But I, as Tori, will feel what I feel, and see the pictures I see, and the songs have always allowed me that as long as I retain their DNA integrity.

It can even come back to parenting. I will do something, say something to Natashya, and I'll just realize I have created a space that I did not want to create for her to walk into. Say she was very naughty and I said something like (and I am cringing as I write this), "Because you did this, this is why Mommy's going to London this weekend." So then she thinks that when Mommy leaves it's because she's naughty. I saw that happen once, and it was as if a thousand prisms were shattered—I began to see in my own being how the tape plays, what I hear when somebody makes a rhetorical move like that. I did something that I'm going to have to deal with and work with now a lot, whenever I leave her. So when I sing "Winter," sometimes now I see a girl walking over that hill with a mommy. Yet the pictures can still be of my Poppa, and my father. It's not always an either / or when I'm singing a song live. I can liken it much more to snapshots or Polaroids that I can flip through in a book, that tug and pull on my emotions with every turn of a phrase. But now other experiences affect me when I sing, "When you gonna make up your mind? When you gonna love you as much as I do?"

ANN: *Before she can gather perceptions onstage, Amos must create a framework. She does so through an unusual approach to compiling her set lists. Most pop musicians rely on repetition to please a crowd hungry for familiar hits, and to make their own night's work less complicated. Contrary to the myth of ecstatic release, an arena rock show now is much more likely to feel like a Broadway show, slickly plotted and perfectly rehearsed. In Amos's view, this common approach serves neither the artist nor the audience. Her fans, who often follow her tours, would grow bored; worse yet, so would she. And the great resource of her voluminous songbook would grow musty with disuse.*

Varying her selections each night over the years, Amos has slowly developed a way of creating a story through set construction. The songs she selects (aided by Chelsea Laird, who sits by her side with a large black pen each night, modifying the list) speak to one another, falling into an imagistic narrative reflecting the particular time and place of each performance.

TORI:

Where am I . . . ?

"You're in Chicago, lady," answers a voice in front of me in a coffee shop line, as Chels jumps back into line after answering her cell. It's nine a.m.

I try to find a corner table. Okay. Where am I? I close my eyes and start scanning my memory banks, the memory banks that hold the lockboxes that hold the keys to the place called Chicago's memory banks. I've played here many times . . . First at a place called Shuba's in 1992. Yes, I remember. I can see that girl / woman / banshee playing for her life at the piano. Playing before the two Marys knew they had to marry within my Being for me to tap into the Feminine without my circuits being blown to bits. These two would have to integrate inside my Being for me to one day be able to play the hebe-jesus into the piano, shake those insurmountable mounds (don't I wish) above and below my navel line, have a sensual whisper with Husband before the buses leave, and be feeding a slightly-later-than-midnight bottle to my two-year-old.

"Hey, they didn't have your usual, so I got you this instead," Chels says with a devilish grin.

"I'm desperate. I'm sure it's heaven."

Chelsea's weapon is open and she's ready to type.

This is our ritual. Every day.

Okay, so *where am I?* This is the core question we must weave into our net before we cast it out into the information pool. Before the set list can be written, there are things I want to know.

"So, Chels, let's get a rundown of what's on at any kind of museum in or around the city—a rundown on any other event or events occurring here this month, from the mundane to the strange. Let's get a synopsis of the week from the *Tribune* online, the last twenty-four hours from the BBC (since we have the previous twenty-four from the day before and so on and so forth . . .) and a National Read in the last twenty-four. The past and the present are the threads that together will give us the clues to what our Chicago tapestry should be."

With a trustee Americano at her side, Chels will ride like Brunhilde as Valkyrie on her laptop to Valhalla in Asgard and back to Chicago by sound check.

Chels reminds me that we already have a history of this area precontact (pre-European contact).

"So let's pull that up, and a bullet-point history of Chicago."

"Do you want an update from the Smoking Gun?"

"Oh, yeah, the more the merrier. We've got two shows here, right?"

"Yep, today and tomorrow. Are we focusing only on today's set list?" (I see that hopeful Chelsea we-are-so-up-against-it-girl-Friday look in her eyes . . .)

"Both. They go in tandem."

"Thought so." And off she goes.

CONVERSATION BETWEEN TORI AND ANN:

Every night the set list is based on the things that cross our path, and we work with a palette. You're given what you're given. Cities have different essences, colors, smells. Letters come across to us that we read or don't read. The time of year matters; maybe we're near a holiday like Easter, and that means certain songs are appropriate. What's on the news figures in. Sometimes what happens is sad, you know—Tash fell down and scraped her knee and called for Mommy and I didn't know what to say. And she said, "Make it go away" and I couldn't, and I glanced at the television and was reminded that there's a war going on. Narratives arise in moments like that. We consider using everything, and some things we discard.

There are also musical considerations, of course. I know how the key of each song connects with the next; I chart out the rhythms in my mind. We also have to keep stations—there's the Wurlitzer station and the piano station, and the Rhodes, and I have to balance the time at each one. I also need to provide time for Matt and Jon to adjust to each song, you know, reach for a tambourine or quickly tune down. It has to move—I do not like lag. The last thing I want is for the show to turn into, you know, "The Best of Ricki Lake and Tori" with the audience between songs.

That approach has no flow. I want each performance to be like a sonic film.

Some consistency is important from show to show, because people just want to hear certain songs, but it's also crucial that we don't seem as if we're repeating ourselves out of thoughtlessness. Many artists work toward one show; they do their homework and spend weeks on their set, like a seminar. But I have a big catalog and don't see the value in doing the same thing every night. I mean, what is this? Like, our seventieth show? Or eightieth, since November. Each night I have to be somewhat different. What worked six weeks ago in Radio City won't necessarily work for Santa Barbara, which won't necessarily work two shows later in Albuquerque. We're different people now, here in the moment, at every show.

The only thing that started being consistent was that we would have the metaphorical fire at the beginning every night. The Apache woman calls all of us to ceremony with "wampum prayer." That's not Scarlet singing. They're different women. She's calling me and the musicians and everybody to the fire. We're burning the sage; it's very much a place for us to kind of shed, I think. Shed the outer world, our habits, the rational. And to walk into the world of metaphor and symbol and story.

ALISON EVANS:

There are certain nights when Tori lets the audience know what's behind the construction of the set list. On the *Scarlet* tour, she dedicated one set to Lori Piestewa, the first woman to die in combat in the Iraq conflict, who was a member of the Hopi tribe. Tori mentioned that during the show. The show was in Boise, Idaho. Other times the theme is not obvious at all. It can start with one line extrapolated from one song that on this night relates to a certain subject. On a different night when there's a different thread running through the set list, that same line could have a totally different meaning.

DAN BOLAND:

The biggest challenge is that she has such an arsenal of songs, and I don't know what she's going to play on any given night. I have to keep it fresh no matter what she chooses. With most artists, it's the same set over and over. You create your theatrical piece and it goes from beginning to end. But with Tori—the Austin show on the *Scarlet* tour is a perfect example. The entire first half of the show, she played all amber and red songs. One of my friends who was there was poking me—he's like, "Don't you ever use blue? Don't you ever use green?" "Yeah," I said, "that's what I use for all the songs that are in the pool that we're not playing tonight!"

CONVERSATION BETWEEN TORI AND ANN:

Sometimes I play a song a lot and I just need a break from it. Especially when we've been on a long tour, certain ones pop up a lot. Sure, we'll do the better-known songs, but it might also be a B-side that recurs. "Take to the Sky" was very much a part of the *Scarlet* tour. Especially with that nod to Carole King, when I break from the original song and put in a bit of "I Feel the Earth Move." But for that tour, I would change it to, "I feel my earth move under my feet" instead of *the* earth. I was going back to one of the major themes of the album, that relationship to the land, getting people to realize that this is something they must claim. I wanted to communicate the idea that your relationship to your nation, and to the earth, is very personal. When we toured in the summer, I wanted to be outside as much as I could be. I wanted to get people back to the land, to their relationship with the land, with music that's working with the land. And Carole King's song, just like the outdoor settings, would also take people back to an innocent sensuality—kissing on the lawn on summer nights. I'd been there.

We were also doing "Sweet Dreams" a lot, because I wrote that during the first Gulf War, when we were in very similar circumstances. I wrote it in 1990 about another George Bush and another Middle Eastern war, and more than a decade later people were requesting it again. It became relevant, a commentary of the time.

I was performing at DAR Constitution Hall in Washington, D.C., of all places, when the Afghan war was announced. I remember that the whole city was in a vise, in the iron grip of a choice that was bringing up all kinds of emotions in people. The backstage was filled with union members— they had pulled Andy Solomon aside and asked him if I would play "Raining Blood" (my cover of a Slayer song) that night because a few of them had boys that were heading out and they didn't know if they would see them again. A lot of them felt as if this one was the beginning of the end of days, whatever that means to people. I was about ready to take the stage in a couple hours, a few blocks from the White House, having to hold a space for a crowd with mixed emotions. Anger. Grieving. Retribution. Reticence. All these being the components of the evening, to name a few. I've played many shows, and this one was one for which I had to remember my training from Poppa. How to make the music like a stream of clear water for people to come drink. Then have their thirst eased by that drink of music and harmony and words in a discordant world on a discordant day, whatever their political beliefs were. I did play "Raining Blood" that night for all the fathers and mothers who were going to have to let their flesh and blood go. To have their flesh and blood exposed.

After the *Strange Little Girls* tour in 2001 and the Afghanistan War, after having the medicine woman come backstage, she spoke to me about how as Americans we have a true mother. That mother is "she who we call America." This medicine woman said to me, an hour before showtime, "Do you feel that the soul of our land is in the right hands?" I was saddened and quiet. Then she said to me, "Would you turn over your physical mother to those who are in control of she who we call America?" I said,

"Well, of course not." She looked at me with piercing eyes, despite her humble appearance. "Then how can you turn over your spiritual mother so that they have made Miss America Misrepresented so that she has been pimped out for the gain of those who can gain from her?" She changed the tone of her voice. Without moving she rose up like a pillar and seemed to speak for all the ancestors from ages past. "We, the caretakers of she who you call America, are giving you a key to the healing of this land. A generation must rise. That generation can be from two to one hundred and two. But this generation of which I speak must form a bond. They have an opportunity to have an intimate relationship with the soul of this land. The European Americans, the African Americans, the Latin Americans, the Asian Americans, and the Middle Eastern Americans must now become caretakers of their Spiritual Mother, or they will be takers of their Spiritual Mother. Caretakers or Takers—you're either one or the other. If the masses keep taking and not caretaking, then your grandchildren will have very little to nurture them. The songs will be coming to you and others who have heard the beating of our drums—you will need to listen. You must find your own relationship with your true Spiritual Mother. Your loyalty should not be to anyone who claims power over the land at any given time, whose intentions can change on a whim, depending if they've been seduced by power and what it brings. You must see the signs, even in yourself, dear one."

Scarlet's Walk was a tour that brought all of us a little bit closer to the realization that the land has a spirit and She is alive. Our buses rolled from California to the New York islands, from the redwood forests to the Gulf Stream waters; this land was made for you and me . . . to take care of. Our buses rolled from Glasgow to Frankfurt and everywhere in between through the *Scarlet* tour, as the drums of war raged louder and louder. By March 20, 2003, we had played through protests and vigils and in cities that were hostile to Americans, and yet we played. We played in towns that could see only vengeance even though they purported to be Christian. We played nights when people would light candles and weep for those going overseas. We played for those who still believed that a peace could be struck.

The furor over the Dixie Chicks, when Natalie Maines made supposedly anti-Bush comments onstage that basically blackballed the group, made it clear that by the time we rolled into Texas I would have to acknowledge what had become a huge issue. So I played Fleetwood Mac's "Landslide," not just in honor of the Dixie Chicks but to affirm freedom of speech. But I made sure that I did my own cover of "Dixie Land" before I did "Landslide" that night in Dallas, because being a southern-born woman, I wanted to make it clear that Dixie could not be about censorship, whether you're from Dixieland or a Dixie Chick—and if you break it down, every woman south of the Mason-Dixon line is a Dixie Chick. So the real point I was making was that a woman from Dixie has the right to speak her mind, no different from a politician from Maine having the right to speak his mind without the threat of being blackballed.

Every night, through all of this, the old Apache woman, singing through me to start the show, always had her say:

In our hand an old old old thread
Trail of Blood and Amens
Greed is the gift for the sons of the sons
Hear this prayer of the wampum
This is the tie that will bind us

CHELSEA LAIRD:

We begin every show with a preshow ritual. It starts in the dressing room: there is always sage burning, then everyone gathers and we all go out to the side of the stage together. The particular approach she chose to begin each show on *Scarlet*'s tour emerged on the promotional tour for the release of *Scarlet's Walk*. She wanted to create this metaphorical fire, as you've heard her talk about. We brought sage with us—it would be Tori and I, Andy Solomon, and Jenni Clarke, who used to do hair and makeup. For promotion there was only us, just the four of us, naturally becoming the four directions (although technically it's six because of Father Sky and Mother Earth which we always acknowledged).

She'd say the prayer before every show. She was working off a Southwestern Medicine Wheel ritual by entering through the south (as opposed to the Lakota, who enter through the east), then going to the west, to the north, to the east. We each represented a direction and an element of animal medicine—for example, the eagle, the mountain lion, the wolf, or the dolphin, to name a few. It would change every night depending on what animal medicine was needed to assist in bringing the songs forth. We'd smudge each other individually with sage in order to clear and release anything from the day—business, bitching, etc. Then she would end the prayer and walk out onstage. I think she always insisted on starting each show this way as a means of focusing everyone. No matter what had happened to anyone that day, this was the way we could all be drawn back down to the ground, onto the stage, and into the show that night. A real method of focus for those on- and offstage.

When we went on the full tour, others needed to be included. In the very beginning Tash wasn't around for the nightly ritual; it was past her bedtime. She and Tori would say goodbye in the dressing room. As the tour continued, Tash became curious and wanted to see what was going on out there. When she started joining us the ritual evolved to include a song like "Ring-a-Ring-a-Rosy." Then we do our own prayer, calling forth the four directions. There's always more than four of us now. You may have three people holding the south, two the west, three the north, and two the east, and we all commit to holding our own direction and all that goes along with that (the animal medicine that each direction is carrying for the night, which Tori has usually figured out because of the show's narrative and what native tribe is close by—what their clan animals are. She has books and books on this stuff; it takes up most of her bus. But all of us include Father Sky and Mother Earth; male and female essence balanced. Still, we make our circle to contain the spirit of the Four Directions, that ancient way of creating a sacred space, as the old Apache woman sings "wampum prayer."

ANN: *A rock star casting the Four Directions—it sounds pretentious and self-serving. In fact, it's a practical move. For Amos, whose life has been so heavily marked by religion, ceremony draws a line between the chaos of life on tour and the order of performance, which must be defined before it can become open and free.*

TORI:

If I close my eyes, then I know where I truly am. I am on some kind of precipice. I'm on a rock that seems to go up and up and up or down and down and down. I'm not sure what world I'm in because around me there is this beautiful darkness. It is everywhere. I can see exploding suns in the distance and I can see quiet suns just there, twinkling. And I hear the voices of the daughters pull me into this beautiful darkness that has light in it, but it's not as if it's what I'm used to on earth. As I stand on this precipice with toes barefoot over the rock, I want to dive. I want to dive into this beautiful darkness where everything exists for me at this time. I hear the crowd in the distance, stirring, restless. I hear voices around me, back in the other world. The world called New York or Paris. Or Red Rocks or Seattle. And I know that they are calling for a show, some kind of experience, they want to take a journey. Part of my mind understands this, but I really don't see them: I see them like a slow-motion film. It's present, but it's almost as if I'm watching a film of it. What isn't a film and what feels real is that my toes, my feet, are standing on this rock, this precipice, and the songs are calling me to join them. I can see a few of them below me, above me, around me, and they are immense. They are these light creatures, and, as you get closer, you begin to hear their song. I want to go into these . . . I don't want to call them structures because they are completed. It's as if I could walk into color. As if I could walk into paints, as I would see on shelves as a little girl, but it's more like a paint box the size of Saturn.

When I was lonely in London I would try to find art shops and find all the chalks and the paints, and I would (if I had the money in my pocket, because I didn't have a checkbook back then in London) buy these chalks and paints, although I can't draw or paint. I would look at them and write songs and sing to them, and see if they would come alive in a song . . . and then maybe, just maybe, I could walk into this world of combined color in lonely Londontown. Worlds that are made of shapes I've never seen—granted, I'm no geometric whiz—and in colors that I have never seen combined before. And that is what pulls you in—when you are standing there on that precipice, that rock, and you know you must dive; you must dive in order for the restless out there to take the journey that they want, and, let's be honest, the journey that I want to take, the journey the rest of the musicians want to take. Then I must dive off that precipice and let go of this world. I must leave it behind yet still be in it. Only I am in it as a musician playing—but I'm playing / translating these song creatures that are definitely from another dimension.

They live and exist, but their house isn't off Melrose somewhere—that would be The Bridge Entertainment Group. Their home isn't off the coast of Cornwall somewhere—that would be Martian Engineering, where we record. Their house isn't what you and I know of as a house. Their house exists I guess when I look up at the sky, when I'm walking in Cornwall with my Welly boots on, all bundled up in one of Mark's big Diesel jackets. Then I look up and sometimes I wonder; is that where they are or can I not see where they are? Can I not see the galaxy they come from? If I had something that could travel the speed of light I wouldn't know how to find them. They find me and I'm taken to their realm. It's almost as if I couldn't find them any other way. So when I play I'm able to return to this place of peace, this place of male and female balanced. The opposites balanced—they have me to take in the harmonization of tone that changes the inside of my body, my mind, and my heart. It is showtime. And I jump. And I jump off the precipice. And there is no bungee cord.

ANN: *Beyond the players visible onstage, others collaborate. Mark Hawley translates the sound the trio makes for the audience; his role is highly visible, behind the big board in the middle of whatever room the group occupies. Yet few know of the other players involved in turning Amos's concerts into rituals— Marcel van Limbeek, the man behind her own monitor, and Dan Boland, who creates the stage set and lighting environment.*

MARCEL VAN LIMBEEK:

I'm right in line with Tori. This is her personal mix, what she hears as she's performing. Mark's doing essentially the same thing out in the crowd, for the audience. Tori's mix is coming to her through a surround-sound setup. She has four speakers, two speakers on either side of her, and with that she gets her own voice in stereo. A normal monitor would just give her one vocal, and it would be static. I'm adding effects, reverbs, whatever suits the song, basically. Every song has its own sounds and its own needs. I'm also doing a few things Mark doesn't do, to guide Tori's singing a bit. She's obsessed with good-sounding audio. She calls it her "audio porno," which I find hilarious, but she's dead serious about it—maybe that comes from her classical roots, but give her shit audio and she'll give you an eyeroll as if you are a primitive, barbaric, piece-of-shit engineer. She'll say, "Uncut diamonds, sounds that can be rough and raw—that can all have its place on a record. Intentional distortion has its place, yada yada yada, but shit audio is not counterculture, Marcel, it's just shit audio."

Mark and I created this setup so that Tori could have an onstage sound that was much closer than usual to what the audience could hear. For me it's become a very highly personalized, beautiful thing. Mark is dealing with much more, such different issues. He has to cope with the sounds of different rooms, different environments. I have my own little world with Tori. She has all these people helping her on tour—Duncan, Chelsea, whoever—but onstage it's just her and me. It's as close as a sound technician could come to being a member of the band.

DAN BOLAND:

The environment I'll create just sort of drives itself, really. I listen to the songs a bunch of times and I'll just start putting stuff up and painting the picture with light and think, *Well, that doesn't work* or *Maybe it should be this,* and then eventually it sort of comes to me. And it takes a while sometimes, but it happens. It starts with listening to the album itself. And talking to Tori. In the case of *Scarlet,* there's a thread—it's a story of travel, and it's how everything kind of threads together and weaves together. And from there I draw what I call a visual concept. In this case we tried to represent the idea of how everything is always in motion and at the same time we're all standing still. That relates to the painted backdrop of mountains that we had. If you're ever driving along in a car in the Southwest, you'll notice that you've always got mountains on your left. And then Scarlet's in the background, the Earth Mother always overlooking everything.

I look to the songs for inspiration. With "Wednesday," for example, the line that stuck in my head was "Stop for a coffee." My idea is, somebody just sitting there listening to the things people say at a coffee shop, and there are overhanging trees and a warm autumn kind of feeling. Sometimes it's the name of a song that will trigger an idea, like "Pandora's Aquarium." For that song, I tried to create a water backdrop flowing along. With "wampum prayer," the idea that came from Tori is that we celebrate the eternal flame. So the song, and that tour, opened with only a red flame, as if we're all sitting around the fire and breathing it all in.

ANN: *The degradation of archetypes within contemporary society has made serving Dionysus a sloppy affair for many. Taking this familiar god seriously is also a risk; humans have gone so far in exploring their indulgences that the idea of liberation as an experience that awakens the soul can seem like little more than a romantic dream. Exploring the Dionysian realm onstage, Amos has come to discover that modern-day liberation comes from rediscovering limits: the hard work of musical virtuosity, the sensitivity required by collaboration, and the self-awareness that leads an artist to realize she is a mere attendant, and not the embodiment, of the divine.*

CHELSEA LAIRD:

It's how she walks out there every night, however she might have felt earlier in the day or whatever events, good or bad, that may have occurred. By working off various archetypes, she can actually be that person that I think everybody needs her to be. It's not necessarily who she is day in and day out. You can't tour for an entire year at a time and have that person onstage—the one giving of herself for the sake of everyone that has come to the table—be the same person you eat breakfast with. It's not going to be.

I think it's how she maintains this level of energy and intensity. She can do this day in and day out, year after year, because she can be somebody else onstage and feed off that energy, no different from what anyone in the audience is doing. Then a split second later she can walk offstage knowing that she's left that person out there, she's Natashya's mommy now, there is a joy for her in that. That other person onstage is this mosaic (yes, Tori and her alter ego are both in there somewhere), but this mosaic is formed of all these archetypes she pulls from, which is pretty much any that she can get her hands on, from any culture, male or female. When we're speaking about performance even Tori will sometimes refer to herself in the third person, and the combined strength of Tori and the archetypes she pulls from are what garners such a powerful reaction.

TORI:

The hum of the bus is what makes me know that I'm home for the night. I can make anywhere home—well, almost anywhere—if I put my mind to it. When you're on the road, the bus is your home. Days off in hotel rooms can be like rendezvous nests, a little getaway. I look at the hotels as a holiday from the bus. But as with any vacation, I always return home. When we come offstage, sometimes Matt and Jon and I do running races through the back of the arena because we are so high and unbelievably amped—we are recharged yet completely spent all at the same time. There is no problem that we couldn't solve in that moment. As we bask in the sweetness with our heart still pounding and our body languid, we begin to come down. It's a soft comedown, not a harsh one like when you do Ecstasy; instead you're ready to curl up in your bunk. We all head to our separate dressing rooms. With a quick makeup touch-up, my performance dress still intact, we welcome back all the after-show guests despite the ticking of the clock, reminding us that we don't have long to get to the next town. Jen has the shower steaming, and I've taken off the dress and high heels, waving them goodbye until tomorrow, knowing that they won't sleep tonight. They'll be dancing with the other high heels in the wardrobe cases. I truly believe that my shoes have their own independent sublife when they are all together, alone in their cases. Getting into the shower, I use my favorite soap. Then I put on my bus clothes (very important note: bus clothes are a very personal thing and the definition of bus clothes is different from crew member to crew member). I don't wear PJs just in case the bus has to stop suddenly and I have to be ready to jump in a car and go wherever I have to go. I usually dress in something comfortable—cargo pants, a T-shirt, Adidas, and a zippy. I sleep in that. I probably shouldn't know this, but I have heard that one of the girls on the band bus won't go to sleep without her fuzzy blue bear slippers and one of the guys on the sound bus sleeps naked but must have his socks on, which I don't think get washed but once a week. I think it's causing a bit of an issue on that bus resulting in extreme and desperate behavior, such as sock-napping and ransom notes. So when I get on the bus, in my bus clothes, I sit down at the little table that I always sit at—usually Mr. Joel sits across from me—and Dunc has whipped up some succulent after-show magic. Before the show he and I will have discussed the menu, so I will have selected the perfect wine to complement the Dunc's Diner Infusion Experience. Dunc sits down and we share his idea of what real food is. At that point, feeling a bit like Goldilocks and the three bears (although naturally it was all low-carb), I know I have a few good hours before I have to get up to do morning promotion. With that, I trundle back into my bunk and prepare for Natashya night duty. In that hour on the bus, I've reentered my body as mom, wife, and friend. And the person who can plug in and do that "thing" onstage has gone back to wherever she goes— and I know I will see her again by showtime tomorrow evening.

CHAPTER SIX

SANE SATYRS AND BALANCED BACCHANTES: THE TOURING LIFE'S GYPSY CARAVAN

TORI WITH BAND MEMBERS MATT CHAMBERLAIN AND JON EVANS ONSTAGE AFTER AN ENCORE

The road. The friendships. A way of life that I hold very dear to my heart. The crew doesn't notice that I've popped in this morning—off the bus, in a hoodie. I'm up early, just walking around with a cup of tea. We're not in a hotel because we're doing a quick show today and we're off again right afterward, so the buses are parked up in the backstage of this cozy outdoor woodland where the show will be tonight. After years of coming up with a good team of people who could probably do this in their sleep, I see they still give 100 percent because, let's face it, it's their love, too. The coffee machines are going; I can smell the beans. Catering travels with an espresso machine. This is one of the most comforting smells that I know. I hear the kettle boiling for the Brits. I hear laughter along with a lot of clanging and banging. Although it's not exactly "whistle while you work," we definitely have our own version of Grumpy. We call the head of sound "Grumps," fondly. He wouldn't have it any other way. The lampies are always up early, along with Mark and Mike from the sound side of things, picking their points, where they are going to hang the big PA. I hear production with its machines making an odd kind of music, but music nonetheless. Music to *my* ears, anyway, because it means that we are up and running.

If Andy knew that I was snooping around he would probably have heart failure. But I do this just to make Chelsea laugh. Of course she has to laugh quietly, or she'll give the game away. You see, the crew doesn't know it sometimes, but I watch over them in my own way. I hear Dunc playing opera—that's a good sign. That means he's making me something, probably Mediterranean, tonight. And being since we are in the middle of nothing Mediterranean, it's definitely a treat. Dunc brings his spices and works off local produce, but we have a wine cellar to pull from to complement his creations. The other caterers always seem to be whistling and the catering tent draws you in, no different from those kitchens you see in the movies and wish you had in your own house. Well, of course, this isn't exactly a house. Anything you could ever want is in this space—call it a tent, a place to gather . . . I call it paradise. This is our little world on the road, and we take it with us. Wherever we might find ourselves tomorrow, the one thing I can guarantee—the coffee will be brewing, the kettle will be boiling, sound and lights will be laughing as things clang, then of course there will be shouting and obscenities hurled back and forth endlessly, Dunc will be playing opera, catering will be whistling, I'll be smelling the soup they'll be putting on, and I will know that I am home.

ANN: *Artistic performance is always planned enchantment, even when its energy descends like a mad god's whirlwind wake. Dionysus, that original rock star, traveled with a road crew: the male satyrs and female bacchantes who attended the god not only enjoyed his glories but organized them, accomplishing the practical tasks that must precede any communal rite. Antiquity offers images of Dionysus's followers as mad, driven to ecstasy by divine intervention. But how did they behave in their off-hours? It's amusing, but realistic, to ponder them essentially on tour—moving along the road in a sleepy caravan, setting up a space for their revels each night, and afterward striking the tents, cleaning up their mess, and moving to the next town, where the publicists among them would have already raised interest for the next ritual.*

In the contemporary world of digital sound and virtual reality, many artists have lost interest in the power of public performance. The hassles of the touring life can outweigh the benefits for musicians whose art really only finds its ideal space in the recording studio or the promotional video. For Amos, on the other hand, touring is essential. Her songs present themselves as intimate communications from the universe to her audience, and she views herself as a conduit, entrusted to bring their news. Her musicianship, rooted in improvisation and the physical feel of hands on a piano keyboard, also demands live performance. Long after many of her peers have pulled back on their commitment to the concert circuit, Amos continues, getting fed by offering sustenance to her fans.

Since her late twenties, Amos has spent easily half her life on the road. So much wandering leads many like her to all varieties of self-destruction. Yet despite the hardships of a lifestyle that shaves decades off the lives of many entertainers, Amos has somehow managed to preserve her health, her creative spark, and her personal life. She has been able to do this because of those attendants who, like levelheaded descendants of Dionysus's crowd, ensure the smoothness of her journey. The few cherished hours Amos and her band spend each night in music making's free zone are supported by a vast constellation of boring details: the usual gas / food / lodging concerns of any vagabond assemblage, augmented by the technicalities of transporting sound equipment, costumes, lights, and a stage set, and the need to maintain harmony among the hundred-plus creative souls who belong to this cavalcade.

Learning the art of the road has been a gradual process for Amos. When Little Earthquakes *first brought her mass success, she performed solo due to limited resources and the desire to build a close fan community. Eventually her musical ambition led her to seek out collaborators, and her entourage grew exponentially. With husband Mark Hawley already onboard as chief sound engineer, Amos was ready when it came time to add another layer to touring life, and she has brought her daughter, Natashya, on every extended sojourn taken since her birth. As Amos's daylit family life merges with the night logic of the road, she is playing a role in the reconfiguration of rock and roll as a life's work.*

TORI:

Breathe. Remember.

I can go back. Back to 1994, playing shows every night for months and months and months. Playing then was really the only time when I was alive, present, and in tune with my Being. When I would come offstage, it was as if I had been unplugged. As if my Duracells had been taken out to be put into another toy.

Johnny looked at me and asked, "Why are you so sad?"

I said, "Because when I play, I'm included in what's going on around me onstage. Backstage, I'm part of a tribe, a team, but after the show I get put back in my box, *The Singing Puppet,* and left until a couple of hours before the next showtime, just feeling empty."

He had tears in his eyes. I saw them.

A couple of weeks ago Johnny asked me if I remembered saying, "I don't just want to be a puppet in a box to be taken out and put away."

"Yes. I remember, vaguely."

Then he said, "And do you remember the rest?"

"Fuzzy. Kinda. It's 2004. That's a lotta remembering."

"Well," he said, "after the anti-human-piano-doll speech, I asked you what you wanted and you said, 'To be treated like a friend,' and then do you know what you said? You said, 'Can I be your friend?' "

I looked at him and said, "What did you say?"

He hugged me then, saying, "You daft sod. You've been my friend since the beginning, and I will be your friend through the end."

The Alpha and the Omega. Right here. Live performance began with friendship. The sacred marriage. First with the piano, when I was two and a half. Next with the Beings who become the songs. And then finally with the people who have become the crew. Sometimes the crew is Mark, Marcel, and myself, slogging it out in the control room. Sometimes the crew is Chelsea and Johnny at a restaurant, clarifying all the components that must be planted, fertilized, and watered before the creative harvest will be ready to be presented. With Johnny's friendship I understood that you can deal with *matter*—money—let's face it, money must be dealt with. It's one of the things that brings a show to fruition. But along with *matter* there can be spirit, intellect, knowledge, and honesty—sometimes brutal, but honesty nonetheless. Johnny brought me the road crew; some are still with me. It works because when everyone is juggling and striving for the balance of matter, spirit, creativity, mutually respected knowledge, and honesty, we have the six directions listening to each other. In other words, all the different departments recognize one another as part of the circle, which makes the wheel turn. When this breaks down, blaming, internal struggles, verbal shit slinging, and out-and-out mutiny can drown the whole caboodle. We are a little city traveling on wheels. But we need wheels or we don't roll.

I toured Europe opening for Marc Cohn in 1991. My record wasn't out yet. The EP was coming out. It was an opportunity; he was huge at the time. We went through Europe and through the United Kingdom and Ireland. I had two different guys, production managers I was out with. Three altogether in the end. There was this really good guy in the end—the other two were cokeheads, I think. I'm not quite sure what they were doing, but they were out of their minds. I just remember missing the ferry from Ireland to Wales. We missed the show in Birmingham. You can't buy experience like that. I understand what it's like to drive across Europe with a cokehead and miss a show and navigate with the maps myself.

After I started releasing records, I was just touring with a crew, no band. There were many times before the buses, when Johnny and I would drive everywhere in a car. Then we would fly and drive, or drive and fly, and meet up with the crew. Our budgets were tight, but we made it work. Now I have hair and makeup and people who can pack my bags, but there was a time when Johnny, my security man, Joel, and I did everything by ourselves, with a sound guy and rented pianos.

It might have been at the end of the *Little Earthquakes* tour when we had a Yamaha CP-80 E electric grand piano we were taking around with us. In those early years, sometimes the gigs were in these rat-infested, crappy bars. I'd already spent eleven years of playing in bars when I was a lounge performer. My only rule was I never ate the cheese that they would put out in my closet/toilet of a dressing room, in case my furry friends were hungrier than I was that night. I played on all kinds of pianos, usually good ones in the hotel lounges, the nicer hotels. Usually crap ones in the bar days. I played the gamut, and I think that is one of the secrets to my success. When it comes to live performances, it's not easy to shock me.

JOHN WITHERSPOON:

I first met Tori when I was still tour managing, as the result of an argument with my then wife. It was January 1992. Tori was playing her first big show in London, at the Shaw Theater. *Little Earthquakes* had just come out. My good friend Ian Thorpe was doing her sound and he'd told me I should come down and see her. I'd just got off a tour and wasn't really interested in going out, but I was having a bad day at home. My soon-to-be ex-wife and I were having dinner, a glass of wine, and the usual argument. I had a choice: drink the rest of the wine and go to sleep or get out of the house. I decided to go out. I actually left the house not really knowing who I was going to see, as I couldn't really remember what Ian had told me about Tori. I sat and watched the entire show. I had not done that for any artist for many years, but like everybody else there that night I was completely blown away. Afterward I went backstage and ran into Tori's European agent, Mike Dewdney, who asked what I was doing the next week. I said, "Nothing. Why?" He explained that Graham Cooper, Tori's tour manager, was leaving to go out with They Might Be Giants and they needed someone to fill in for two weeks. I said, "Yeah, why not? I'll do it." And so the next week, after a few transatlantic phone calls, I rented a car and drove from London to Munich—no budget for cozy flights in those days! Before I knew it, there I was, checking into my first of many hundreds of hotels with Tori.

My first meeting with her consisted of me knocking on her door, her saying hello and all in the same breath asking to change rooms, due to the stench of the previous occupant's cigar-smoking habit. I also have a hatred of stale cigar smoke, so no sooner said than done. That first meeting was one of only a handful of room changes Tori ever requested. We had such a blast those two weeks in Germany, but I had to head back to the United Kingdom to manage a big orchestra tour with the late jazz pianist and actor Dudley Moore. As soon as the Dudley tour finished, I signed straight back on with the Tori tour.

In the early days we used to fly all the time, or drive around in rental cars. If the distance between shows was less than 150 or 200 miles away we'd drive. At that point it was just me, Tori, and Ian on sound. We were out for months and months and months. When we started we had no idea that it was going to be almost a year before we finished. We decided to do some more shows in June and then a few dates in July and then maybe we'd go to Europe and come back to the States, and then before you knew it, it was December. And the record kept going and kept going and kept going. There wasn't a show on that *Little Earthquakes* tour that wasn't sold out.

ANDY SOLOMON:

When I first started going on the road with Tori, when she was touring for *Under the Pink*, she was a Mrs. Fields cookie freak. Instead of stopping for Starbucks every day, we were stopping for cookies. And she was not a bus girl at first. She got sick when she tried to ride on it. So she and John would fly. The crew would already be at the gig, setting up, and they would fly on the morning of the day of the show and rent a town car and drive to the gig, then after the gig drive to the airport, or if it was far they'd drive to a hotel, fly the next morning, do the same thing again. I don't think it was until 1996 that she finally got in the bus.

JOEL HOPKINS:

We did like a little trial run with Tori on the bus. I think it was Philadelphia to Washington, D.C.—a short jaunt. We were discussing the possibility that on the next tour she might get her own bus, you know, instead of flying all the time. And the first ride just didn't go that well. It was touch and go there for a while, but I think that once she had her own bus and realized it was a little bit better than what we started off with, she adapted.

There was one horrible time when Tori's apprehensions about the bus really proved right. We were going from Munich to Florence, over the Alps, something like that, and we had just left the venue and made it out of town. We were on a double-decker bus, as you often get in Europe. Bunks upstairs. We were all still downstairs and Tori was having her meal after the show. We came to this covered bridge, and the driver didn't read the signs right; he didn't see that we wouldn't be able to clear it. We slammed into the top of the bridge, and it took all the skylights and every-thing right off the top of the bus, and all the glass and bus parts just came streaming down in shards. I jumped on top of Tori to protect her. We got through all that, and we're off on the side of the road, and what do we have? Open the door, and I've got a fan standing there—*Can Tori sign this for me!*

I said, "You've got to be kidding, get out of here." So what we had to do—we got Hefty bags and that sort of thing. Of course it was going to snow and rain that night, and we're up on top of the bus pathetically trying to make a new roof out of plastic bags. Imagine a convertible bus—there wasn't much of anything we could do. The flight options to Florence were limited. We wouldn't make it in time to do promotion the next day, so we decided to bite the bullet. It got very, very, very cold that night, and rainy, and the wind had the Hefty bags flapping like birds on drugs. That was a scary night, to say the least.

TORI:

Once I was in a position to provide us a better way to tour, I did. I'm a good businesswoman—even with just five dollars in my pocket, I've never asked anybody for money or borrowed money in my life. Even when I was playing for weddings and funerals at age nine. Call it pride, call it a woman who brings home the bacon, but there's a level where you go, "Yes, we can support these people, we can feed them, we can put petrol in the tanks, we can sit there and calculate to the dollar what it's going to take." Sometimes, because of the level of comfort I create on tour, we only break even, after months and months and months on the road. Meaning me, I break even—sometimes just . . . everybody else on the tour gets paid. Does it make things tight sometimes? Sure. So I'm saying, I don't need to do this the way I do it. I don't need to tour at all. But honestly, I do it because I love it.

I have to play. And if I do it at age forty, I'm not staying in the two-for-one motel at the corner of Bargain Boulevard and Friends-of-Flea Avenue, when I have three beautiful homes where I could be. If you want to be harsh about it, what's in it for me? Tramping my kid all over the fucking world?

ANN: *Like any complex organism, Amos's caravan requires structure. Road crews are often deeply hierarchical, with authority radiating outward from the protected inner sanctum of the artist. Special circumstances have tampered with the usual order of things on this tour: not only a personal life that has put her in intimate contact with the quietly acknowledged champion of the crew, Hawley, who has brought a lot of them into the Tori camp, but also Amos's own untrammeled generous streak, which she's had to learn to balance with a leader's assertiveness.*

TORI:

Because Johnny, Mark, Marcel, and I basically came up together and became friends, and because I didn't have a band in those early days, I bonded with the crew. Some crews you might not want to bond with in that way, just because they're living a whole different experience. But I've seen artists who are so far removed from how the organism works that they get duped. They're controlled and they don't even know it. I have sometimes known what was going on with an artist more than the artist did, just because crews talk when they cross each other's paths. And if I know what's going on with another artist's tour, then he or she does not have the right team. So I made a decision to be involved. Being married to somebody who's from that side of it has made it very difficult for anyone to shine me on. There's no hiding the information. I'm democratic in my approach, but at the same time I know when I need to be the boss. It doesn't make me feel strange or make them feel strange. But we all treat it as shifting the gears on a car. The term *boss* has such weird, jacked-up connotations; I see it more as allowing the Artemis archetype to lead me with her bow and quiver.

As I've grown older, I've realized that problems are going to happen. How can they not with so many people? But maybe because I married Mark, I realized the crew is my backbone. Many crew members come back time after time. I try to be fair, though sometimes I'm tough. To be a real leader you have to be able to deal with confrontation. You have to be able to say, "Dude, this is uncomfortable to talk about, but we need to deal with it." And if you can't do that, then you have to turn that role over to somebody. Usually I don't have those conversations. They can be embarrassing for the crew member, so they are delegated to someone else. But if things land on my plate, I've got to deal with it. And I will deal with it.

Too often, artists turn over their power when they go on the road. I've seen it firsthand—managers and tour managers taking a bribe (a backhander, as the Brits call it) from the equipment companies, from the sound company, so its equipment will get on a big tour. It might not be the best thing for the artist; it might not be the best sound you can get, or the best lighting rig you can get, or the best bus and truck company, or the most reputable tour accountant. I've seen tour managers fire crew members who might have been good for the artist but were getting too close and might have shared too much confidential information about what management was up to. I made a decision to be aware of what was going on with my support system. I've kept my ear to the ground. That means knowing things that aren't necessarily going to make my day happy. But if I'm paying, I want to know what I'm paying for. There are people whom I do trust, but ultimately I trust myself. I trust myself to say, "This support person lost it today and can't make a clear decision. If I'm the one who can't make the decision, if I'm too emotional, then I'll delegate to whoever I think can make it best for me. I delegate a lot. I give a very wide berth. But there are rules. There is a discipline.

For the art to be taken out into the world, you need people around who can help you present it. You create a tribe around you. We have to see what everybody's abilities are and understand how to use those abilities. But the thread running through all this is *how we treat each other.* When someone starts treating others offensively, then there are consequences. The whole tour can suffer if it's not dealt with.

ALISON EVANS:

On this tour, there's a really strong family vibe. I think we all appreciate the level of maturity. Not to say we're all over the hill, but everybody kind of has a life somewhere. People have houses and spouses and girlfriends and dogs, and the camaraderie extends from the general understanding that this tour is just one part of our lives. We take care of ourselves. We don't stay out drinking all night; we really want to get our sleep so that we can enjoy the next day.

It's almost like a lesson, just living this close to people, many of whom you didn't know before. You can't be a bitch; you can't be difficult. On days when you want to be that way, you just have to go and hide. Because you've got to make it work. Everybody's too close and depends too much on one another to make the show happen.

ANDY SOLOMON:

Mark keeps tabs on the technical side of things, and John is the final word as Tori's manager. My job is to keep the details in line across the board. What I've learned working with Tori is that if you put together the right team, you can give people space to be responsible. My personal style is loose reins, big pasture, and when you're at the fence you know where it is. That seems to work with this group of people. We've all become very, very, very close friends, but there's a line you don't cross. I've known Mark for fifteen years, from before either of us knew Tori, but I'd never use that connection to slack off. People on this tour understand how to balance their personal connections. You have to stand up and perform, and you can't use anything as a prop. This is a very performance-oriented tour, and though it may seem odd to say this, in this business I don't think that's the norm.

TORI:

When there's trouble I'm there in the trenches, but at the same time I have no problem saying, "We must get rid of this person, this one and this one, goodbye." Because I've seen what happens when you don't. I've seen how one person can pull a whole crew down, a whole tour canceled. Over. Bands splitting up. Not on my turf.

I provide a lot of freedom and a place for people to express their opinions. But there is a protocol and a way you treat people. If you're passive-aggressive I'm going to smell you out quick. And if you think that you're going to manipulate things, then you get to meet the lioness. Not a problem; I will rip your throat out. I've made it here with myself and my piano, against all odds, having pissing matches with chairmen of Warner Brothers. I have no problem facing a lighting guy who happens to have the Bitch from Hell Mother complex.

Attitudes can be contagious, like colds. People start reacting to a mood and they don't even know where it comes from; sometimes they're taking it personally when things aren't addressed. I have found more often than not, people aren't even aware of how they're treating others. They're going through something, or somebody said something and they just reacted. Loose cannons, dangerous things. It's different when you can go home from work, when home and work are separate. But month after month after month after month of working and living as a group, you can't have the cancer within. You'll bring the whole thing down.

"Okay, when did you talk with them about it?" I ask as Keith, our tour manager, pulls up a chair.

"I spoke with them about the bitching and moaning exactly four days ago."

"Let's get them in here, pronto."

"You have radio promo."

"Yeah, yeah. Okay, ladies; let's take ten for you to get a coffee, and Keith, let's get the guys in, and I want you, my friend, to witness what is about to transpire. After all, you will be overseeing sending these two out and bringing their replacements in. How long till the big shows in a row?"

"You got five days, T."

"So only two days to train the replacements?"

"That's it."

"So Keith, do we have them on hold?"

"Their tickets are already booked and I've already brought them up to speed. They want to come."

"That's the right attitude. That's what I like to hear. But they realize it isn't a done deal, right? Not until our guys have failed the final test, which I'm hoping they won't do, but the glass carriage is already part pumpkin and the clock has just struck twelve."

"It's all been made very clear that there is one more chance, but it is the final one."

"Let's go. This can take only seven and a half minutes from the moment you shimmy out the door."

"I'm shimmying, and T . . ."

"Yeah?"

"It's well overdue. They've had plenty of chances."

(Door opens three minutes later with Keith and the other two.)

"Hey, Miss T." "Hey, Tor."

"Hi, guys. So, you two were asked to sort your differences out and it continued. So then you were asked to sort your shit out. And now your alls' shit has made it into my dressing room. Your alls' shit has now, today, become the center of this tour."

(A bit of throat clearing.)

"Look, T, we're cool. It won't happen again."

"No, get clear—you may think it's cool, but I am boiling here. You've heard of a sleeping volcano? Well, she just woke up. By tomorrow's sound check, if you two haven't sorted out your negativity, your bitching, and your attitude, although I'm going to miss your creativity, you gotta go."

"But, Tor, we're all a team."

"No, get clear—we are all a team until we do things that bring the team down. Then we are a team divided. Instigated and held hostage by certain individuals—who will be taken off the team so as not to facilitate the whole group to self-destruct."

"But you need us. The big shows are next week."

"Yes, and no. I don't need anybody. I came into this world with a piano and I will leave this world with a piano. I *chose* to need you, and right now I'm ready to *choose* to need someone else. The ball's in your court, guys, but the clock is ticking."

At this point Keith politely says, "Five minutes to sound check, lads. Tea, then?"

And off they go.

ANN: *Amos has developed the strength to intervene if a crisis hits the tour, but as important is her commitment to communicate with crew members on a daily basis. People tend to remain on her crew for many years, partly because she believes in offering technicians and support people a chance to fully realize the creativity of their positions, in collaboration with her.*

Artemis, the Greek goddess of the hunt

DAN BOLAND:

There's more to working with Tori than just playing music and getting the paycheck and getting out. There's a whole idea of communicating things. Tori has things to say onstage, and I try to accent it with lighting. I listen to her music, I've talked with her about her ideas, about the songs or the overall space of the tour, and then I just try to create more environments on top of it.

I'm going out with Eminem after this tour is over. I'm more of a hired hand there. If I'm ever called into the dressing room, it's a bad thing. It's not that he doesn't care how the show looks, but we're not going to sit there and share ideas. It's more like he says, "This is how I want it." That's the usual reality on a tour. But with Tori, there's collaboration. If she starts to play new songs, even during rehearsals, I'll just throw lights up to just try to create something in my head that goes along with what she's playing, and she'll stop and say, "That's pretty, what is that?" We'll have a back-and-forth, and my work evolves from that.

ANN: *Despite everyone's best efforts, conflict is inevitable on tour, especially when it comes to the daily schedule. More than most audience members know, every minute counts.*

TORI:

Even well-oiled machines need tune-ups. Very simply, if a squabble on the road has made its way into my jurisdiction, then obviously it hasn't been dealt with correctly. And once it's on my radar, then I will be putting in my two cents. All the crew members learn this quickly, and some learn it by being handed a plane ticket—I don't mind where, but off my ship. Do we run a tight ship? Yes and no. I don't care what you eat or how you sleep or with whom, as long as everyone is consenting. Some bands have security cops that follow people around on their days off and watch what they eat—vegan watchdogs. If a band has members in Alcoholics Anonymous, some tours will employ antialcohol cops to make sure that the crew remains sober, so that if the musicians go out with them then they are not tempted to drink. Frankly, I don't care what people eat or drink, but I do care if you can't do your gig. If I start doing your gig, and you will know that I am because Andy Solomon will come and tell you that I am, then it's not going to go very well for you. We are out here to be the best. Now, we are not the only touring act that is out here to be the best. But we are part of a privileged group of troubadours that have a reputation so that year after year people will come. If you are on my crew, you have to love touring because I pause for very few reasons. If you can't cut the pace, then you need a slower tour.

You're only as good as your crew. Let me repeat myself . . . you're only as good as your crew. Hear me, young future superstars—even if only in your own mind. If you are a good performer (not great—let's be honest here, radio gods and goddesses) and you have a great crew, the perception will be that you have a great show. If you are a great performer but have a mediocre crew, it'll sound shit and look shit, and it's hard to shine through shit. Riveting stuff, but very simple. I ride the crew hard. But I'm fair. And I reward them. You've got to reward your crew. Sometimes we're rolling on six shows a week with shorter, radio-sponsored shows on the off day. If some "genius suit" (from the business side of my world) suggests that the crew doesn't need the most expensive lager on their buses after load-out, then, through my "favorite suit" (Philip-the-Good, officially Phil Holthouse, my beloved accountant), this "genius suit's" suggestion will be knocked on the head during a business conference call with the words "The artist, whose money it is, incidentally, reminds us that the crew is doing six shows a week while some of 'us' are having a cozy week-end sitting on our fat asses. Next?" "The suits" have their role, but they don't always make the right call for the right reasons. The crew must feel as if "said artist" respects the fact that they are breaking their balls. So if the best lager or better after-show food helps to make broken balls happy balls, that's important. Do the crew members think I'm a motherfucker? You'll have to ask them. If so, hopefully they think I'm a fair one.

CHELSEA LAIRD:

There are a lot of elements being juggled on any given day. We might be a few performances into a tour already before Tori even runs into some of the crew members. The pace can be manic—radio shows, meet and greets, interviews, and more. Tori's had a full day before she even walks into sound check. She doesn't expect crew members to cover her side of the day for her, and in return, she expects the technical side of the show to be working. One of the most important things for her is rehearsal. She sound checks every single day for at least an hour. For her it has to run like clockwork. That is the most important thing to her. The hours are long but when you have a good show everybody feels it, from the stage to the sound board to the production office. It's why we all ultimately do this, for that payoff.

TORI:

Because a tour is essentially a flow, and it has to keep rolling, time is often the biggest area of dispute. There are two areas on tour about which you can't negotiate, timewise. One is a child's schedule, and the other has to do with penalties. In many venues, because the staff is unionized, if a show goes past a certain hour, you have to pay a large overtime fee. The penalty can also include running over your designated sound-check time. If we're running fifteen minutes behind, sometimes we're fighting to get that fifteen minutes back all day. And if it's just one of those days when you're doing radio or telly and we're behind because the driver was late or Tash got sick that morning, it can be harrowing. We're playing catch-up. If we don't make it, I'll have to choose to cut the show down or take a financial hit.

Sometimes I'll take that hit, and sometimes I won't. I might say that instead of doing three eight-minute-long songs, we'll do three four-minute-long ones. Songs that I know people really love but will still let us meet our time. So I'm sitting there fiddling. That's when you have to know time, but not just clock time. You have to have an internal sense, which includes improvised live song timings. And those obviously change from night to night. So you have to have a sense of your own rhythm, the band's rhythm, the crew's rhythm—is it a blue day? Is it a triple-espresso day? All of this affects tempos and could change the show by ten minutes, which is a huge amount in penalties. This timing is something you either develop or don't. It's not something that can be taught. Over the years, either you gain the skill because of a certain intuitive mixed sense of rhythm time and real clock time, or it just doesn't click. I can't really write music out and I can't count very well. But I have a sense of the time of each song, to the second, almost.

For acts that blow their schedules all the time, that can be a $5,000 penalty, at the least, night after night. Poorly made decisions can cause a tour to shut down. How many acts do you know that have had to cancel their tours recently? I'll tell you why. It's because record companies, who typically extend no-interest loans to artists to finance their tours, say, "We cannot shoulder this anymore. We just fired a thousand people this week." These days the touring artist isn't allowed to run up a ridiculous bill. And tours are costly, with trucks, buses, food, salaries, venues—you're talking lots of money. The record companies are hurting because of changes in the industry, and they can't afford even the loaned support they once offered. Now, I've never taken tour support. But the economy's downturn has an impact on my organization, too. Times are tight, and this is affecting everybody: the labels, the artists, the crew, sound system suppliers, bus companies, truck companies, catering companies and all the employees—and the fans, of course, who would like to come to the show but can't afford the tickets.

Tori the businesswoman and Tori the performer are both included in the decision to cut a performance short. Because my performances are more than two hours long, I don't feel I'm shortchanging anyone if I play for ten fewer minutes. Sometimes you can't get sentimental. You have to make a decision very quickly. You're rewriting set lists, time is eating away. You know how long the show is. You already know you can't make it. Above all, you have to keep things running. I've always believed in the balance. Why can't we live like human beings on tour *and* pay our bills?

ANN: *Despite the daunting economics of touring, Amos makes choices that others might consider luxurious—and not only for herself. Creating a nurturing environment, she allows for everyone in the caravan to maintain health and inner harmony.*

JON EVANS:

Playing music is hard work, you know! There are so many things going on during a performance, and you have to be able to concentrate. Getting sleep helps. Tori never drinks before she goes onstage. Matt or I might have a beer or a glass of wine or something, but we never really indulge. Especially with all the travel—this tour is so much traveling, often on really bad roads. You can end up with serious sleep deprivation. Like you'd actually get shaky and your insides feel like they're just trembling; it's the worst feeling. But you have to keep up with this pace. You can't stop and say, you know, "You guys, I'm going to go to a spa for three days and regroup." You have to keep going. You can't get sick. You just have to take care. So you try to sleep when you can and eat as well as you can. Sometimes it's just not possible to keep the regimen going. You know when you feel run down, you just want something that tastes good? That plate of fries is not necessarily what you need. Later you feel even worse. So you go through these little cycles, and it's really hard. There's no easy answer on that.

ANDY SOLOMON:

A tour is a long race, and if it takes a personal chef and a nanny to help make your life better so that you're not so beat up, hire them if you can, because this will beat the hell out of you. Whatever it takes, really, to preserve Tori so that she can keep doing it, that's what we need to maintain. Look, if she cancels a long tour because she's burned out, or gets ill, then we're all out of maybe one year's work and salary. Most tours get a crew signed on months before they go out, so you can't just get another gig that easy. She's made some really smart choices in that. She knows it all hinges on if she can maintain. She knows what she wants to eat; she knows what she needs to keep going, and she puts systems in place that help perpetuate the whole thing.

People ask me if Tori's a diva. What is a diva, anyway? I don't know. Tori has always been very particular, which some people have a problem with, but I like it very much. At least I know what she wants—because *she* knows what she wants, right? And if there's anything to go wrong between the execution and the request, it's just a communication breakdown. So no, I never saw her in that way.

TORI:

Back when I was just a girl with my piano and a small crew, I would make the tours pay for themselves, but when you get a huge entourage, one more bus, one more truck, the costs multiply. Matt and Jon count for more than two people—they have techs who look out for them, and with their gear we need another bus, and now we have a nanny . . . It's big, you know.

I guess there are some very successful artists who don't have their musicians staying in the same hotel as they do. I can't do that. That's not right, especially if you can afford it. Now what does "afford it" mean? Does it cost a lot of money? Are you kidding? Of course it does. Would I save thousands and thousands of dollars—six figures—if I had my band and crew stay in a Motel 6? Substantially. But it's worth it. We also have catering on the road, which a lot of people don't have. Most tours pick up local catering. With your own catering crew, you don't have the same old fried chicken and Sloppy Joes every day. You try to have salads and soups, healthy food. A vegetarian option, a fish choice, some meat, whatever. I'm trying to treat people as I would want to be treated.

Mark tells me what the crew goes through when you pick up catering locally; it can be bad for their health. I'm hearing that local caterers are raising their standards in order to compete, which is good news. But I saw some of the women who work with me getting sick on *Strange Little Girls* because I didn't have catering; some of the financial guys advised against it. I regretted it, because everyone walked away really not well.

MARK HAWLEY:

After touring for a decade, I've come to really value catering as a big part of the team's social day. The kitchen staff knows each person, and we have all formed a relationship with them. They've got your tea the way you like it and you go in there and have a moment and establish a home away from home. It's the kitchen. Always the most beloved room in the house.

ANN: *The kitchen is particularly important for Amos herself, whose fairly delicate constitution sometimes balks at the demands of ongoing live performance. A touring musician is very much like an athlete, asking more from her body than an ordinary person would deem reasonable, needing to keep her system well tuned as she repeatedly pushes it to the maximum. Yet for most artists, diet is a minor factor, haphazardly approached. Hotel restaurants and truck-stop diners offer what fits into a busy schedule. Amos lived this way for years, until a lucky encounter with the chef Duncan Pickford led her toward a path that now sustains her.*

Pickford's approach to road food balances healthfulness with culinary delight. Fresh vegetables, fish, and lean meat form the center of his flavorful palette.

Pickford knows where the organic groceries are located in every major American city, and he has created a portable kitchen that allows him to prepare unprocessed ingredients in whatever crazy corner a venue offers—an extra dressing room, a closet, even the hallway. An interest in medicinal herbs allows him to add another layer of nourishment to Amos's daily routine, as he prepares teas, tinctures, and tonics to soothe whatever ailment might afflict her, her bandmates, or crew members as they endure constant changes in climate and atmosphere. His special "Duncanade" keeps Amos's throat in shape for the daunting calisthenics of each show. He also prepares a customized essential-oil blend for Amos and her bandmates to wear during each performance, reflecting the elements of the region, the time of year, the weather, and whatever circumstances the set list addresses. Amos considers Pickford a lifeline on tour and off, and their intimacy is reflected in the fact that after he cooks for her, he often shares in the meal and her before-show confidences.

TORI:

Before I met Duncan, I wasn't a junk food junkie. I thought I was eating healthily, but I wasn't feeling great. That's because I hadn't found what was right for me. I tried all sorts of things—vegetarianism, health food, the macrobiotic diet. You hear from other people what's working for them. I couldn't quite figure out how to get the energy I needed to perform night after night. Often during a tour, we roll on three shows on, one day off—that's six shows a week, month after month after month. I'll also have a full promotional schedule, with press and radio appearances usually scheduled from the early, early morning. Radio shows are all about "drive time"—seven until ten in the morning. On my early tours, I didn't understand that certain things for me just don't work. I've learned the hard way that to maintain energy, I need to separate my carbohydrate consumption from my proteins. I don't eat rice or potatoes or bread when I'm having protein, because it doesn't make me feel good. I have to live in this disciplined way to meet my scheduling demands.

Duncan makes the discipline delicious. He is ethnically Welsh, though he was raised in England. He's very much a modern Druid type of guy, and there's all of that pagan beauty in his creations. His heritage really brings him back to the properties of food and herbs. And he's been doing so much research on what, say, cardamom does, on the power of different herbs and how different combinations work off each other that build the immune system. The throat is an instrument. A guitarist or a drummer can get a cold and still play; I get a cold and sound like a wet mitten trying to sing you a love song. Charming.

CHELSEA LAIRD:

Tori is really drawn to Duncan, not just for his culinary skills but also for the healing aspect of his craft. By preparing tonics, aromatherapy potions, and drinks, as well as meals, he provides care of the throat, the stomach, whatever it may be. He's definitely a healer. If she's not feeling right in a certain area of her body, she'll tell him and he will go after it. Of course, having a chef on the road is a good perk, but it's not just a luxury. It's part of a regime. On the same principle, she'll do abdominal exercises in the dressing room before a show just because it makes her feel so much better, and we try to do some stretching. It all helps relieve a physically challenging situation.

Being a mom on the road is really difficult. Tori hardly ever gets any sleep, and there's really barely any real downtime for her to retreat inside her own brain and just be there for a little while. If it's that five minutes she's got to go into the corner of her dressing room, even if there are three other people in it, she does that and she carves that space out for herself. She's really good at that now, because I think for years and years and years that's all she's had, and you have to do it. She really listens to herself. She really listens to her body.

DUNCAN PICKFORD:

When I'm cooking for Tori, the overriding concern is nutrition. It's my job to make sure that she's eating regularly—I prepare a breakfast smoothie for her every day, plus a preperformance supper and dinner afterward on the bus—and that she's getting a balanced diet. If she doesn't eat, Tori gets low blood sugar and then she gets very, very tired and finds it difficult to concentrate on what she's doing. And she reacts badly to certain foods, which could affect her performance, so we separate carbohydrates and proteins and maintain a certain regimen.

At the same time, the food has to taste really good. On tour, it's extremely important to enjoy how you get through your day. If you're not able to eat the things that you like to eat, then there's stress over that as well as whatever else is getting thrown at you. After five years of our working together, I can sense what Tori needs to eat on a certain day. If she's a little down, I know what she really likes. She has her comfort foods, though they're not the usual mashed potatoes and fried chicken; more like caramelized baked tilapia with chili, ginger, and lime wrapped in a banana leaf.

Sometimes you look at her and she's so tired. You just think, *God, this woman just needs to lie down for twelve hours.* Yet you know that afternoon she's going to go do three radio station interviews. And she's not screaming at people, she's not jumping up and down, foaming at the mouth. She just says, you know, it's my career; I'm just taking care of business.

ANN: *Dinner with Duncan is a key aspect of the intimate sphere Amos carves out wherever she travels, a necessary counterpoint to the public exposure of her per-*

formance. Because she protects herself physically and emotionally through healthy habits and the support of her team, Amos can be unusually open to her fans, who have come to expect an unusually high level of contact on tour. Amos herself typically declines to discuss her fans, but even after years of touring with her, her fellow travelers still marvel at her generosity.

TORI:

The relationship with the fans is the area where the least bullshit goes on. There's an agreement. They want this person that will be someone they have a relationship with. I can do that. I know what they need from her. I've got no problem with it.

The key question is, Can you listen? You really learn from people's stories and can see, *Wow, these are the people relating to these songs.* So whatever the record companies are telling me these people want to hear, I have to wonder, what is it based on? Some nefarious demographic exercise that suits and bean counters calculate by monitoring what products people buy at Walgreen's? Not relevant to my crowd.

ALISON EVANS:

Tori knows many of her fans that are at the stage door for the meet and greets by name, and she knows their stories. She'll actually say, "Hi, John, how's your sister?" because she knows his sister is suffering with depression, for example. She's very connected to the ones who keep coming back.

CHELSEA LAIRD:

There is a posse of fans who travel to every show, and she does know them. I've gone so far as to send books to fans whom she's hoping she can reach with something they can relate to. She goes out of her way to make sure these people feel as though there's somebody that cares, that someone is indeed listening. They feel that connection from her so they continue to come back. I think it's just been years and years and years of taking that all in, and maybe, in a way, being one of those people herself—in need of connecting, as we all can be. Just really sympathizing. That's how the whole meet-and-greet tradition came about. It's that one time of the day when the fans all know that they can come and see her, have a chat—she tries her hardest to reach all of them.

To be honest with you, I think sometimes it becomes hard for her to draw lines with the fans. I see her listening intently, knowing she alone cannot reach everyone standing in line, and wanting to desperately. It is hard; it's a fine line. The stage crew is ready for sound check and Tash is ready to spend time with her mom. That's where her great relationship with Joel comes into play. There's a lot of trust there. He's been with her for a really long time, and he's amazing with the fans. He's completely that iron fist and they all know it. Whatever he needs to do to set the boundary, he will do. When Tori has to run, she has to run. But they all take it as complete loving kindness, because they just know how he is and they know he's acting in Tori's best interest. He's got a fan club, just as much as she does. There are people out there giving Tori gifts and they slip him the Starbucks card that they bought him. He is that line between her and the fans, and they love him for that, they really respect him. They'll send thank-you notes to him, thanking him for protecting Tori.

JOEL HOPKINS:

She's always wanted to go the extra mile rather than just coming, playing, waving, and leaving. She wants to have that little extra connection. I've always tried to make that work for her, to make it happen so that she can do that but not feel threatened in any way. I've told her on many occasions that she's my hero, because she never lets her fans down. No matter what else is going on, she makes sure that she can make them satisfied so that when they leave they're feeling good.

In the infancy stage of the meet and greets, a small group would be outside the venues afterward. It grew into where we'd always just come out—I'd always come out first, some kids would have flowers or one would have a note, and then a note would turn into a letter from somebody else, and then on and on and on. In the beginning we'd usually have maybe ten or twenty fans waiting around before I would get her and Johnny to the car. I would always go out and talk to them and let them know what we were going to do, same thing as I do now so that there's never any disappointment with them, so none can say, "We've been out here all day and no one told us and that's not right." They can never say that, because we always have that communication. There's a lot of respect on both ends, and I try to keep a close watch on the vulnerable ones.

A lot of times I don't share their troubles with Tori. Sometimes I do, if I think it's something that's really important that she needs to deal with. If someone could hear something from her that might bring them out of what they're in, and it's something really immediate, then you know we'll talk about it. But you just have to be really careful about how much of that that Tori gets now, because it did get to a point where it was a little overwhelming. It's just too heavy.

Originally, Tori would want to read all of the letters the fans brought, and she just couldn't deal with it and still function on the level that she wants to be on as a performer. You can't save everybody. I often had to tell the kids, "It's great that you guys have this connection with Tori and that it's enlightening for you and it gives you inspiration, but remember that she's also an entertainer. People also come to see her perform." Sometimes some of the kids can forget that—especially if they're fleeing and escaping an abusive life experience.

The feeling with every kid out there is that it's one on one. And they're all tuned in. Every single one of them. The respect for her while she's on-stage, you don't see that with the majority of artists.

DUNCAN PICKFORD:

I remember once we were in L.A. for a few days during a tour, taking a few days off for Thanksgiving. We'd gone to the Newsroom Cafe for lunch and were in the kiddie's bookstore just across the plaza. Tori and Natashya can spend ages in there, just peeking at books and pictures and stuff. I happened to just glance out of the window, and there's this big cadre of obvious fans gathering. I'd been talking to one earlier on and actually walked away saying, "No cell phones!" So when I saw him in this crowd, I walked straight up and said, "Did you call these people?" And he put on this, like, really shamefaced look and wouldn't look me in the eye.

Joel wasn't there; it was his day off. I had to handle things. So I walked over to Tori, and said, "Look, look, there's a whole bunch of fans out there and I don't think they're going to just leave." She said, "Okay, I'll sign two things, no photographs." I said okay. I was just quaking, because this wasn't my thing, dealing with her admirers. I was like, "Listen, guys, she's coming out in a minute, she has her daughter with her, none of us really appreciate you being here, but she's consented to sign two autographs. No photographs. Don't take offense, okay?" So she came out—and she was there for twenty minutes, signing everything anyone wanted, and the cameras are going, *click click click.*

JOEL HOPKINS:

Away from the venue, she's very personal about her time. She's never gone out on the town. Her night on the town is to go to a nice restaurant with Mark or with Johnny and Chelsea, to be able to just talk about stuff, about the show, talk about whatever they want but have that distinction between show life and private life. She's never been one to seek the limelight or the gossip columns. Not a chance. That's nonexistent. If it ever did happen it was something that she didn't have anything to do with.

She's an extremely hard worker, and she doesn't sleep much. Even back in the day she was an early riser. We'd walk around the town we were in, do stuff, see what's out there.

ANN: *Sensitivity to her environment feeds the improvisations Amos explores in performance, as she translates the mood of her locale into music. Yet just as she's learned to protect herself from bad food, negative crew members, and overly demanding fans, she has become an expert in creating an oasis in barren locales.*

CONVERSATION BETWEEN TORI AND ANN:

Sometimes the narrative is so strong in a place that it takes you with it, it takes you by the hand and you step into this magical place. Sometimes you're in a place where you have to pull on reserves because everything is off, from the coffee, to the venue itself, to the smell, to the unkindness of the staff. Sometimes I know why the kids have come to the show, because there's not a lot in that town that is encouraging and they're starving. When you walk into a starving town and you haven't been fed, either, that's when your discipline comes in, that's when you have to be strong and focused.

There are ways you can protect yourself in a place that's not feeding you. My dressing room space has always been something I've been aware of as sacred. It's not only where I prepare for the show; it's where I create the night's set list, which is a composition unto itself. We'll often get into a venue and there's nothing on the walls but dingy, chipping paint—this isn't a place where you want to be licking or even touching the walls. It's just a crash pad, and the night before it might have been the crash pad for a metal band—love you guys, but they will have left the place stinking of vomit and stale semen and pussy oil, still pungent on the couch and floor from the human sardines who had a fuckfest. Yum. The first thing that comes to mind, thinking back on such venues, is my least favorite smell in the world: patchouli incense. But even that would be an improvement over what you get sometimes.

We have to transform the dressing room to begin that transition to the stage. Chelsea and I will talk about colors and scents appropriate to the time of year and the region, and what we think the show might be like that night. It's different every time; you go for different themes. In January, when it's cold, we might go for crimson and lemon chiffon. In the spring, we like sea green and Alice blue, everything very fresh. You can't always do much about the venue itself, the space where you're actually playing, but you can at least create a haven that might help you get through a hard night.

The dressing room is usually where I say good night to Tash on the nights that I perform. Usually that's a great thing, and I can bring a sweet memory of her with me onstage. But, like everything else on tour, it can backfire. I remember one night, in Austin, Texas, there had been some technical problems at sound check and we were rushing to make the show start on time. Tash could clearly sense that we were in a hurry. You know the difference between when a child is kind of just having a tantrum and when a child has lost it? She lost it. She was clinging to me and tears were rolling down her face and she was saying, "I'm not leaving Mummy." Mark tried to take her away; he said, "Yes, you are, Tash," and she just started to howl and scream. This went beyond the usual—her being taken away from me at that moment wasn't the start of a tantrum. This was like, *Everybody keeps taking me away from Mummy, and I've had enough.*

So I took a minute. I just said, "Mark, why don't you go get a cup of tea?" and he really gave me the evil eye. But there had to be a shift. She needed to see that he was leaving and she could stay with Mommy. Then things changed. Mark went out, and the girls came in. By the time Mark walked back in with tea, he got the big "I love you, Daddy," and by then she and her nanny, as usual, started laughing, playing dress-up, and it was back to normal. But this little upset put us thirty minutes off the show's start time.

Everything takes time, and two or three glitches can set you back. But Tash is the main thing to me and to Mark. Time stops with her. So I made the decision within myself that night in the dressing room. I looked at Chelsea and I just said, "We might be taking a penalty tonight."

ANN: *Of all the adjustments Amos makes in order to thrive on the road, nothing has been more complex than the decision to bring her daughter along and remain highly involved in her daily life. Amos and Hawley are working parents who incorporate parenting into their hectic professional lives. The caregiver on the road provides relief in those inevitable moments when both Mom and Dad are busy, but unlike many touring artists who enjoy their families strictly when it's convenient, Amos and Hawley care for Natashya in tandem with the caregiver on a daily basis. In fact, Tash's well-being affects the very shape of the tour—a development that has required attitude adjustments from some longtime crew members, but which ultimately provides a model for a truly feminist and family-friendly rock-and-roll lifestyle.*

TORI:

When I was first on tour, all of those millions of months ago, I didn't know how to exert my authority. I wanted to get on with everybody, which is not always probable, much less possible. When I became a mother, I realized that my getting on with everybody means Tash doesn't get what she needs at all. Now, we arrange certain things to protect her. It doesn't mean that we're bringing up a spoiled brat, but it does mean that certain things can't be compromised. For example, we do day drives on some legs; we don't always do drives through the night because it's too hard on her. We stay in good hotels, and base out of cities that I know are the most comfortable, with fun stuff for kids that has been researched: where there's a park, where she can be around other little kids. Many people on the tour benefit from these choices. But I don't make these decisions to ensure that everybody else is okay. They're based on mother logic. The adults on tour will be okay anyway.

When people are having a bad day you can try to do everything you can, but after many bad days, it becomes a problem. Again, we're not in a van, where you don't get a shower and you don't get good food. Yes, you try to deal with the internal conflicts, you try to be the mothering force, but at a certain point . . . there's one toddler on this tour. And when she's handling things better than the adults, then it's time to make them aware.

CHELSEA LAIRD:

There's a difference between taking your kid on the road and *really* taking your kid on the road and trying to be with them. With Tori, on days off, the nanny is not on duty, ever. It's completely Tori and Mark, and they make a special effort to try to carve out spaces in the day. It's definitely the priority above anything else. If Tash is sick or if she just fell down before we go onstage, the show's going to be pushed back, no question.

MATT CHAMBERLAIN:

It's really different with the baby being out. We're really separate from Tori. I hardly had a conversation with her on the *Scarlet's Walk* tour. The playing is the playing, and there is going to be that connection, but as far as hang time goes, it doesn't exist. She doesn't have any time. We used to be all in the same bus, drinking wine, having fun. It's sad—I miss hanging out with her, but I respect that she's trying to make it work with the kid. Every once in a while I'll talk to her and say, "I understand what's going on—don't feel guilty, please don't. You've got such a great kid and everything's great, and we'll hang eventually, in Cornwall."

CONVERSATION BETWEEN TORI AND ANN:

Mark and I had dinner alone together twice in six months during the 2003 tour. That's because we didn't want our daughter to be heartbroken. She doesn't have a child friend on tour. It's all adults. So we made a choice, but at the same time it can test us. There's not a lot of time to be alone together.

On rare occasions, if there was no show scheduled and I had a different kind of work, like a radio interview, that would put me with Mark and Marcel somewhere and Tash out playing with the nanny, then Mark and I could grab some dinner before we came back to the hotel and put her to bed. This is the only way it could work, as opposed to, let's say, being with her all day and going out at six o'clock—she cannot handle that. She would cry, "Why can't I come, why are you leaving me?" This was a tender age, it's not about reasoning. She only had just turned two when the *Scarlet's Walk* tour began.

Tash gets certain things from being on the road. I mean, she's with her mom and dad every day, more than some kids in some ways. She's surrounded by people who love her. There are advantages to having Chelsea Laird, who was a nationally ranked gymnast, teaching you forward rolls and backward rolls—Tash is learning how to do it right. She doesn't get somebody going, "Oh, don't tumble around so much." Instead,

Chelsea's there to say, "Let me show you how to do it without hurting yourself." It's great to have Matt sit there and play drums with her, and dress-up. One of the great drummers in the world—wearing a feather boa. Tash doesn't care that he's one of the great drummers in the world, but because he is, it affects her. She walks around with drumsticks. She also has a very broad sense of the world. She knows San Francisco's different from New York City, even though they both have a Chinatown— believe me, she can recognize the difference. She knows we're part American and Native American (she always goes for the cute Cherokee look over the Dallas Cowboy cheerleader look) and part British. She is a citizen of the earth.

Now, the downside. She's not around children. There's no playgroup on the road. Her social world is Roz, her nanny on the road; Jen Daranyi, who does my hair and makeup; Auntie A (Alison Evans); and whoever's got a minute on the bus. Or Mommy and Daddy in the pool on a day off. She needs to have her little posse in her life—that's really, really important. When she does, back at home, she doesn't mind so much if Mom's on the phone. On the summer leg of the *Scarlet's Walk* tour, which we called "Lottapianos," having Ben Folds as part of our musical family was great, because every day Tash and his kids, Gracie and Louie, caused wondrous, stupendous, ludicrous mayhem, thereby taking over backstage. That was really good for everybody, especially all the super–ice cool tattooed people.

CHELSEA LAIRD:

Tash is so animated and such an entertainer. I think everybody loves having her around. With her in the mix, there's been a shift in understanding among everybody on tour; we all know there's more at play in the day now. Before, we were dealing with calls from management, calls from the label, or any number of things that might either cause Tori to be late or something to go wrong or the day to backfire or her mood to just all of a sudden take a dive. But now it's this other factor, and it's much bigger than any of those things put together. Most people on her crew have been with Tori forever, because of the relationship that she builds with people, and now, because of Tash, reality on tour is totally different for many of them. Totally different from the way it was.

ANDY SOLOMON:

There are certain rules and regulations that go along with the baby being on board, but for me she's a joy. I mean, the day can be crap and I've just had the most difficult time, but she just comes in and makes us all smile, just being a kid.

Here's how I put it: Tash is antigig. That's a good thing. She flips the script. We get to see it through her eyes and remember a bit more why we're here and what it really is. It's about the stuff that she sees that none of us can see. Little imaginary things. Tash reminds you that this tour and the music really bring the world magic, what Tori's doing you can't touch. It touches you. But you can't grab it. Most days our jobs are nuts and bolts, nuts and bolts, nuts and bolts, nuts and bolts, but we're all really here for the magic, and Tash reminds me of that.

ANN: *The interplay of magic and minutiae defines a successful touring life. Amos has labored long to get the particulars straight, and the road has rewarded her investment, financially, spiritually, and artistically. The many arts Amos must cultivate to keep her caravan alive—boundary drawing, family building, self-sustenance—can prove exhausting. But she never forgets that all her work serves one purpose: her ability to keep making that impossibly long, dazzlingly short walk out of normal life and onto the stage.*

CONVERSATION BETWEEN TORI AND ANN:

There are people who work within the organization who are backstage all the time and are never part of the show. Mark brought this to my attention—I was complaining one day, and he said, "Well, do you realize so-and-so is tired because he never gets those thousands of people cheering at him?" I'll be looking at Matt and Jon after they have played, and they're energized, as if they're on the rocket trip of totality. And I'll see other people who look as if they've been drained. The relationship that happens between us onstage is this love affair, this journey that not everybody is a part of. Those others may be in some little cubbyhole dungeon in the venue, dealing with how and why the wheels turn, which is vital to the matter.

John Witherspoon and I have really been able to kind of understand this one. One night it became so clear to both of us because we both had the same case of the flu. I went onstage feeling just like he did. A few hours later when I came back offstage he saw me, I saw him, and we got it. I was on fire and had sweated out the ghoulies completely, and he was sneezing and shivering, doubled over. I was moving through it, because music does have the power to move things. And I was able to break through.

TORI:

There is a tradition of traveling troubadours, bards and their companions, that goes back to the beginning of music and storytelling. A small group of people would make its way from encampment to encampment, through wars, through peacetimes, to sing of the news that they knew. Sometimes certain dictums prevented certain subjects from being discussed. That's why a particular set of symbols runs through art during some historical periods. Some people knew what these symbols represented, but because of the threat of being killed, iconography had to be used. This was its own language—pre-gangsta. It was part of a bard's art form, and still is.

I find that today, like the old troubadours, we pick up information on the road. If we're playing Seattle on a Friday night, what we bring to Portland the next night will contain the information we collected in Seattle. By the time we reach San Francisco, we will have added more to our palette. Even though compositionally the palette is ever changing and is at the center of my process, it's not the same as the revolving palette I use when I'm writing new works. What I do use is what I term the Road Labyrinth Palette. It's a thread that remains unbroken from show to show. The performances can connect, so that once you get to Dallas, you can pull from the London show with the snap of a finger. All the set lists are cataloged in a computer, along with the themes for each show—weird, sexual, religious-repressed shows, or hostile, political, in-reaction-to-world-events shows. From the information I've categorized, including every word of every song I've written, I can build a narrative that interconnects within the subtext. This is just an example of how threads are used to weave one night's live performance tapestry. This is what harkens back to going from campfire to campfire across Ulster—what you hear in one village you take with you to the next.

Some things are consistent in this world. The main ones for me are that a mother's love is a mother's love, romance is romance, and that a musician—be it 2005 B.C. or A.D. 2005—must play, and that a road dog is a road dog is a road dog. Hopefully you will have felt this if you've toured with my crew.

SONG CANVAS: "Martha's foolish ginger"

I started writing this one years ago, when I was close to the water, on tour somewhere. I had only a seed idea of it, but it has stayed with me for a while now. On the "Lottapianos" tour during the summer of 2003, when we were in San Francisco, I was by the Bay again. The song began to come back to me. Once I began to understand the female character I needed to embody, I was able to finish this piece, but a real turning point was when I was able to see the character's boat, which she called *Martha's Foolish Ginger*, sailing out of the Bay and into the Pacific Ocean.

chapter seven
venus: creating a public self

ANN: *Venus: the brightest planet in the universe. Venus, the goddess whom the ancient Romans first imagined as a simple, primal force governing fertility, transformed by Rome's encounter with the Greeks (who called her Aphrodite) into one of the most complex characters in the world pantheon. That Venus, the one the world remembers, is exacting and generous, innocent and manipulative, the patron of marriage who tore the world apart by leading the hero Paris and the beauty queen Helen into lethal adultery. The embodiment of physical attraction in all its chaotic power, Venus is unavoidable. She governs what the art critic Dave Hickey once called "the iconography of desire": what strikes the soul as beautiful, no matter whether it's morally proper or politically correct.*

Because she exists beyond the realm of rules, Venus can take whatever shape suits the moment in which she enters. Her name has been given to female figures as wildly different as the squat, heavy prehistoric Venus of Willendorf; the gorgeous, armless Greek ideal known as Venus de Milo; *the Renaissance wraith Sandro Botticelli painted in his* Birth of Venus; *the "Venus Hottentot," an African woman exhibited as a freak to a racist British public in the early 1800s; the Venus flytrap, the sexy southern plant that snaps up its prey in its "jaws"; Blonde Venus, the Hollywood version embodied by Marlene Dietrich and Marilyn Monroe; and even Sailor Venus, a Japanese anime character who flutters the hearts of today's teenage boys. Far from pure, Venus leads us into the thicket of social prejudices, historic assumptions, and personal fascinations where desire grows, seemingly beyond governance.*

In a world where few can agree on the power of the gods, popular culture is where the desire Venus personifies finds a home. Images saturate our consciousness, ceaselessly emanating from movie, television, and computer screens, billboards, and magazines. Beauty, always an asset for artists, is now an unavoidable subject. The challenging task is to take control of one's own beauty, to decide what it can be, rather than just giving in to the whims of the fashion industry and other marketing forces.

Tori Amos has fought to claim her own sense of beauty over the course of her career. A musician first, and always a feminist, she has sought ways to capture desire without becoming its object. What she wears, how she poses for a photograph, the light she emits when she smiles: these gestures are not insignificant. She has come to learn the importance of taking care with even the small details of a public image, as she's spent two decades coming to terms with Venus's whimsical command.

PART I

[TORI:

First I'd like to say that I believe that every person creates a public image, which I address in the second part of this chapter. Because Ann had a very clear vision about wanting to talk about a performer's public self, I wanted to give her "the floor"; I guess, more accurately, I wanted to give her "the pages" to express her view of a performer's public self. Since she has had to interview the likes of hundreds of my kind and kindred, musician/performers, I felt she has a valid perspective on a performer's public self. After all, she has certainly seen more than I have. The first half of this chapter resulted from the ongoing conversation between us; the second half is my considered response to what we discussed.]

CONVERSATION BETWEEN TORI AND ANN:

Every performer has to create a public image, and if you're a woman, you can't pretend it's a matter of small importance to your career. Try slouching around in your gym clothes and the record label will be after you, the press will consider it either a statement or a mistake, even your fans will think you've lost your touch. I had a few choices when I started to find my way as Tori Amos. I could have done what many artists do now, taking whatever was offered from the fashion industry representatives who put those gowns on the award show runways, and in music videos, and on album covers. Or I could take charge of my image as another aspect of my art. For me, the choice was easy. But the implementation of this has naturally been a challenge.

If you're going to put out art that's sonically fresh, why wouldn't you be open to art that's visually fresh? I do consider the designers who make the clothes I wear to be artists. Still, it takes a lot of time and effort. And money. But everybody shops, whether you're a performer or a student or a secretary. It's just a matter of putting the time aside, the money, and surrounding yourself with visual artists whose sense of style fits you like a good pair of stretch jeans. I work with a team for whom fashion is a full-time thing. My advisers on matters of style—Mark dubbed them "the Glam Squad" a few years ago—know things I could never know. I live the musical life, I'm a musician mom, this is all I do. I write songs every day. Nobody will hear most of them. Nobody will see 90 percent of the things my crew suggests I wear. But it's a flow we create.

We take pictures of every performance and appearance so I'll know where we were that day and how much exposure any given piece has had. I'm only taking so many wardrobe cases with me whenever I travel, so I have to make choices. I let only my own stylist buy things, because she knows what we've done. When she's on another continent she liaises with Chelsea, and after all these years that works well, too.

One thing is a necessity—good shoes. Designers and stylists lend clothes all the time, but I don't like to borrow shoes. Because I'm playing, and I'll wreck them. So I have to buy them, and they are not cheap. I need many different kinds of shoes—a certain kind for playing live, a different kind for television appearances (they can't be too low), and then some for just kicking around. If I've worn a pair on a nationally broadcast show, I can't wear them again for a similar show. It's a big part of playing, the right shoes. I reassure my hands of that all the time.

Sometimes the musician side of me rebels against the fashion side of the pop music world and I just want to wear jeans and sweatshirts, the way I did before I made records, the way many male musicians still do most of the time. When I get into that space, I start buying lots and lots of visual art books. I need an entry point back into the visual side of my work. There was a period, in the late 1990s, when I became really tired of the fashionista phenomenon. Designers, brand makers, and models had been taking over the house like cockroaches. You know when you see a house and it's covered in a kind of tent because it's being fumigated? Around that time, I needed to be fashiongated. I did go back to jeans and a T-shirt—though they were always the right jeans and T-shirt, the ones that made a statement, however quiet. It's very hard to figure out the balance.

If you don't keep pulling in from the visual artists who are making pieces you can wear, then what happens is you stop relating to people in some way. Obviously, for a composer the content has to be at the center, but I don't think you can let either slide. After you've been in it for a while your image can become humdrum. Yet many female musicians develop the opposite tendency, even those who are legitimate composers or virtuosos. Too much energy has been put on the image and not enough on the content. Enough already . . .

The people who are performers first, like Madonna, have this sussed, and we can learn from them. They're thinking about the look and the video *before* the content, and their music often originates in direct connection with their image. Madonna's sound was made for the dance floor when she epitomized the New York club kid; it got a bit closer to rock when she started presenting herself that way, connected with R&B when her image became softer again, went New Age techno when she got into spirituality, and so on. Fashion has become a part of the musical exploration and experience. Missy Elliott has done a similar thing; so has Gwen Stefani. Their image is essential and extremely tight. If they get it wrong, critics castigate them for it—they are known for their style.

Sometimes artists get overconfident about their content, and that's their downfall. But musicians can make the opposite mistake. I'm including myself here, too, so let's be clear. They put on an image without thinking of how it relates to their music and forget that live performance is also visual. If they are uncomfortable with this side of things, sometimes they go out there trying to make a joke of it all. Sometimes you wish these guys would just try pushing a "Krusty the Clown" image, because at least that would be funny. You can't run away from visual expression. You can't hide behind the "I'm all about the content" line forever. You may get away with that for one record, if you're hot. But style will choose you if you don't choose it. And it takes even more energy to have a nonstyle, because you have to work very hard to be the paradox of what's in fashion. If you can pull this off—this "all about the content" look—then you could become known as an anti–fashion victim.

ANN: *Amos doesn't use the phrase "fashion victim" lightly—she has lived it. During her first stab at stardom, in the band Y Kant Tori Read, Amos convinced herself that she could take on the "rock chick" image popular in 1980s Los Angeles. Gallons of hair spray, a leather bustier, thigh-high boots, and porn-star makeup turned Amos into everybody else's archetype, but she was clearly suffering beneath the glamour. Trying to please the music-biz "experts" who seemed to control her fate at the time, the budding virtuoso and composer was nearly smothered within heavy-metal cliché.*

CONVERSATION BETWEEN TORI AND ANN:

If I had grown up wanting to do cock rock, if that were my aspiration, then maybe it would have been different. I would have been happy in fishnets. But you see, I was brought into music with Bartók. I was brought up in a tradition of musicians. I did not think I was a bimbo when I first heard Led Zeppelin at age five. I could see and hear how deep it could be. But clearly I got it very wrong in the 1980s. I think when you chase somebody else's notion of success, you're bound to fail.

I thought if I didn't succeed, the consequences would be deadly. How many girls have had a dream of who they really are and been rejected so many times that they can't believe it? If there are not people to catch you at that point, you're lost. I had my father, but he was driven. So was I. I thought, *I have to succeed at something here, no matter what it is.* You go after what you think the record companies want, and you change the music, you get the dicks hard, you find a way to do it. And you know what? You're sitting there puking in the back. My good friends will tell you—I was the angriest dog on the block back then. Didn't know why. Or wouldn't admit it.

What was most difficult was that some women had been able to keep their integrity while I was sacrificing mine in the name of getting cocks hard. When I was making *Y Kant Tori Read,* my executive producer was David Kirshenbaum and across town he was producing somebody called Tracy Chapman. He exposed me to her, and I couldn't understand—wait a minute. Wait a minute. How come I'm the cheap hooker and she's the poet? Then I looked at myself in the mirror and I said, "Well, you look like a cheap hooker."

It all culminated in an incident I've talked about a lot—my accidental epiphany. The record had been reviewed in *Billboard,* and I had been called a bimbo. [The exact quote was, in fact, "Unfortunately, provocative packaging sends the (inaccurate) message that this is just so much more bimbo music."] I was at Hugo's restaurant in Hollywood, and I overheard someone I knew slightly talking about me—"Oh, that's that girl over there with a review in *Billboard* magazine this week where they called her a bimbo." The humiliation of that. This was the very moment in my private life when I'd started to play piano again, and I'd met some women who were turning me on to all sorts of poetry about sexuality, stuff that captured how people could burn inside, and I was burning, too, I was burning alive. That night I realized that when it comes to sexual expression, unless there's a certain initiation, it's like a woman dancing in a strip club and saying she's liberated. Maybe she feels liberated, but she will also have to be clear that she is an object for most of the onlookers. Not the subject. Now can you hold the duality of being an object for many while being the subject for yourself? If you fool yourself and you are not able to hold the duality—which is extremely difficult to hold—then you will become just another object in their subjugation of women. What I'd been doing with my image was more akin to degrading sex . . . that's no way to honor the Sacred Prostitute.

ANN: *The failure of* Y Kant Tori Read*'s debut album, which sold only about seven thousand copies, revealed to Amos that success was inseparable from self-governance. Still, Amos would have to find the songs that became* Little Earthquakes, *leave Los Angeles, and meet the inimitable stylist Karen Binns before she could capture a public way of being that felt real.*

CONVERSATION BETWEEN TORI AND ANN:

I had to change, but at first I didn't know how. Obviously the music was the easier piece of the puzzle to change—I just reached out for my piano and she was there. My outer appearance, as I remember at the time, became very plain in a way. No makeup, no hair spray, no tight Lycra . . . I got rid of all of it within a few days after that *Billboard* article. I was doing demos with Eric Rosse for what would become *Little Earthquakes*. We're talking 1988, when I started writing all this music on the piano—"Silent All These Years," "Crucify," etc. *Little Earthquakes* didn't come out until 1992, so as you can see, I spent a few years just playing the piano and writing these songs.

Yes, this album was written from a deep catharsis, but also there was a reclaiming of the five-year-old little girl I had been at the piano and her view of music. I finally started to figure out that the "public image" issue would have to be addressed when I came to properly record *Little Earthquakes* in the studio with Davitt Sigerson. He was one of the album's producers; he's real music-industry sage material. He said to me, "People can feel it when an artist is wearing clothing that isn't hers, literally." It's like claiming a false lineage. He got me back to my lineage. That was his greatness. He reminded me. We would talk and he would ask, "How can somebody with your pedigree as a musician end up where you did?"

By this time I was in London, and I was already in my metamorphosis. Lee Ellen Newman, head of press at East West Records UK, became my first friend, my compadre, and partner in crime on the U.K. side of Atlantic Records. Because of our deep friendship, she was able to talk with me in a way that no one else could, thereby getting through. By the time Elyse Taylor was brought in as head of marketing at East West in 1991, Lee Ellen and I were confident enough in our friendship to open our circle to her, thereby making a triad. With Elyse we created an equilateral triangle: Lee Ellen presented to the world what Elyse and I spent months developing. This was the original creative think tank under the watchful eye of Max Hole. Lee Ellen and Elyse knew that we would need to pull in visually talented people who understood what I was pushing sonically.

First I would meet Cindy Palmano (a photographer brought in by Elyse), who changed how I saw imagery, and she, in turn, turned me on to Karen Binns, with whom I've worked ever since.

We didn't have a lot of money at that time. It was exciting, though, and you're seeing what's out there and trying to figure out what you're doing and who you are. We would pick stuff up from the open-air markets in London. Karen still does that every weekend. It's great, because what you find is one of a kind.

When I met Karen I couldn't understand a word she was saying. She's a professional now. In those early days she was not. She was doing weird art stuff; she'd been involved with the downtown art crowd around Michel Basquiat in New York. Cindy had suggested her, though, and I trusted Cindy. I don't know why, exactly, but I just said okay. And the great thing is, Karen and I developed the look together and then Karen had other clients and her look became influential for them. She'll say to me, "Girrl, you're my muse," and I'll just laugh. I'll laugh my head off, because everybody else is my muse when I write songs.

KAREN BINNS:

I was living in London, having moved there from Brooklyn, where I grew up. Cindy Palmano contacted me about this new singer. Don't ask me why Cindy called me—maybe because I wasn't at the top of my field at that time, so I would be available for someone new. Cindy said, "This is a girl you can grow with. I know you have something in you that can work with this girl." I have to give it to Cindy, for her to see that I would connect with Tori was a shock, because nobody else in the fashion field would have imagined us as a pair. I mean, just look at us. Tori's style at the time was different. She was obsessed with Patagonia, that outdoorsy clothing line out of California. I became obsessed with Patagonia too. To the point that

I had André Walker design her a glamorous fleece Patagonia-like gown for the 1994 Grammys, which was stunning. Could you believe it? André made fleece look sleek.

Coming to England did change Tori's style. The record company wanted to style her as this English rose type of girl. Tori told me she listened to Led Zeppelin. She wanted to look like Robert Plant. So she got to wear jeans, but with something more exciting, like a vintage swimsuit, on top. I think I started her off with vintage clothes and jeans—with a flare leg, of course. Which was a good place to start in 1992.

ANN: *The impact of* Little Earthquakes *not only allowed Amos to define her own style; it established her as a pop icon. Though the look she explored in partnership with Binns, beautifully recorded in Cindy Palmano's album photographs, was thoroughly modern and bohemian, many still called her a "fairy princess." The crystal-clear artwork for her second album,* Under the Pink, *reinforced her dreamlike image, though on a deeper level it reflected the introspection of her art.*

KAREN BINNS:

Under the Pink was a record Tori made, metaphorically, inside her room. I had to show the purity of what she was trying to do. The purity of her work, of her music, and where it comes from. White, of course, is the best color to convey that essence, and as you remember she had really natural makeup for *Under the Pink.* The designers she was wearing at the time were quite earthy and ethereal. Which was what was happening at the time.

CONVERSATION BETWEEN TORI AND ANN:

I remember Cindy, Karen, and I having long, long talks about how to represent emotional danger. Cindy came up with a glass world with a lone woman—Tori—having to navigate it with bare feet. Karen came up with the idea of white. I dug it because if the lone woman missteps, then there is nowhere to hide all that blood on such a pretty white dress. I found that expression more in the vein of Artemis, if you're looking for an archetype. Artemis—the lone huntress, who finds other women to help her achieve what must be achieved as she tries to protect those creatures that she cares for.

ANN: *Though she remained a musician first, by this time Amos fully recognized the value of approaching her public image as another aspect of her art. Her next album,* Boys for Pele, *leapt into fiery territory utterly removed from the relative calm of* Under the Pink, *and Amos and her partners in style devised a new visual approach to match its intensity. The photo session for that album's cover produced the most controversial image of her career: Amos, in southern belle dishabille, apparently suckling a piglet. In another shot, she brandished a rifle and a coolly defiant gaze. Amos has anything but regrets about this session, though many found it utterly distasteful.*

CONVERSATION BETWEEN TORI AND ANN:

I've said it before—that was a Christmas card for my dad. It came from a real place for me. It's not *What can I do to shock you?* It started with the fact that my dad was really getting on my case; he was asking how I could stray so far away from Christianity and my roots that I couldn't even do a Christmas song. I told him he could get me to do a Christmas card. And this was it. Maybe it was me saying, *I'm going to give all the good Christians something to think about.* People didn't get that image, because most aren't raised as intensely Christian as I was. Those who were might have understood that this was a Madonna and child, but one that brought in the non-kosher, the unacceptable, back to the fold.

I don't really think that everybody involved in the shoot necessarily got what we were trying to achieve. Obviously Cindy understood the necessity of a photograph that forced the question to Christians: Do you truly practice the Golden Rule, "Love Your Neighbor As Yourself"? "Judge not that you be not judged. For with what judgment you judge, you will be judged; and with the same measure you use, it will be measured back to you." "First cast out the plank in your own eye; and then you shall see clearly to cast out the stye that is in your brother's eye" . . . I'd been noticing a shift away from a liberal way of thinking, heading toward where we are now. It was the beginning, just on the periphery. I was experiencing the hypocrisy of people who would say they were liberal thinkers but were making comments about "bitches" and "fucking faggots." The backlash from an openminded culture to a mob mentality—with no regard for another human's basic rights—was hard to take.

I took a lot of heat for that photo, I guess, but I didn't care. I was laughing my head off. I knew the power of that image and exactly how it would hit.

KAREN BINNS:

For *Boys for Pele,* Tori was a witch doctor. Cindy did all those great photographs. New Orleans is where it went down. I mean, with the pig and the drama of that shoot. We talked about it. Tori said, "What do you think works style-wise for this music?" I said, "Let's take it back to the range." But it wasn't a Western thing; it was more of a *Gone With the Wind* thing. You know how those Southern belles had to hold on to their homes after the disaster was over? We all go through a Civil War in some way. So we just took it to the Civil War theme and made it trendy. We noticed afterward that the trend stayed at least for a few years. The Edwardian thing. Going back, getting the heirlooms that your grandmother actually wore, bringing them into modern society, making them hip, which is quite Gothic. You can always move in and out of the Gothic scene, because at least you're understood by the kids. Once you start going the other way, if you start wearing pretty dresses and trying to be like the nice wife thing, then you lose the kids. Gothic is strangely flexible. It's quite a classic rock look.

ANN: *The period that produced* from the choirgirl hotel *and* To Venus and Back—*the double album Amos actually named for the goddess with whom she'd delicately dance for so many years—was not an easy one. Confronting her own mortality, fearing that she would never be able to bear a child, Amos had to renegotiate her relationship with her own body. A time of tremendous personal growth, her midthirties demanded much rethinking from Amos regarding the face she offered the world.*

CONVERSATION BETWEEN TORI AND ANN:

I had done all kinds of photographs with Cindy from the box on the cover of *Little Earthquakes* to the gun and the pig on *Pele*. She'd been an important part of the team for a long time. At this juncture, she was delving into different artistic projects, some that had nothing to do with photography, which I had to respect. And when we approached *Choirgirl*, I had just come to a place where I was stripped, brought to my knees about my image. I was going through my miscarriages and the pregnancies and the gaining of the weight and the losing of the weight—I mean, it's not like I was obese, but I was in a pregnancy process. Once I had Natashya I was back on track again. Then, you lose your weight and you get healthy. But when you're in that middle zone trying to get pregnant, miscarrying, you're not on a low-carb diet. I mean, my real crisis in life came from thirty-two to thirty-six, until I was able to carry a full-term pregnancy.

During the *Sneak Preview* tour in early 1998, the first tour with the band, which seemed colossal and endless, I still felt that to show up in jeans and a T-shirt wasn't enough, but I did it. That was Mark's suggestion. He said, "You're part of a group of musicians just playing together right now, your persona is more stripped down, and to wear some kind of gown looks silly to me as a guy." It was very casual then, and it was about the music. And honestly, all I could really do was wear what I wear to get up in the morning and then be in it and change before the show, but basically change into the same thing. I don't even think I wore makeup. There's a time in every performer's arc where it's just about getting back to the music, and that was the case for me during that tour.

Karen was very understanding about it. I said, *This is what I'm doing right now,* and she said, *Whatever,* and she just waited until I came back around. She didn't beat me up for it, as my friend; instead, she'd bring in these beautiful flowers to the dressing room and I'd feel beautiful. Even though my body was tired. And then soon after that for the *Plugged* world tour she came up with the glamour aprons—these cutaway dresses I would wear over the jeans and T-shirts. I was crazy about them; they were a little like a body helmet. And they were funny—I'd always had a waitress fantasy, so a glamorized apron worked perfectly.

Before that tour, recording *Choirgirl*, I'd had to nurture myself. I was eating whole grains, lots of protein, because I'd lost so much blood. I'll be honest—I put on more weight than I'm comfortable with, and maybe that was ten pounds, but for me that's a lot. On the one hand, I did feel sexy because I was with Mark and very happy, but as far as putting an image out into the world, I didn't feel so good.

So my image then had to connect with how I felt as well as the music's content. I'd been talking to Elyse, as I always did before any visual artists could be chosen, about the girls in the songs: How could we use photography to capture girls who'd been lost, who weren't there? The daughters and mothers on that album are no longer in their bodies. Elyse brought in the artist Katerina Jebb, who creates photographs using a Xerox machine, very ghostly, ideal for the project. We were able to create a strong visual, avoid the problem of conventional glamour, and stay true to the text. Lesley Chilkes was a pillar of strength, as she had always been, having done my makeup more often than anyone in the world since 1991.

Cindy had brought me Lesley and then Karen, and as I'm writing this I have just completed a shoot with them and will work with them on the cover for *The Beekeeper*, with Kevin Mackintosh at the helm as photographer and Shona Heath as set designer. Having women developing seed ideas from the womb makes them the midwives in a way. This is the ninth project for which Lesley and Karen are the two women who consistently have been there with me—in the womb where the sonic world and the creative world have intercourse, in a way, to create what I term "the project child."

Through the years many women have been very influential in the changes and the choices that I, as Tori, have made regarding my public image, thereby influencing my private self. In 1999 Lesley brought in the hairdresser Cim Mahoney—the three now, Lesley, Karen, and Cim, are the latest configuration of "the Glam Squad." Before Cim came into the picture, the hairdresser Jimo Saleko had been part of our visual groove. Cim and Jimo offer a needed male perspective.

At the time of *Choirgirl*, there were two photo shoots. The Martina Hoogland-Avanov shoot involved the team of Karen, Jimo Saleko, and the late Kevyn Aucoin. The Katerina Jebb shoot, which included the cover shot, came from the teamwork of Lesley, Karen, and Jimo.

When we decided to make a live album from the tour for *Choirgirl*, I called the photographer Loren Haynes. He came to Pittsburgh, where we were live on the road. I felt the shots needed to be about us, the band, because we were doing a live record. Berta Camal (who, with Tony Lucha, made up the American version of the Glam Squad) came to Pittsburgh to do makeup, and in this instance hair as well, because Tony couldn't make the shoot. Loren, Berta, and I really did fly by the seat of our pants on this one. I didn't choose to have another shoot once we added the new music; I looked at the photographs from Pittsburgh and felt they were as close to the truth as could be captured, so I let it stand and it became the *Venus* double-CD package. Of course, I did press shoots with different photographers, naturally having Lesley, Karen, and Cim there with me, stirring the visual potion in the cauldron.

I love Loren's art. We've made powerful covers for magazines, particularly one for *Spin* not long after *Little Earthquakes*. He's good at capturing me at my most sexy, and I guess I was feeling sexy that day.

LOREN HAYNES:

I've been working with Tori for years; I shot her the very first time she was featured in *Spin*. Then the next time it was for a cover. Her popularity had just exploded. At that point, I felt that Tori had really given enough to that quirky princess fairy identity and image, but she was still being photographed that way. I've always thought and still do think Tori's incredibly beautiful and sexy in photographs. I said to Tori, "I want sixteen-year-old boys to drop to their knees when they see this photograph." And Tori got that. Kevyn Aucoin did the makeup, and we were shooting in the studio and I was playing the Latin jazz artist Gato Barbieri. She fell in love with one song, it's called "Ruby Ruby"—sexy saxophone. And boy, did she feel it! But she was already a professional at this point.

When I joined her late on the road, for the tour that became *Venus,* I saw her change gears. I directed the video for "Bliss," using live and behind-the-scenes footage. What was interesting was that, judging from the comments on my web site and various Tori fan sites, her fans felt that "Bliss" was her best video, because it was the most honest and self-exposing. I think it was very smart of her to lead me in that direction with the video. People were getting tired of the whole surreal, quirky Tori, and her image at that time gave her fans a sense of her as grounded.

ANN: *After the earthiness of the* Venus *period (ironic, in a way, because of Amos's invocation of that heady goddess) and the birth of her tiny muse Natashya Lórien, a rejuvenated Amos was prepared to take on the most ambitious image-oriented work of her life: the covers project,* Strange Little Girls. *For each song she recorded on this album of songs written and previously recorded by men, Amos conjured an anima, a female voice to recast the song's meaning. Working with her creative partner in crime, the novelist Neil Gaiman, Amos invented biographies for these "girls." Then she brought them to Binns and the late, legendary makeup wizard Kevyn Aucoin, who worked with her to make each girl flesh. The fashion photographer Thomas Schenk immortalized Amos's anima on film.*

CONVERSATION BETWEEN TORI AND ANN:

You cannot come up with this portfolio until you know the story of each girl in each song. So it was character building in a lot of cases. I had my think tank, and I talked extensively with each member of the team about each character before we staged the shots. Neil Gaiman wrote stories for each of the girls; they're great. They were published in the *Strange Little Girls* tourbook. Neil, Mark, and I really felt, as I was nursing my little girl child in my arms right before Christmas in the year 2000, that a generalized image of the antiwoman, antigay heterosexual man had hijacked Western male heterosexuality and brought it to the mediocrity of the moment. At its core, this perverted male image was filled with malice and getting high off swallowing its own violent ejaculation.

I did huge research on these songs. I didn't just sit down and record them. I knew the characters. Before I sang them I walked into who these people were. No different from if you're talking about theater. We take it to Emma Thompson doing *King Lear,* playing the Fool. It's the same thing, but sonic. Instead of becoming an actor, you become a "singtor," because those songs represent roles, not pieces of me. The female characters in my songs do become a part of me, when all is said and done, but I approached songwriting differently after working with the men's song children. Not only were the songs changed on this "covers album," but I was changed by having these songs hold my hand.

I was able to channel and work through the anima of these songs, so it became important that I bring in somebody that could transform my physical image to emulate them: the makeup artist Kevyn Aucoin. He could determine how each woman would express herself with makeup, and then physically I would move into who this was. Karen, imaginative as usual, had a different look for every single character, which we'd been working on together almost daily for months and months and months. I had my interpretations of the men's music there in rough mix form, and during the photo shoot, the woman that I was trying to embody would have her song played over and over and over and over while I was getting made up. I was preparing myself to walk into her, physically, spiritually, and emotionally. Karen and Kevyn were there the whole time. I loved the photographer, Thomas Schenk, who brought in Ward Stegerhoek to be the hair and wig master. Thomas held a wonderful space just knowing that I needed to do this. He made the choice to do each photo on a blank background. We felt that props weren't the point. It was more like these women each came in and did a sitting for a photographer. And I was moving from anima to anima very fast, though it was at least an hour between each shoot.

Kevyn and I talked on the phone about this project three times a week for six months before doing it. I'm so thrilled that we got to do this before he died. I'd never spent so much time working with him and his genius— he transforms people, that was his genius. It wasn't necessarily bringing out something from the person. He could work from his subject's own psychology, but more often, I think, he could transform you into an archetype. That was his genius, to turn you into a 1930s film star or a Native American princess. Into somebody else.

I sent Kevyn and Karen the songs early on. I'd call Kevyn and say, "I'm thinking about doing this one, let's listen." Karen would come down and listen, because she was in England, while Kevyn was in New York. Sometimes I would just tell her about the song. Kevyn had to hear it. Karen sometimes doesn't need to hear it. She can say, "Tell me when she was born, tell me what's her love life." They would both ask me questions and we'd be bouncing things off each other.

I had a sense of what each visual would be when I tracked the songs. I knew the girl in the Stranglers song "Strange Little Girl" was the daughter of the mother character whose voice we hear in Eminem's song "Bonnie and Clyde." The daughter of this horror—her mom killed by her dad, sings "Strange Little Girl" as a young woman. Lennon and McCartney's song "Happiness Is a Warm Gun"—that's the call girl who visited Mark David Chapman before he killed John Lennon. In Neil Young's song "Heart of Gold," those are the twins; they're up to all sorts of shenanigans. The person in Joe Jackson's song "Real Men" might be a lesbian or a transsexual, I never was quite sure. I knew that Lou Reed's song "New Age" represented that moment when the girl takes her glasses off— my god, you're beautiful. She's that girl who does research in New York City, the smart publishing type. But she has fetishes. I knew the showgirl in Depeche Mode's song "Enjoy the Silence"—she was an older woman now, and a mother presence; she was not the victim. She understood things because she's been there. I loved her nurturing. We needed a nurturing presence and she was it.

With Slayer's song "Raining Blood," I chose to do the song partly because of what was going on with the Taliban destroying ancient sculptures of the Buddha in the Bamiyan Province of Afghanistan. Like many people, I had tears in my eyes that day. I had had a personal experience with bloodletting and just the information of what was going on with women in Afghanistan . . . the image was so clear when I heard the Slayer song.

I just immediately thought it was a wonderful feminist song, and I saw this huge vagina ring of blood and fire, swallowing the Taliban. I thought Slayer would love to be part of that, whether they knew it or not. Because talk about alternative—*that's* alternative, let's get a big old pussy. Then in the visual image, we went for a World War II French Resistance heroine posing as a German agent, representing a different reign of blood.

Finally, with Tom Waits's song "Time," I knew she was Death. Until we knew she was Death, Kevyn did not come up with the gold makeup. She has that Swedish thing going on. But we loved the Victorian aspect— you can't negotiate with her. Still, she's very compassionate. She would say, "It's time" to you, in a very gentle way.

ANN: *The extreme transformations of* Strange Little Girls *prepared Amos for her next character, the titular heroine of her 2002 album,* Scarlet's Walk. *This persona is the most sophisticated yet for Amos—fully fictional and yet partly herself, naturalistic while still embodying the mythos of America itself. In the artwork accompanying the album, Amos realized an image that would carry her forward into the next phase of her career.*

CONVERSATION BETWEEN TORI AND ANN:

For the *Scarlet's Walk* cover, we worked with Kurt Markus, a very American photographer who's made great images of athletes, cowboys, and the Wild West. Lesley wasn't involved in the cover art for *Girls* or *Venus,* although she was right there with me through all the press shoots for those particular projects, so she was ready to dive into this next project, *Scarlet's Walk.*

Lesley, Karen, and I were in New York City, Midtown, on September 11. Karen stayed with her family in New York while Lesley and Tony Lucha came down to Florida with me so I could see Tash briefly before driving back up on a tour bus again with me twenty-four hours later, if you can believe that, to do David Letterman. Because we were the first musical guest after the attack, I thought it was essential to work as a team and express ourselves as a team since we had lived through it as a team. That particular configuration was Karen, Lesley, and Tony, so you can see that Lesley and I had a lot of time together.

While I was writing *Scarlet* I would call her and talk with her about Scarlet's relationship with her spiritual mother, whom we call America. After seeing some other photographers, she came up with Kurt Markus. She felt we needed to go with a photographer's photographer. We needed to go with somebody who had his own relationship with our spiritual mother, America. We went to Montana and the juices were flowing, and John Witherspoon was there along with art director Sheri Lee and this posse of new girls from Epic, my new record label. We were there for four or five days. Montana is Kurt's stomping ground. We had thought about shooting in different places across the country, but finally we settled on one day of Scarlet's journey, one moment.

KAREN BINNS:

Those are 1940s-style dresses Tori's wearing in the *Scarlet* photographs. It's like the girl on the prairie, but not like any prairie you've ever known. That was the look for that year.

CONVERSATION BETWEEN TORI AND ANN:

I loved being Scarlet. I'm not an actress, but I let this form inhabit me. And Mark doesn't have any problem with it because he enjoys, you know, being monogamous and having relationships with all these different women in that way. Because when I'm in the thick of it, I'm in the thick of it. I wear it around. Tash has forced me to jump out of it real quick, so she's teaching me. I have to be Mommy. But I'll tell you, there's even a wardrobe that I buy for Mommy. I've always done that. Meaning for the homebody person. Sometimes I have to be able to be clear with myself, and clothes can help.

We go back to the idea of pieces, and the pieces of Scarlet, some of them have stayed with me. All the records have changed me, all the songs have touched me, but certain songs stay with me more than others. Some I visit. Like "Leather"—I really enjoy her. She might have been something I was walking with when I was starving for that kind of experience. Now I understand her in a very different way.

ANN: *Amos continues to perform her duet with Venus as it evolves with every new aspect of her art. Whether posing in glamorous midcentury garb for the compilation* Tales of a Librarian *or taking on the role of a torch singer in the film* Mona Lisa Smile, *collaborating with the photographers she admires and the clothing designers who lend her inspiration, Amos now heartily enjoys putting her own mark on the iconography of desire.*

KAREN BINNS:

Tori can connect with the rockers, she can connect with the couples who stay home and listen to their stereo, and she can connect with the radical kids who want to shoot the president. She can connect with everybody, you know. The way she dresses—I think it's important that she connects but still is one person. There's a way to do that. You look open, you look like you're in touch with what's going on, you look like you're in touch with social issues. I want to make sure Tori looks as good as anybody that you're going to see on the cover of any magazine, cause she's got the right things on for that year. They're not the trendiest, but they're the right ones. So if a seventeen-year-old reads those—all right, Tori's the girl with the red hair and she's kind of ethereal, but she's got it, too.

LOREN HAYNES:

Here's an anecdote that gets to the heart of Tori as a photographic subject. We were driving to a radio show one morning when I was on tour
with her, and she was being interviewed by a journalist during the drive.
I was taking pictures of her from the back seat. She was talking to the
writer, but she was still very aware of my presence and her duty in that.
There was one moment when she put her head onto her arm and sort of
leaned on her arm and I ran out of film, I couldn't get the shot. Then we
got to the venue. What I found fascinating is that later when we got back
in the car, she very quickly went back to that pose, meaning she was completely aware, even though she had been talking to this reporter the entire time, in a deep conversation about the state of the world, which was
very important to her—she remembered I didn't get that shot and she
was able to take me back there and give it to me again. That's where you
go, *Wow*. Even I had forgotten that shot. I mean, she's not a model. Most
musicians are more consumed in their own trip, what they're saying or
doing or what's next. With Tori, there is an element of care and concern.
She cared enough about me and what I was doing; she knew I wanted
that pose and she remembered that and had enough care to put that into
full process.

CONVERSATION BETWEEN TORI AND ANN:

When I'm posing for a photographer, as with music, it has to be improvisational at a certain point. For it to work you have to allow yourself to
dream, to walk into a painting. If you establish an inner dialogue while
you're being photographed it can be a bit more revealing. I might remember a conversation with somebody that takes me to a certain space. I'm not
inhabiting a different character—I'm inhabiting myself, although this
might be a piece of the self that even I am just meeting for the first time.
That's what I like to see in a photograph. When somebody's just blankly

staring out at you, or seducing the camera in a really obvious way, it just doesn't have the same resonance.

Though I'll use fantasy as a motivator, I let fiction stay fiction; this is just a place where we can play it out a little. The characters and events I'm playing with change. It could have been my husband today, it could have been something an acquaintance said to me, it could have been somebody, I don't know their name, and I saw them and they did something that intrigued me. There's a moment that you're drawn to these people and you allow yourself to be drawn. And the photographer is watching it happen. I'm letting him see me getting drawn into someone. You and the photographer agree to let something take shape. It's a safe place to let your mind wander.

Having Tash playing dress-up has made me see how much we all love playing dress-up. I got to a place where I could understand all facets of it. And this is the fun side of it—why can't I enjoy it?

You do have to be careful, though, about using your sexuality in forming your image. It's very much like Frodo and the Ring—don't put it on. If you reach for it, it's very unlikely that you won't be seduced by it. When you start valuing your body, you start valuing whom you let into it. You realize there are consequences. I know some people who seem to be focused on how many people they can get into their room. Their whole M.O. is "How many locks can I pick?" Some of my guy friends in the music industry are really into that. I don't know if it makes them feel more powerful or what. But I've been able to mostly avoid being intimately involved with men like that, unless I just made a mistake, not realizing I would just be another scalp on their belt.

It goes back to that balance between forming a public image and being a musician. Because I have an instrument and because I connect with the tradition of musicians, I can go back to that. I'm in relationship with something onstage. I serve it. The great players will tell you they serve their instrument. I'm an extension of my piano, and it plays me as much as I play it. You know, this is not a possession of mine; it's just abhorrent to think that this is a possession. When you refuse to possess your instrument, you yourself can't be possessed, either—you can't fully be reduced to an object of desire.

INTERMISSION

Tour Body Roll Call:

Hello, Glutes.

"Hey, T."

What jeans should we wear today?

"Any, T. We are your touring Glutes so we can fit nicely into all your jeans this week."

Hello again, Glutes.

"Hello, T."

What jeans should we wear today?

"Sorry, T, we are your composing Glutes, so we are more interested in assonance than ass."

Do I miss my touring body when I'm off the road? Oh, yes, yes, yes, yes. What does a touring body feel like? Because I eat pretty healthily—lots of greens and protein—food doesn't slow me down on or off the road, but on the road my body is forced to breathe in ways that normal living never asks of me. When I train for the road, I have to practice singing while I row on my rowing machine. Otherwise, I never build up vocal tone control while doing heavy aerobics. The live show is heavy aerobics with breathing, tone, abs, and glutes all having their movement. But breath control is essential or I'll sound like I need an oxygen machine. Can you imagine buying a ticket to see some forty-year-old woman pass out? When you get it right and when the body is moving with the music, while I'm playing the keyboards—my internal organs feel like they are also getting played. This is an unbelievable high. Not just physically, but emotionally and mentally—I have to be present, so as not to burp or miss a step in some way. Because all the different pieces of my being are giving their ultimate: the physical body (south), the emotional body (west), the mental body (north), the spiritual body (east)—together, all the pieces can create an activated medicine wheel within the being. Do I miss this when I'm not touring? Of course. But to have the songs that create an exciting live narrative, I must go into the quiet, I must go into the depth: chop the wood, carry the water, practice the piano, get out my palettes, sharpen my pencils, turn on my crap tape recorder, and embrace my composing glutes.

PART II

THOUGHTS FROM TORI ON THE PUBLIC/PRIVATE

SELF . . . RUMINATIONS ON THE CONVERSATION

Do you watch people, people whom you know (or you think you know) when they are out, out around people? They have a public persona, right? Something different from when they are lounging around at breakfast— if you know them well enough to have seen them waking up, pulling themselves from that very private dream-sleep, or from that restless-nightmare-lack-of-sleep, riding back on ghost mustangs so that they can make it back into their bodies, back into their bed as the sun rises. What we call private must ease into becoming exposed to the real world, with the opening of our bedroom door . . . and so it begins. Then opening the door to your house, and then there, in that moment, another level of what is truly private is becoming an echo.

Okay. A BBC newsreader. Do you have any idea how and what she would be like out on a Friday night? I have no idea, having sat in the BBC many times, thinking about just this very subject while waiting in the queue for my chitchat with the extremely professional, well-trained interviewer who is interviewing that day. I'm writing this and I'm thinking, *Tony Blair is sitting where my 5 Denier stockings have been*. I wonder if he thought about these people who are questioning him—interrogating him, somewhat—and what makes these people tick. Do they blow-dry or towel-dry while conjuring prehistoric Paleolithic critters in their bathmat pre-sunup, pre-mask-on, preinterview? Tough questions. Do people like Tony Blair sit there and size up: "Okay so this newsreader, this interviewer, has an airtight public image—impenetrable." Well, they definitely have the upper hand, and I have discussed this with this book's cowriter, a journalist herself, in depth . . . the media always has the upper hand. That's the case if a writer is worth his or her ballpoint when it comes to interviewing the subject, because of one simple point—this person, the interviewer, is not in the hot seat, is not having their personality or their work peeled back like Eve's apple to be exposed and—let's face it—if not eaten (embraced), to rot.

Over the years I have found I enjoy finding out who is interviewing me, because once I understand the symbology that person favors, his interests, etc., I can use different language so I can somehow, in twenty minutes, try to relate to this stranger. Then the interviewer gets to go and edit our conversation in any way that he wants. He can present an altered image to the public. For example, an artist might have all of her humorous or self-deprecating comments edited out. This way the writer presents the character he was determined to present even before the interview took place. Yes, there are some journalists who welcome being proven wrong about their interpretations of an artist's personality. But some are conjoined with their preconceptions, and fulfilling them becomes their objective. Upholding their intuition, even if it isn't right, is the hidden agenda. Sometimes they're not even aware they're doing it. It's a crapshoot. For both sides, I guess.

Every person has a public face. The woman who works on Wall Street, the soccer mom, the college student at NYU. My niece goes to NYU, and we have talked quite a bit about this: When can you let the mask down? Especially when you're living in a college dorm, essentially living with strangers, similar to a road crew. But a road crew should be professional and know the rules of the game. Students who in some cases are away from their bedrooms, their personal spaces, for the first time in their lives aren't supposed to be professionals. And yet they're thrown into such a lack of privacy, where they may find themselves rooming with a gay-hobbit-porno-web-site fanatic—that would test even the most experienced road dog. Remember, most road crews get at least one day off a week, and on my tour you usually get a room to yourself to regroup and have some privacy. At the worst, you get your own bunk where the curtains pull shut, with your own drink holder (wow), TV set, reading light . . . yeah, it's a tight space, but it's your own space with the curtain closed, where nobody dares to pull your curtain back unless they're on some vodka-crazed rampage and they want you to be the donkey in a game of pin the Velcro on the donkey. Honestly, if that's the least that happens to you on tour, then you are truly loved. But students don't even get anywhere near this privacy.

There is a strange way at work here, or at play. If you have an image of yourself and want to be "in that skin," to walk in those shoes—how can this perception of you be questioned by others, and maybe even by yourself? Why? I don't know how or why. A strange set of coincidences can converge to bring your perception of you and other people's perception of you into a questioning state. A state that can have a set of rules or laws that may and can be broken, intentionally or completely unknowingly. A state that can have a sheriff. The act of breaking these unspoken laws set into place in this public-image state can end friendships, sever acquaintances,

and cause overall mayhem. You could also possibly be taunted and humiliated if you don't follow the views of the "image connoisseurs" in your social circle and be who you should be, according to them.

I have to catch myself drumming up preconceptions of people: I pinch
myself and say, "Just observe without making judgments too quickly."
There have been guys who on first glance and meeting come across as
maybe your worst nightmare. Basically sporting a chauvinist, shaved-
head, arrogant stance—I'd say pretty much pushing a prehistoric "I'll
drag you back to the cave, and I've got computer-nerd weenies on the spit,
grilling."

And then, sometimes, a strange circumstance presents itself where I see
this guy's "stance / demeanor / personality / self" change right before
my eyes. The gears shift. Then a laugh, maybe. And sometimes you find a
big grizzly bear that, yes, can be ferocious, but can also be protective and
even, once in a while, cuddly. If you don't have enough time with your private self to sit down and catch up with the voices inside, then how do you
know who you really want to be? Not just who your family wants you to be,
not who your lover needs you to be, not who your current crowd hopes you
will continue to be . . . but who you want to be. I've constantly had to battle with the issue of what kind of woman I wanted to be. Sometimes I've
given the complete opposite impression to some people. Why? Sometimes
it was intentional. Sometimes it wasn't. There have been those around me
who have equated the meaning of compassion with the definition of
weakness. Because you want to give people another opportunity to prove
themselves, you can get the reputation of being a softie. Then if you
choose to break off the relationship after having been compassionate, you
get the reputation of being a motherfucker. One extreme to the other. I've
begun to firmly believe true compassion is a tough skill to wield and it
takes a strong resolve to listen, be understanding, and then still be able

to say, "We've given this relationship chance after chance after chance of working together, of creating together, but it just isn't working out." There doesn't have to be animosity over this—choosing different trails up the mountain—but if there is animosity, then there is. As hard as you try to be diplomatic and fair, other people may not see you as fair at all but as a manipulator, a crusher of their dreams. But what was their dream based on? A fantasy combined with an image they had of you (as a girlfriend, as a working partner, as somebody who could fix their life . . .). Did you buy into this image they had, because, frankly, for a while, it pulled you in? Let's be honest. You let yourself be pulled in because it felt good to be wanted, needed. But then it went too far, as projected images always do. If it's not a real image, but one that has been projected onto you, then you can keep up the masquerade for only so long before the mask cracks and the paint on the mask peels away.

After our all-around household coordinator Deb, fondly known as Super Debs, my niece Cody, and I spent a week in Ireland together, getting the house ready for the summer holiday, the three of us came to a conclusion. Even though we'd all been working together almost every day over the previous weeks, waking up with each other in Ireland took us to another awareness of one another's personal selves. I've worked with Deb for more than four years now. And Cody is my sister's daughter, so if you had asked me two weeks ago if I knew these two women on a personal level, I would have said absolutely, without question, I know these two women personally. But on this trip to Ireland those "public masks" got stripped away. Stripped away with every day—a few layers closer to what each of us considered to be truer to her real, private self.

The three of us, Cody, Deb, and I, were convinced that if anybody really thought about it they could pinpoint when the private self and the public self join hands—in the morning before you go to work, in the car before you arrive as that wedding guest—who is in the driver's seat, the private self or the public self, depends on where you're going. In England, when we first boarded the plane, the public selves, for Deb, Cody, and me, took over in order to deal with ticket-counter check-in, security lines—we all know this dance—so we had our private selves protected somewhat by the public self. We all do this in order not to take so personally the cold, hard reality of such interactions. Because so much of life these days is impersonal, we all basically put on a protective coating, similar to Scotchgard on your dining room chairs, so that when somebody squirts their emotional ketchup or mayonnaise on you, intentionally or not, you can wipe it off without too much of a stain being left. By the time we woke in Ireland on the second day of our trip, with phone calls coming in that were personally affecting one of us, the public selves were ushered out the front door and mugs of lattes and Kleenex boxes were more the order of the day.

I've often thought that the people you become close to depend on certain circumstances occurring. For instance, sometimes you are with someone during a crisis: by chance, as I was with Lesley Chilkes on September 11 in New York City. Other people were there, but because Karen Binns went to deal with her family in Brooklyn and because Lesley's friends were stuck in Miami, she and I gravitated toward each other. Marcel and I also had a moment at the rehearsal studio that afternoon; while all the horror of the day was occurring, we seemed to find another depth to our friendship. I've been working with these people since 1991 and 1994, respectively. But during that time, because I was with them in circumstances when our private selves were completely on display, I saw sides of them, and they of me, that strengthened an already existing friendship by a hundredfold. Now I know these two people really well. I would say they know me extremely well. I realized my depth of love for them and I felt their depth of love for me as I had never felt it before.

People are the most fascinating mysteries I've ever read. I'm sure someone reading this has had another experience like the one I've had: You meet someone's public self and choose to work with them because you've had a good feeling about them. Then the nightmare begins. And familiarity sets in, the masks droop and slide, and you see the heart of a monster. What has blown me away is that some of these people retaliate if you don't choose to accept their monster. I have found that the only way to tour with the many different personalities you deal with backstage, as well as onstage, is to truly know the scope of your *own* monster. If you don't, you are a walking time bomb. Before a world tour starts, my private self always takes a long walk with my public self, and the protective clothing of the former and the masks of the latter are packed together in the suitcase, ready to board the bus. "All aboard" takes on a new meaning these days.

SONG CANVAS: "goodbye pisces"

I'm a sucker for a good love song. One of my friends had sent me this book called *Sextrology*, mainly just 'cause she's into that kind of stuff. Anyway, I was thumbing through it one night, as you do, and I started thinking about how in a relationship you can't stop yourself sometimes from putting your lover's attitude about something down to their sign. I don't necessarily think that the male character I'm singing about is a Pisces; he might have Pisces in his chart somewhere. But more than anything it's about the end of an age—whether that's the end of a relationship or the end of the Piscean Age, which has been the last two thousand years. And sometimes a relationship can feel like it's been going on for two thousand years.

chapter eight

The Lioness: surviving
the music business

ANN: *Feminine power is not only a warm, nurturing thing. Furious goddesses have transformed the world since ancient times, laying waste to man's corruption, wreaking havoc until justice is served. From the wild dance of the Indian deity Kali to the rampage wrought by Tura Satana in Russ Meyer's exploitation movie* Faster, Pussycat! Kill! Kill! *stories of women on fire with rageful power have taken hold of the culture's imagination. "No more nice girls!" these archetypes scream, reminding us that what is right is not always easy, and that kindness has meaning only when fierceness is its counterpart.*

One of the oldest deities of Egypt was an angry goddess: Sekhmet, red-haired and lion-headed, hot as the sun. According to her legend, Sekhmet burst forth from the eye of Ra, king of the gods, to punish humanity for losing faith. She relished her path of mayhem so much that Ra had to put a stop to her by leading his thirsty daughter to drink a lake full of beer and lose consciousness. Awakening, she saw the error of unwarranted destructiveness and lived on, transformed, as a righteous punisher of wrongdoers.

Sekhmet survives today in the imaginations of modern-day women battling the lingering forces of sexism. Despite enormous gains made in the past century, women's equality remains tentative and circumstantial; old-boy networks still dominate most areas of public life, while in private many women still fight to maintain confidence in their talents and authority. Nowhere is equality more paradoxically fulfilled than in the entertainment industries, where women artists are expected to present themselves as strong and independent, despite the fact that few actually control the nuts-and-bolts aspects of their careers. All artists are at risk of exploitation within a system founded on the sale of something as intangible as talent. Women, whose contributions have historically been underestimated, from the hearth to the hospital to the secretary's desk and beyond, are at the greatest risk of being used and discarded. With so much emphasis placed on youth, beauty, and novelty, the female popular artist has no choice but to tap into fury to demand the right to a full career.

Tori Amos learned the need for anger's energy early, when she wrongly trusted the "experts" who led her into the ill-begotten artistic and physical makeover of the Y Kant Tori Read *project. Reclaiming her identity as Tori Amos meant learning how to say no to bad guidance. Since those early years, Amos has never stopped fighting to maintain control of her art and her image. Battle after battle have taught her to wield her fire with uncompromising grace.*

TORI:

I'm in a tight corner. Is it serious? Yes. Let's say that if we were playing the final chess game in the world, WWChess, then my opponent has just looked at me across all the chess pieces and said, "Check."

I have one move left to save my soul. My mind races to a similar quote by Dr. Faustus made in 1592 (in a book with the same name written by Christopher Marlowe). Dr. Faustus wanted all the knowledge that there was to have. He made a pact in Blood. He made it with Lucifer, the one called Satan in the Bible. Once he realized the extent of the agreement, he wanted to break the pact, but it was too late. If only he could have his soul back . . . He studies the pact. "See, see, where Christ's blood streams in the firmament! One drop would save my soul, half a drop: Ah, my Christ!"

I have one move left to save my soul. Here I am saying this today, four hundred years later, from where I sit on this craggy Irish hill, looking out to America and the Power Seat of the music industry. I am reminded that today I am writing from what was once the Power Seat of Munster about 2,300 years ago. The Seat of Power changes. Yet those who wield the execution of power rarely act with a sense of fairness and integrity. Fairness and Integrity are more akin to Maat, the Egyptian goddess of Law, Truth and Justice. The fact that power in the wrong hands corrupts is a tricky one. Because when we place power into the hands of those we have deemed worthy, in that moment they seem worthy. In that moment it does not seem that we are putting our faith into the wrong hands. Little do we know, the person we think to be just and fair will be seduced and corrupted by the shadow side of power. We all think we are above this seduction, but I guess no one is. Then the other side of the coin is the character in this little story who could be you or who could be me, who could not believe we could be fooled by or drawn into this power epic. No, we do not think we have the need to be the power hungry, the addicted-to-the-hunt and close-of-the-deal-type PHC personality. That would be "Power-Hungry-Crazed" personality. And no, maybe we don't have this PHC personality, but that's not where it all goes "tits down," as they say. It becomes a real-life game of cat and mouse when you, or when I, in this little story make an agreement—a pact—with this power-hungry-crazed type of individual. Sometimes you don't find out who they are until you're in so deep, so deep to where the struggle of trying to get out of the situation can drive the hooks in even deeper.

In the music industry, like Dr. Faustus, you sign your pact in your own Blood. This contract can be with the record label, the manager, the business manager, the music attorney, the publishing company, or the agent. Or let's say you have no contract at all, yet you still have a massive fight on your hands because of the precedence that has been set in the years that the relationship has been going on, and yada yada yada, blah blah, puke. I have known too many people in the music industry, from label honchos to publishers to publicity assistants to accountants to managers to publicists to journalists who, when push comes to shove, will let you down and lower themselves morally down even further so they can cover their ass by doing it.

He enjoys watching the fall of a colleague. The self-destruction of another. The physical defecation. His fingerprints are never on the person's state of mind—hard thing to measure. It makes him hard. Aroused.

"Yes, Mom, it turns him on."

"How," she asks me, "in Jesus' name, how can someone that has been, let's say, not an enemy but even called friend, a good acquaintance or business associate, how can they become like this?"

"Because, Mom . . . he likes the blood."

"But he doesn't seem like an evil person when he talks, dear."

"Yes, and bin Laden lives behind my trigeminal nerve—that doesn't mean I won't play fair. Some people you think you know until push comes to shove. The Day of Reckoning. It happens in every relationship; the friendship gets tested and it always comes down to one thing: Do we both want a win-win? He's the type of creature who in order to really win then needs someone to lose. Someone must pay. Someone must be yelled at, humiliated. A pound of flesh must be paid to feed his inflated sense of himself. Insatiable need."

"What need, pray tell, does he have? He has so much power, darlin'."

"I know, Mom. But so did Napoleon. So did Hitler."

"You know, Hitler was a vegetarian, dear."

"Yes, Mom. Never hurt an animal. But they have the same ravenous need."

"Need for what?"

"An endless need to possess. You know, Mom, benevolent and malevolent are only a couple letters off."

"Yes, dear. I would say these two misguided tyrants, who remind me a bit of your friend somewhat, were six letters off."

"How's that, Ma?"
"That would be Russia, dear."

this House is like Russia
with eyes cold and grey
you got me moving in a circle
I dyed my hair red today
I just want a little passion
to hold me in the dark
I know I've got some magic
buried deep in my heart
but my priest says
you ain't savin' no souls
my father says
you ain't makin' any money
my doctor says
you just took it to the limit
and here I stand
with this sword in my hand
you can say it one more time
what you don't like
let me hear it one more time then
have a seat while I
take to the sky

I've been playing that almost every night on the *Scarlet* tour. Reclaiming something. Russia's landscape has changed since I wrote that in 1990. But my landscape has changed, too. Conflict and the pain of conflict come up in every show, in every record. At least somewhere.

CONVERSATION BETWEEN TORI AND ANN:

The music industry does not deal in music. It deals in moving product. There are a few terms you will need to know and understand to be involved in this world. The first one is actually two words: *NET* and *GROSS*. When it comes to you as the artist, you will want to know who is getting paid on the net or on the gross. Virtually in all cases the artist is paid on the net—that means after everyone has taken his or her piece of the pie, so to speak. Record companies take their piece first, and once you the artist have paid back all your expenses and some of theirs, then you finally get what's left . . . if there is anything left, sometimes there is and sometimes there isn't.

Now the dangerous question here is, obviously, Who is getting paid on the gross? Who is getting paid before all the expenses are deducted? Who is getting paid on your creative work before you are? There are a few managers who get paid on the gross because they are responsible for manufacturing an artist, but I have found through the years that many managers who don't manufacture artists still want to be paid on the gross and will take that option if they can get it. I find that grotesque. That is why I set up The Bridge Entertainment Group with Johnny and Chelsea, because I inherently disagree with the philosophy of more than a few management groups. It's less complicated to define how net vs. gross impacts an artist's financial future when it is explained in terms of touring. Here's an example of how paying on the gross could affect an artist. Whether the number in this example is $10 thousand or $10 million, the result for the artist in this scenario will be the same. Namely, that the artist will potentially be in debt after a year of touring. Being In Debt is Being In Debt no matter how you get there. Let's say this artist is involved in a deal where the manager is being paid on the gross, and after a year of touring the artist has grossed $10 million on tour. The artist will then realize, to their shock, as they start having an eczema attack, that before all the expenses have been covered, the agent and the manager are taking their share. What this means is simply that if the agent is on a 10 percent deal and the manager is taking 15 percent . . . well, you do the math. The agent would take $1 million and the manager would take $1.5 million.

Now let's imagine your Accurate Accountant calls you and says, "Excuse me, Artist, we have a problem." They then drop the bomb: "Because your expenses in themselves were eight million, with the added commissions of one million for the agent and one and a half million for the manager, you are now a half million in the hole, in the red, in debt." "I am what?" you stutter in absolute horror. The very grave answer from the very Accurate Accountant: "I hate to say this, Artist, but you are a half million In Debt." Then the artist starts to freak out and says, "This can't be happening, I've been on the road for more than a year of my life . . . how could this happen?" "It happened because apparently you agreed in the contract to pay your management company on the gross instead of the net." Now usually agents get paid on the gross. Agents book the gigs. Some agencies get 10 percent, some get 7.5 percent, and some get 5 percent on the gross of an artist's tour. This must be negotiated with the agency. I've been with Carole Kinzel over at CAA since the beginning of my career. She's one of my dear friends, and yes, she knows how I feel about any agency taking such a huge percentage. In my opinion, the percentages for agencies are still out of line. However, it's a ballpark standard for an agency to take from 10 percent negotiating down to 5 percent of the gross of an artist's tour, depending on the artist's pull in the industry.

Management companies, however, do not have a ballpark figure. Some are taking 15 to 20 percent off the gross of what an artist generates. Some are taking 15 to 20 percent off the net of what an artist generates. Well, obviously there is a massive difference in these two options. Net pay for

managers off a successful artist is a pretty good payday, so can you imagine a gross payday off a successful artist? I feel that management companies receiving payment of 15 to 20 percent of the gross is extortion. The
manager will be making more than the artist because, you must remember, the artist has to shoulder all the expenses, unlike actors. Actors are not
responsible for the costs of the movies they are in, whereas musicians are
completely responsible for many of the costs that go into the manufacturing and promotion of a record, including the funding for their own tour
and quite possibly the party the label is throwing for the launch of their
record. Don't forget the word *recoupable,* because everything is. The words
recoupable and *nonrecoupable* will be mentioned more times in this industry than the words *good luck.* This is one of the reasons that you'll read
about certain musical artists who have sold millions of records of their
own music and yet are broke. I mean actually broke. No house. Move in
with a friend. Move back home. Try again. Sing in the shower, it's safer.

Now for our next word that I think is quite important, and here again
it's more of a phrase than a word: *YOUR FRIENDLY MUSIC ATTOR-
NEY.* Do I have one? I have two. They are known to our team as "the
good guys." They would be Jamie Young and John Branca at Ziffren,
Brittenham, Branca, et al. Does it matter who your music attorney is?
Well, let's put it this way: the first thing out of the mouth of "those who
are they" at the record label will always be, "So, you have good represen-
tation?" Now, that is not a question. Is it a warning? Well, in a way.
Partially because if you don't have a powerful deal maker, your attorney,
then you are toast. The record label likes toast, even those on low-carb di-
ets. Toast is popular but something that you or I really do not want to be.
Have I ever been toast? Yes. With organic honey and smooth peanut butter dripping off it. And I've also been toast that has no Dutch butter
spread on it, that doesn't even have margarine on it, for chrissake. Just

toast left on the counter fighting not to get stale and moldy while waiting for the attorneys to get back with a counteroffer. There's a natural question at this point: What does this music attorney get paid? I would say, loads and loads. They can make tons. Sometimes, they can even make more than the artist. I did not say all the time. But I'm trying to impress upon you their importance. Or should I say, the importance the music industry itself has placed on some of them. I'm only talking about the Big Guns. So if you're not a Big Gun, then you won't be offended by what I'm about to say. And if you are a Big Gun, then go on, bask in your Bigness—this is quite glorious.

These folks are the power brokers for the whole industry. A very few represent the whole kit and caboodle. For example, an attorney who represents "you," let's say, could be talking about "your" issues with the chairman of a record label, whom this attorney might also represent. And if your attorney doesn't represent the chairman, they could be golf buddies, or this attorney could be described sort of as one of the label's guidance counselors. Or the attorney could be doing The Big Deal with "such and such" merger that the chairman of your record label wants your attorney to finesse . . . In another instance, if the firm with whom your attorney is with has a stable of artists, this adds to their flexibility in making deals. Mainly because if you're their only client, then if and when you fall out with your record label the big Cheeses that run the label won't need to take your attorney's call. But an attorney who has many irons in the fire, on the other hand, will always have his call received because the label cannot risk pissing off the firm who has all the horses running in the Kentucky Derby. So when your record label has stopped giving you any oats or carrots, and your stall has been completely left to rank and ruin, then it's not a bad idea to be with a firm that has a big enough stable so that even if you have to get carrots from the Arabian next door, at a certain point it doesn't matter where the carrots are coming from . . .

Let's talk about payment. Some attorneys will want percentages on all income because they feel they have negotiated it. Others will take a fee. You're talking about hundreds of dollars an hour here. The simple truth is, though, that artists need music attorneys as much as soccer players need a ball. The other simple truth about this matter is that because most of Congress is in the back pocket of the powers behind the majors (there really are only four major labels now), these barbaric laws have been able to stay in place. Laws whereby artists can be "owned" by a record label for fifteen years or longer. Yes, these laws are still firmly in place. Yes, they are antiquated laws that say that once you sign a contract you have signed it in blood—you have handed over all your power whereby if you disagree with a major label, they can obstinately refuse to let you go. Hear me, young artist: You cannot even quit. You're not even allowed to quit your job. And if you try to quit . . . are you kidding me? Quit? They will sue your ass if you even think about trying to make music and distribute it on your own. Why? Because if you sign a standard artist's contract, then they think they own you.

The theatrical community has laws in place that protect them against this kind of ownership. The music industry and the film industry are completely different animals. Now. The next layer of this music business cake is obvious. If there were clearer laws in place, not only would the label have to adhere to certain parameters (legally set in place by the government) but—and here comes the clincher—but the need for music attorneys, these power brokers, these deities, would diminish. So, who has a lot to lose here? As much as I may adore and respect my music attorneys, I still have a responsibility in writing the "Music Business" chapter to question the music attorney community as a whole, as well as their intentions. Now, I'll be honest with you: if I were a music industry attorney, I would be torn. That's just the truth, I would be torn. It's a double-edged sword knowing that your place in the industry would lessen if artists were more protected by the government. If these laws were put into place, then the place of the attorney in the music industry as the Tony Soprano of this little music industry drama would become more like Tony Danza in *Who's the Boss?* Let's face it, folks: Tony Danza has always been cute, but between Tony Danza and Tony Soprano, who's the boss here? If I were wagering money on this one, I would say most of the attorneys in the music industry still want to be Tony Soprano.

TORI:

Power. Delicious Power. Herein lies an unknown. Will the judicious voice of the goddess Maat be stronger inside the soul of those whom we call music attorneys, or will the voice of delicious power drown Maat's voice out? It would be great if there were laws in place whereby we as artists aren't at the mercy of what goes on at the eighteenth hole on a golf course. A couple years of my life have been decided at the eighteenth hole. "C'mon, Emmenthal, c'mon Stilton," my music attorney says to the big Record Company Cheese at the end of the eighteenth hole. "Just let her go," suggests my attorney, who with much duplicity is just trying to get everyone to think with a clear head. "Is that what she wants?" asks the label Cheese. "Hey, you know, you can sell her, make a profit, and get rid of the headache. Stilton? Emmenthal?" "Is that what she really wants?" asks the Cheese again. And your attorney, as he thinks he's closing the deal, says, "You know it would be best for both parties." And then the Cheese's putt misses the hole. He looks up from his ball and says, "Fuck her."

It was raining, not that refreshing spring-in-New-York kind of rain, but that it-should-be-snowing-not-raining miserable kind of day. I'd flown in;

I was on tour. I'm now a member of the PLE (post-limousine era), but at the time I was a member of the PSUVE (pre–sports utility vehicle era). In the limo there was a variety of suits: one of my lawyers, John Branca, my manager at the time, Arthur Spivak, and my tour manager at the time, John Witherspoon (now one of my managers). At this juncture with Atlantic Records there were things that needed to be said. We were at a crossroads. It was no longer just a given that I turn over these song Beings to people who might be in a job that they just should not be in. Should not be in because the definition of this job would mean that they are capable of receiving an artist's music compositions. Assuming that once they receive these music pieces that they would know what to do when putting them out to the world, without denigrating them in any way. Imagine that . . .

Everybody who had been there when I signed with Atlantic had moved on to other ventures, such as Jason Flom, who heard me sing in a little bar back in 1983 in Georgetown. Although Jason signed me to Atlantic in the eighties, at this juncture he was no longer in my jurisdiction and I wasn't in his. Doug Morris, who really got my career off the ground, had jumped out of the equivalent of a Warner Zeppelin (and I don't mean the band, I mean the big air transport device). He had jumped out of this Warner Zeppelin with his golden parachute, taking Max Hole, who had facilitated the breaking of *Little Earthquakes,* with him over to Universal. So that day my team was focused, sitting in that limousine, and agreed that yes, if there were changes made, then a relationship could be workable for both sides, but issues had to be confronted. Now was the time.

We left Johnny to make calls back to the crew at the venue that was hundreds of miles away, making sure everything for the show the next night was in place. We went in, the three of us, meeting with "those who were they," the Cheeses representing Atlantic. Branca led off with our grievances. So, just to clue you in as the reader, very simply, there were seventy right answers to our grievances. But the response we got was as far away as it could possibly be from one of the seventy right answers they could have given. Their argument was, "Look, we felt we did everything we possibly could, from our point of view." That was it. It was war. The die was cast.

I took the floor and said, "A lethargy has set in to this company by which the stock shares of each person at this company seem to mean more than the music." The retort was, "We disagree." I said, "Do you disagree on who is running this label?" And they asked, "What do you mean by that?" I said, "It's clear that no one here can seem to agree on who is running this company. I feel I've gotten caught in a power play here." They responded, "Well, we don't see it that way at all." I said, "There isn't much to say anymore, but I will do everything in my power not to hand over as many of my musical children to you." To me they were the Hand That Rocks the Cradle.

At this point, one of them stood up with a piece of rolled-up paper in his hand, pounding it in the air like a judge's gavel, saying, "I own you, Tori Amos, I own you." I walked out of the room, leaving the other two to gather their coats. Found Johnny, found the limo. I said to Branca, "Get me off, sell me, sell me to somebody." He said, "Let me see what I can do." I said goodbye.

Johnny and I got on a plane headed for the gig. The label would have never known if I had made that gig or not, because they had nothing to do with the live performance and nothing to do with making the records.

A few weeks later I was in New York again. Somebody from the label asked to meet me for coffee, privately. He told me he was sorry that the meeting hadn't gone the way I'd wanted it to. I explained that I thought it could have gone well for both sides. They could have acted as if they gave a shit and I would have gone on giving 100 percent like I always do. Instead they pretended they continually give 100 percent, when we both know they had refused to genuinely promote my work. It should have been standard practice, for example, for Atlantic to purchase a block of tickets to my concerts and distribute them to the higher-ups at various radio stations, to interest them in promoting my work. Atlantic was buying tickets to my concerts, all right, but instead giving them to the radio honchos and saying, *Here's a little handout—as a return we'd like to promote a different* (newer, more "potentially moneymaking") *artist in exchange.*

He was shocked that I knew anything about that. I asked if at least this strategy was working to break the other artist. He couldn't look at me when he told me that Atlantic didn't think my song was a radio hit so they used the tickets they had received for my show as a trade for another artist's career push. I told him I was glad I could help out.

He asked, "Do you know what you did by questioning who holds the power at Atlantic? Do you know that you stirred up a hornet's nest?" I said, "Everyone who knows anything about the situation at the label is also questioning who is holding authority to make the decisions there." He laughed as he put down his espresso, saying, "Yes, but this is the first time Atlantic was confronted face-to-face about this particular issue, especially in a power meeting like that." I said, "It doesn't matter; Branca is going to sell me."

Silence. "Hey," I said, "are you okay?" He waited, reached for both my hands, which wasn't his style, and whispered, "Oh, Tor, I don't think Branca can bail you out of this one." "What do you mean, 'bail me out'? I didn't think I was in prison." He looked away and said, "Call Branca." "Right now?" "Soon." "Okay, I'll call him, but not until you say what your instinct wanted to say to me just then. Jesus, c'mon, whose side are you on?" "Look, Tor, Warner, Atlantic, AOL, whoever the fuck, they write my paycheck." "No, old friend, I write your paycheck. Robert Plant writes your paycheck. All the artists on the label, even those who have been fucked over by the big Cheeses, write your paycheck." "Okay, okay . . . The Cheeses, as you call them, have chosen to exercise their option and keep you under wraps, so to speak." "Oh, Merry Fucking Christmas—what are you talking about? Speak American, for Chrissake." "Tori, wake up. It's over." Silence. "What?" "They won." "What?" I said in shock, in a walking nightmare kind of voice. "They won. They've got you sewn up for three records. I'm sorry, I'm so sorry, Tor. I think they want to bury you." "How can they bury me?" I said, somewhat dazed. "I can play a full house at Madison Square Garden with or without Atlantic." "Yes, but they've got you sewn up for three records and by then they say you'll be . . . " "What, be what?" I said, now with tears running down my face in this small little café, with the waiters bringing me napkins for the dam that was about to burst. "Be what?" I whispered, through tears. He lowered his voice and said, "Oh, honey—too old. And then . . . " "And then, what?" I demanded. "And then no one will want you." Dam burst all over me, all over the coffee, all over everywhere. Flooding the little table. "Too old," I cried. "Well, of course I'll be older, fuck them, fuck all of you."

With gasps of hysteria in between teary, slobbery breathing, I was able to warble two words, "Tina Turner." He just stared at me, and I said, "Was she too old when she showed all the cool chicks how to be hot? Was she too old when she captured the hearts of all of us? Did she break the chains of her own kind of prison? Was she too old?" Response: "Tor, they are not expecting you to survive this, to even think about being around as long as Tina. You know that in this industry Tina is one of the only ones in the history of the music business who at fifty started her solo career." By now the café was getting rained on by me, so I started to grab my things. He grabbed me and gave me a hug and said, "You know, in my own way, I've always been there for you, Tor." I looked at him and said very quietly, "This is guerrilla warfare. You know that, don't you?" He just stared at me and said, "What can you possibly do? Believe me, they know the contract." And in that moment the only thing I could think of to say was "Just you wait, Henry Higgins"—I blew my nose—"just you wait." Another blow. I left first. I guess it was a good thing nobody in there spoke English, not even us.

I got back to my hotel room and called Jamie and John. "Hey, guys." On the conference speaker I hear two somber voices saying, "Hey, Tor." I proceeded to tell them everything that had just been revealed to me in that little café in New York City. The phone line got quiet for a moment, and then the two of them said, almost simultaneously, "Tor, they won't let you go." "What?" I was sure that they would be able to conjure something up. "John, Jamie, get me off, if somebody tells me they own me, then fine, sell me to someone else." The somber voices answered back, "We've tried. We've really tried to show them the advantages to selling you, and they have just dug their heels in. They won't let you go." A thousand guns were pointing at my song children and me in that moment, as I heard the drums summoning all of us to the record company guillotine, me and the songs together, in a line. I held the phone to my head in disbelief, asking John and Jamie, "Is this revenge?" John responded, "They won't look at it that way, even when pressed. Their strategy is tight. Their response is that you are a valued artist, so why would they want to let you go . . ." "John, Jamie, c'mon: the marriage is over, there are no conjugal rights, it's a dead marriage. I want a divorce from them." "Yes. Tor, we understand this. But they are saying they won't let you get a divorce, and your contract says that it's their option." "So I'm their prisoner, in actuality." The somber voices drummed on. "They want your product." "Yes. I understand they want to take my product, hoping all this will diminish my value on the street." "We're sorry, but we didn't do this early development of your recording contract." "Yeah. Yeah. Yeah. I know the drill, guys. I know when I've been put in check on the chessboard. So how many years of my life do they own from today?" I was having this conversation in December 1998. "You're looking at around four years of your life, based on your past productivity." Jamie said this trying to be brave, but I heard the sadness in her voice. "Then, Tori, in four years, you should be free to go." Free to go. Free to go. "Free to go where? In four years, with no promotion of my work except on a minimal level, we all know the interest will diminish . . . and then I will diminish. I'm not totally stupid." There was silence on the end of the phone, and I knew that they knew that I knew that my future looked very bleak indeed. And John, as a last-ditch effort to cheer me up, said, "I've warned them, Tor, that you could do what Prince has done." "Yeah, and what aspect of what Prince has done have you warned them I will do?" He said, "By performing on television and writing 'slave' on your face." And, without any emotion in my voice at that point, I said, "Of all the moves I can make right now, guys, and there are not many, some white girl with red hair who has a bank account with at least something in it, who writes 'slave' on her face, will not only have no career left, but won't have any friends left, either. I mean, for Chrissake, let me have some friends here." Believe it or not, they laughed. Believe it or not, I laughed back. I thought to myself in that moment, *If the Cheeses take that away from me, then they have won. If anyone can take that away from me, then they win.* I thought for a second and then I said, "Listen, you two, I need to think. I need to go see the medicine women. I'll call back in a week to restrategize."

I did go to see the medicine women. They all said the same thing. Then I saw my friend Lorraine Neithardt, a mystic. Whether I like it or not, what she reads into a situation, for good or ill, is always spot on. So I knew the grim walk that lay ahead of me. Although I could hear the information that spoke of this grim walk, I felt more shattered than capable of taking on my jailors. And for all those spiritual skeptics out there: I don't disagree with your skepticism, but you know what? Logic had failed me. The law had failed me. Any sense of loyalty from the record label had failed me. Using my trump card, which is my fan base, was something I could not do, because to drag them into this is like dragging others through shit and puke. You can ask that of somebody once, but it had better be worth it. And, frankly, these people were just not worth it. They weren't worth risking that relationship. So I called on the warrior goddesses and I started to construct a shape that I would step into to combat this malevolence. That kind of vitriolic posturing that you get from insecure power. Looking back, it's kind of amusing now, only in that I can see the difference between raw male power being exerted with a clear intent and distorted male power that at its root is a record company Cheese with erectile dysfunction.

I remember Branca and I having a coffee over breakfast not so long ago. We were having a laugh about the past after the success of *Scarlet* in the States, and he said to me, "I know you miss Polly." He was referring to Polly Anthony, with whom I partnered at Epic Records once I left Atlantic. And John Branca sat at that breakfast and said, "Donnie [Donnie Ienner, head of Sony Music, the new Cheese I report to] is a powerful guy, and you will find he has a different style than Polly." And John looked at me and said, "I know you and Polly had become friends but are you open to the changes at Sony?" And, as ever, I smiled at John and said, "Why wouldn't I be open to the changes at Sony? I have never had an issue with powerful men. I usually get along with them quite well. It's the men who aren't powerful that become little tyrants because they don't know how to exert their power—that, I have an issue with. So if Donnie is truly a powerful guy, then I'm sure we'll get along like wine and . . . Cheese."

But back to our story: So after I hung up with John and Jamie after they told me I was in for another four years, I became despondent for about a week and did what I never do. I closed the door, did not let any light in, and watched TV incessantly. Okay. So you know when you're just lying on the floor on top of a blanket with a scrunched-up pillow and you just stare at the TV? And then all of a sudden you look up at this black-and-white movie that's been playing as you've been spaced out, trying to work out your own sticky predicament, and there she is, Barbara Stanwyck staring right at you. And soon you come to realize that it's Barbara Stanwyck Week on Turner Classics, or whatever the hell it is. For many days I had Barbara Stanwyck staring me down in black-and-white and in color, challenging me to stand up to these cattle rustlers, these hustlers of humans, who will try to completely ruin and destroy another human being. From her movies as a young woman to her role as matriarch in the long-running TV show *The Big Valley*, this woman became one of my archetypes that I began to create in order to play the chess game of my life.

Sekhmet, some would say the shadow side of the musical goddess Hathor, was another piece of this female archetype that I was building, an archetype who could take on the music industry. Though my adversaries at Atlantic believed that they had me cornered for four years, I began to dissect every side, every facet of the chess game, and I made my next move.

I called Branca and Jamie. "I have an idea, guys," I said. They responded, "You know, Tor, we've been going over the contracts, and you owe them three more records." "Yes, guys—I've been trying to come up with a concept for all three that will honor the music and yet at the same time circumvent the need for Atlantic's promotion machine." John and

Jamie interjected, "On the strength of your touring and especially with the financial success of the *Plugged* tour, we were able to get Atlantic to count the live disc for two if you will generate two discs." "Guys, I can generate ten discs, but the question here is, will two live discs not promoted by Atlantic go platinum [500,000 copies sold for a double disc]? Because if it doesn't, it will do what Atlantic ultimately wants—which is to effectively cause other potential record labels I may consider going to to question if I still have value in the marketplace." "Tor, just come up with two discs that will go platinum, and then you won't lose your value in the marketplace." "Thanks, guys, for your genius ability to come up with a concept. I mean, if it doesn't go platinum, we're fucked. And it's not about if it will be brilliant—brilliant works get buried in the music business quite frequently. So it's not about whether it's good work; neither is it about whether I can capture the imagination of the public while I'm fighting my own label, which stands between me and the public." "Look, Tor, both of us sitting here know that you will come up with a concept. We know you can do it, we believe in you."

The double disc of *Venus* did go platinum. As we were developing *Venus* at Martian Engineering Studios in Cornwall, the concept came in a simple but beautiful way. I was taking a drive with Marcel, and I was jazzed about the live tracks from the *Plugged* tour that we were mixing. He said something to me that had a huge impact. "Tor, I've been hearing some of the new songs you've been writing, and I think they have to go on this record." "Yeah, but Marcel, we have a live concept for the double disc." "Yeah, but Tor, why don't you make one disc live and one disc with these new songs that I want to keep listening to?" "But I don't want to give Atlantic any new material." "Yeah, but Tor"—in his Dutch accent— "you need to give these songs to the people, not to the record company." "Jeez, Marcel, I need to think about this."

So I took a long walk in the dark that night, and I looked up and I thought I saw Venus looking down at Earth. And as we were coming into the millennium, I started to think about how Mother Earth must be feeling in the face of so much violence. And Venus seemed to be generating this light, almost like a hand outstretched in friendship. And I started to think that Earth could probably use a girlfriend. And *bam.* There was my concept: one disc for Earth, which would be the live music that had been created definitely on terra firma. Then another disc for Venus, which would be the new music that was feeling like a sonic outstretched handshake to her girlfriend Earth . . . recorded at, of all places, a studio called Martian Engineering.

ANN: *With one project still due Atlantic Records, convinced that she could not offer original work to a company she now considered purely adversarial, Amos found herself in yet another dangerous spot as the twentieth century expired. A dream her mother had shone a light on the escape route: the project that became* Strange Little Girls.

CONVERSATION BETWEEN TORI AND ANN:

After *Venus,* I still had one more record to deliver to Atlantic. Everyone wanted to know what I was going to do. I knew that whether I gave these executives a full-length disc of new material or not wasn't the most important issue in their lives. It was to me, at that time. I knew there would be a night when each of them was at home in bed, comfortably thinking about their families and their lives, and I would be out there with my music. I believed that my contract specified that the record I delivered in 2001 had to be original work, and I didn't know how I was going to deal with that a second time. While I was stewing on it, I got a phone call from my mother. She'd had a dream. Even though she's very Christianized, my mother has always remained intuitive and aware of the world of visions. She told me to call my lawyer. She claimed that my contract didn't specify what the music had to be. She told me that the ancestors had shown her. My mother really, really believes that if you need a warning, the ancestors will come and provide it. That was what her father taught her, and what she taught me.

So I called my lawyer, and Jamie my attorney and Jamie my friend with calm kindness said, "Tor, come on, we've gone over the contract. Don't make me do this again. It's just too painful for you." I said, "Just do it to make my mother happy. I can't call her a loony bird. Please, Jamie, just do it for her sake." A few hours later I got the call back and Jamie said, "In fact, the contract does not specify original work, which in itself is extremely unusual—just that the work has to be of the same quality as what has defined you as Tori Amos." Clearly the ancestors seized on the one element in the contract that sometimes the Cheeses miss but that can come down to interpretation. So I asked if she could defend me legally if I pushed the definition. She said she could. But most important, she thought my concept of an all-male reinterpretations record was a powerful one, and she has always encouraged me to play to my strengths.

So I came up with the plan to give them some of the greatest songs that had ever been written—just not by me. And I put my heart and soul into it while keeping the oath to myself to not give Atlantic any more of my song girls. Yet because of the concept of *Strange Little Girls,* we generated the kind of project we wanted to, which generated the response from the public without the support of Atlantic. As this work was getting ready for release, and when other labels wanted it because they were excited about it, I had to laugh. Because even in the final hour, when they could have made money by selling *Strange Little Girls* to the label I was about ready to sign with, which was Epic/Sony, I began to see the light at the end of my tunnel. No, They, the Cheeses at Atlantic, couldn't be gracious, even in the end.

Through almost three years of guerrilla warfare, we were still able as a team to produce three CDs—with involved concepts—that we believed in musically. Through it all, in the face of extreme adversity, we kept our musical integrity. To this day I still feel the need to thank those people who held little torches up for those of us trudging through the constant confrontations that tried to rip us to shreds down there in the Tori Tunnel. And as *Strange Little Girls* came out and made the top ten on *Billboard*'s album charts, I was able to finesse, alongside John and Jamie, certain aspects in the new Epic/Sony contract, which I signed forthwith. And as I held my daughter in my arms backstage at one of the shows on the *Strange Little Girls* tour, I thought to myself that my inner circle and crew had come through as a team and intact. And I looked out from England across the Atlantic Ocean to the white-collared dragons in the music industry and whispered, "Checkmate, Motherfuckers."

JOHN WITHERSPOON:

When Atlantic failed to reach a settlement with Tori after all those meetings, the writing was on the wall. After Tori had released *Strange Little Girls,* therefore fulfilling her contractual obligations, Atlantic issued a press release that included Tori among various artists they had

sekhmet, the egyptian lioness goddess

dropped from their roster. As we have already explained, this could not have been further from the truth. It is sad that some of the executives involved felt the need to justify their actions by doing that. They lost a great artist who had not only sold millions of records for them over her twelve years at the label but had also drawn other credible artists to their roster. Then they felt the need to cover their tracks.

With the sale of Warners in early 2004, some of the major players who were involved in the negotiations were escorted from the building after being let go by the new owners. Even if they did walk with huge buyouts from their contracts, there is still some sense of justice that these people were removed. There were a great many members of the Tori Amos family who had worked their collective asses off during those last two records who were let go also. Some of them are still there, including Jason Flom, now co-chairman and CEO of Atlantic. Had this happened a few years ago . . . who knows?

With her newly gained freedom from the Atlantic shackles, Tori released *Scarlet's Walk*, which included her most successful radio hit to date, "a sorta fairytale."

As that song gained momentum at the radio format of Hot AC and Triple A, I got countless phone calls from some of the "family" at Atlantic, crying, "Why now?" "Why has she written a hit now? Why not four years ago, before she left the company?" I think, without exception, they all got it after the circumstances that brought about Tori's exit and subsequent move to Sony were explained.

With the release of *Tales of a Librarian*, we thought Atlantic really had a chance to show that maybe they had made a mistake and to prove that they, the people in charge of the label, were worthy of working for the famed Atlantic name. Unfortunately, we were wrong.

With the early meetings, all the normal gusto was there. We were hearing stuff like "We want to show Sony what we can do" and "We will make this record one of the top five most important records ever to be released on Atlantic." Well, that meant nothing. Without a checkbook, there was little they could do. And the checkbook had been locked away with the whiskey until after the sale of Warners to Edgar Bronfman Jr. In fact, the staff's T&E (travel and entertainment) accounts had been suspended without preapproval from the Warner accountants for anything over fifty dollars . . . along with the private cars and jets to the Hamptons. There was the Press and Promotion Department, terrified for their own jobs and scared to book anything in case it cost them money!

This was not entirely unexpected, and with the formation of The Bridge only a month before the release of *Tales,* Chelsea and I went into overdrive to put together a schedule worthy of a career-long collection of music. As this book is published, we are developing a relationship with the new holders of Tori's back catalog and hope that, in new and safe hands, this work is forever treated with the respect that it deserves.

TORI:

If you take away only three terms from this book about the music business, then take the three that I'm about to give you. *Controlled composition. Recoupable. In perpetuity.* These three terms can lose you your artist's soul. Remember these terms similarly to the way you shudder when you hear "666, The Mark of the Beast." These three terms are the 666 of the music business.

Simply, *controlled composition* means that if you are a contracted artist who writes your own songs, then your record label is allowed to cheat you out of what any other songwriter, who isn't under the terms of your deal, would get paid. Songwriters should be paid on the statutory mechanical rate set by CARP (Copyright Arbitration Royalty Panel), which, as of

January 1, 2004, is $.085 per song in the United States. Record labels in the United States traditionally pay on only ten songs, up to twelve, per CD. You, as the signed songwriter to a record label in America, do not receive the statutory mechanical rate if the record label puts a controlled composition clause into your contract. Some songwriters have actually owed the record label money every time a CD of theirs is sold because of this devious controlled composition clause. This clause is far more complicated and menacing than I can explain in one paragraph. Now, why is this allowed to happen? This is not allowed to happen in Europe. Why do Congress and state legislators not protect the artist from the controlled composition clause?

Recoupable. Okay, just think of it this way. The record label charges you for pretty much everything. So if you get sent flowers, which my last record label did, don't be surprised if you get charged for them in your next royalty statement. I did.

Publishing is one of the most important aspects of the music industry. If I had listened to some of my former advisers way back when who are no longer advising me, I would have sold the publishing for my first seven records. The first record that would have counted would have been *Little Earthquakes,* so as you can count I would not have fulfilled the terms of the contract until 2006. Therefore, this contract would have included from 1991 to 2006—from *Little Earthquakes* through *The Beekeeper.* To put that amount of time in perspective, my twelve-and-a-half-year-old niece just said, "Oh my God, that's older than me!" And the crazy thing about all this is that I would have signed over fifteen years of my song girls for about the price of a Toyota. Now, I like a Toyota, but give me a break.

Signing that deal would have made me financially broke. I mean *broke.* So the question you have to ask yourself as a songwriter is whether or not you think that you are going to have a successful songwriting career. If you do, then you need to think long term. If you don't, then you might want to take the money and run. Now what I mean by that is, if you're getting offered a big advance and you desperately need the money, then I know and you know that you're gonna take that money. But you see, there's a huge hook—the biggest chorus ever—in this song called the publishing contract. There's a little phrase that can even hook, catch, and grill the cleverest of mermaids or mermen . . . and that phrase would be *in perpetuity.*

Okay, for anybody in the music industry or anybody thinking about getting into the music industry, these two little words can change your whole life. Change your whole life. These two little words mean *FOREVER*, so just to explain it, let's talk about a for instance. Let's say that Tori signed that publishing deal back in 1991. Even though she would be getting out in 2006, which would mean that *The Beekeeper* would have been the final work for which the publishing company could have taken all her publishing money, that doesn't mean that she gets these songs back. If Tori leaves the publishing deal, this means only that she starts getting paid for the publishing on her next work, which could be in 2007 or 2008. *In perpetuity* means that the publishing company that Tori "signed with" will get all of the publishing money from all of her songs from 1991 until 2006, forever and ever. These songs do not revert back to Tori. The revenue from these songs does not revert back to Tori.

Now I will say here that if you're hot, you have more leverage during publishing negotiations. But I was far from cold when I was offered my publishing deal right before *Little Earthquakes* came out. If I hadn't had Al Stewart (*Year of the Cat*) jumping all over my case, and my mom and dad begging me not to sign my publishing away, then I would probably be working at Nordstrom in the shoe department. And I'm not dissing a job in a shoe department. Me? Are you kidding? That could almost be heaven. But it's not heaven if you've sold millions of records on the back of your own songwriting, songwriting you would have signed away fifteen years previously to buy the equivalent of . . . what??? And for whom??? I certainly could not have secured myself a place to live. So remember those two little words, *In Perpetuity*. Believe me, they can cost you a hell of a lot more than those other famous two little words, "I do."

SONG CANVAS: "Hoochie woman"

This is very simple in the world of chicks: some are hoochies, some are not, and some should never try to be. It's no different from the idea of sports. Now, I can go on my little rowing machine four times a week, twenty-two minutes a time, and I can feel as if I flirt with the sporting world. Similar to the idea that a woman can put on something cute for her man, for those moments, and flirt with garments that a hoochie woman might be pushing. But never for one moment should you get confused. My little rowing machine and I cannot consider ourselves athletes. Wearing the same garment does not a hoochie woman make. So if you are a true hoochie woman, may garments below the navel always be in your future. If you are not, then please don't throw away your cotton zippy jacket.

TORI:

As some of these songs were coming to me, I asked the gospel choir arranger, Wayne Hernandez, to come down to Martian and lend his vocal magic. He and his singers, the girls who I call "the gangsta-rinas," are on four songs on *The Beekeeper*, including "Witness."

Betrayal happens in strange ways and comes from strange corners sometimes. Some days life can feel pretty normal, so to speak. Then there are
other days that make you think you've walked into something sinister,
into a Hermann Hesse novel. I wish I could tell you that nothing sur-
prises me anymore. But unfortunately that isn't true. Fame and money
expose people for who they really are. Some are willing to do anything
to keep it. "Witness" is a song written about this betrayal, and betrayal
is always one of the seeds in the Garden of Sin-suality . . .

Phone rings.

"Hey, T."

"Hey, you."

"I need to give you some news."

"Give me the bad news first."

"It's all bad."

"Okay, I'm standing. Shoot."

"They want —— from you." (Some issues are locked up in confi-
dentiality agreements.)

"Hmm."

"Are you there?"

"Yep."

"What's our response? Do you want your team's advice?"

"Yes, I want your advice, but not today. My response is—tell the
team no one responds. I will not dignify their insult."

"Understood."

"I suspect they'll call back within six days."

"Six business days?"

"Yeah, weekends count only for musicians and crew."

"And accountants."

"Fair enough. But never suits. I haven't seen a suit at a gig in a long time."

"I wear a suit," says Philip-the-Good.

"Nothing personal."

We say our goodbyes and I hang up. And, sure enough, within six business days I get a call from Philip-the-Good.

TORI:

Having been in the music business since I was thirteen years old, there are things I've been exposed to that I haven't seen, or that the accountants and investment bankers I've worked with haven't seen, in any other business. Which leads me to something I'm quite convinced about, and it's very unusual for me, but in this case I must argue with the playwright Congreve when he pronounced, "Hell hath no fury like a woman scorned." I must rectify this by saying, "Hell hath no fury like a rejected entertainment executive scorned."

SONG CANVAS: "Barons of suburbia"

This song is about takers. We all know them, either as people we have to work with or friends we find out about eventually, and sometimes it's a real shock to realize that when push comes to shove, all these people really care about is what's in it for them. In the end they don't even pretend to care if you're okay. Not if you're okay, or if the friendship is okay, or anything else. Can somebody tell me what is wrong with the idea of a win-win? Why does somebody always have to bite the dust?

Jeez. These days it seems as if it's getting harder and harder to get people on the team who really want to show that they value one another. People might say that they want to, but at the end of the day most of them care only about what they get out of it.

I remember a couple of years ago when one of the musicians said to me, "I think music should be free." And I was just not in the mood to deal with yet another genius, but I did, and I said, "Well, you have made the question about where to send your check easy for me to answer." "Um," said the musician, "what do you mean?" I answered, "We weren't sure whether to send your check to your address or to your girlfriend's address, but now you've answered my question for me." "I'm not quite following you, Tor," he said. "Well, obviously since you believe that music should be free, then we won't need to send you your check." The musician looked at me incredulously, and with shock in his voice said, "But I've just played my heart out." I looked at him very calmly and said, "So you think you should get paid but music should be free?" "Well, yeah," he said. "And so who do you think is going to pay you if music is free?" I asked. And therein lies the problem—everybody wants free stuff but nobody wants to work for free.

The truth is, all the people who have ever told me that music should be free still believe that they should be paid for their job, whatever that job may be. They are completely insulted when I suggest that they work for free as well. People usually get quite defensive at this point and say, "If I don't get paid for a day's work, then basically I'm being cheated." And I look at them and say, "That is basically right."

This musician sheepishly looked at me and said, "I guess I sound pretty hypocritical . . . but Tor, you're kidding, right?" And I said, "You mean about you not getting paid? Of course I'm going to pay you, because I value what you do. But do you want to know what scares me, and

I mean *really* scares me?" And he looked at me completely baffled and said, "No, what really scares you?" "The fact," I said, "that you weren't kidding."

CONVERSATION BETWEEN TORI AND ANN:
It is personal.

When you care about your team, when the bonds have been formed and somehow this big ball of tape starts unraveling and tangling. I weep and would walk to Japan to fix it, but after you walk to Japan and it still isn't fixed, you begin to realize that each person has to want to look at his or her part and say, "Okay, sorry—so that rupture is mine and I don't want you all tripping over something that only I can fix." Unless you have the inner desire to walk the extra mile with your creative circle, then the circle will be breached. It will break. The circle's breaking aches. And it is personal. Sometimes we enter into a forgetfulness, thereby treating companions, creative compadres, as if they are taking from us when they are giving. And the decomposing of the harmonic structure that was in place has begun. And the cords pull—no, *yank*—in your gut. Oh my God, it feels like your ovaries are being yanked out with tweezers. Then every time it happens, you realize that you cannot make others want to look at their part in the discordance. You can say how it's affecting your relationship and what you're willing to do or not do. Then it's out of your hands. Completely out of your hands.

Kali, Sekhmet, Pele, Oya, Sedna—these mythical goddesses have taught me about not being intimidated by a destructive force. This can be a person on the crew. This can be someone working closely on a project. This can be administrative, management, the record company, or the agency. This can be someone in the audience. I've sat in the stink, the spewing of someone's negativity. The Piss Christ was made of urine. Can a negative experience spark and inspire the Passion that is in us, maybe suppressed inside us, to rise up and out of "their" thoughtless remorse? Can we build something better? You know you must descend to ascend. Pass through the eye of the needle . . . If it's too loud, then turn it up. Yes. Sometimes a negative attitude that has spread can make everyone question and improve and reach for excellence. Value the opportunity. Sometimes it is just negativity in the end. The creative tribe cannot shoulder the negative cancer if at its core it chooses to stay malignant.

The intriguing thing about conflict in the creative world and the business of the creative world is what it brings out in people. You really don't know what a person is made of until conflict enters the picture and people are forced to choose sides. If there hadn't been people who went over and above what a friend should be, then I wouldn't be here writing this book. A lot of times projects get accomplished because of the tenacity, not of the big record Cheeses, but of the girls and guys who do the busywork at the record company. Without the Vicky Germaises, the Elyse Taylors, the Lee Ellen Newmans, the Linda Ferrandos, the Patti Contis, and the Matthew Rankins of the world, it would have been a very different story from what it turned out to be.

I call on Sekhmet when I need to stand in my own authority. She is the one who acts until certain policies are changed. Her spirit leads me when it comes to being able to have force—and I don't mean like Obi-Wan Kenobi. I think the patriarchy would say that Sekhmet's plan of action was a rampage, whereas I say that it was about saying no to wrongdoing. If someone who already has power is going to hold people hostage, well, two can play at that game.

I am always willing to discuss things before laying down the line. If you don't want to take the high road, it doesn't mean I'm going to go away.

If you don't want to come to the table and define terms, which I feel Sekhmet was willing to do, we can play another way.

I can definitely be a battle-ax. That's a side of it. Madonna has that side; so does Chrissie Hynde, even successful women who project a sweet image, like Sarah McLachlan. The women who have impact must be willing to pounce when it's appropriate. If you're going to take on the music business, you need to find that red energy somewhere in you.

The aggressiveness and strength I've cultivated can make me open to criticism, and not just from the men I've had to confront. Women have also challenged my decisions. I've run across a certain attitude from women who took another path. Feminism did not really make it okay to have it all. I've met women who've essentially said to me, *Tori, you have the houses, you have your empire. It might be a small empire, but you've got one nonetheless. You don't have to look to a man to provide. You can bring home the bacon. You made that choice, whereas we chose to be the nurturers and the mothers, and you have to respect that, too. Admit it—you can't have it all.*

At times I did feel very guilty that I went after the chance to be the best and to negotiate with the big boys. To someone who's not an artist, the fights I've gone through might seem unnecessary. And this business doesn't necessarily reward compassionate behavior. I know women in the business who are very competitive, and I've been very competitive. But now that I have a little girl, I see how in popular music, where all the lads get to have their chance, there can be room for a win-win among women, too. There can be room for more than one of us at a time. Many different archetypes are needed to complete the pantheon. Aphrodite can't be Athena and vice versa. To be jealous of Athena when you're Aphrodite is ridiculous. To envy Artemis' abilities when you're Athena is not the right use of energy—it's emotional cancer. I've learned the hard way.

Being able to determine your own identity—that's what makes the struggle worthwhile. After going through the embarrassment of *Y Kant Tori Read*, letting people who claimed they had my interests in mind turn me away from myself, I said I would never again become something I wasn't. I was playing a role then, and I learned from that. I decided, no, that doesn't fit me very well. There are other ways I need to express myself as a woman and as an artist.

What we have to realize as women in the music business is that the old-boy network wants us to compete with one another. Divide and conquer. And no matter how many times the media declares it "the year of the woman" in music, right now things are only getting worse for anyone who wants more than momentary success. The window is getting very small. Years ago you had women who could go four records deep, like Joni Mitchell or Linda Ronstadt, and continue to be supported by their labels, radio, and the press. But now the corporations dominating music run through an artist in one record and move on to the next one. Stick around and your label will probably try to get you to do something that's a real loss to your dignity, just to make a shock statement. My heart goes out to those women who've exploited themselves. Ten years ago I would have had a smirk on my face about it, but I see now that we're all forced to deal with that moment. It's one of the steps you go through to survive.

Wrath is a force that should be conjured strategically. I'm beyond the fury of youth at this point. I love it when I see young women who are angry—they're our wild mustangs. But if you don't transcend that at some point, you become a very disturbed forty-year-old. You're just mean and mad at the world.

TORI:

Today I turn forty-one. Dunc said something to me today that has got me thinking. He knows I've been writing this chapter for days and days, and he said to me, "Don't you think that it's kind of poetic justice that on to-day of all days you are finishing the music business chapter?" I guess I should have gotten the hint at Tash singing Gloria Gaynor's "I Will Survive" off her disco classics CD. Dunc talked about an idea—you start collecting all kinds of things from the age you're old enough to. You collect rocks, you collect ideas. You pick up these rocks, these ideas, and you place them in a bag that you carry with you wherever you go. These rocks represent events and experiences that you take with you. Sometimes, though, these rocks become too heavy to carry around. After all, there are only so many rocks that you can carry in your bag before they weigh you down so much so that you can't even move, much less walk. Some rocks you just have to take out of your bag.

The greek god Athena

quan yin:
The Art of compassion

ANN: *Archetypes survive because they are both consistent and adaptable. The goddesses who continue to inspire us, even those who have survived the civilizations from which they arose, are no strangers to change: their legends, their outward appearance, even their names, have evolved to serve the needs of whatever communities call upon them. Corn Mother speaks of respect for the land that bears us; Saraswati honors the flow of creativity; Sekhmet stands for the fierce inevitability of fate. In other circumstances these deities had other names: Ceres, Minerva, Kali. But the qualities of the soul each represents remain consistent.*

In Asia, one goddess thrives whose spirit is adaptability itself, as it manifests in the act of extending kindness to others. However you spell her name, Quan Yin, the beloved avatar of compassion, remains the spirit of refuge, the comforter of sorrows whose name means "the one who contemplates the supplicating sound of the world." Quan Yin is called Kannon in Japan, the Green Tara in Tibet, Quan'Am in Vietnam, and Kanin in Bali. She manifests as a male as well: as Avalokitesvara, the keeper of the mystical Lotus, and as Guan Yin, the guardian of the sea. She has been pictured as a thousand-limbed, thousand-eyed dancer and a white-robed queen who rides a celestial dragon upon the streams of life. Consistency in multiplicity is Quan Yin's essence, for compassion must manifest uniquely to suit whoever seeks it, though the gift of peace it brings is ultimately the same.

As above, so below: it is the human mission to become an eye within the storm, to remain grounded while responding to life's sometimes baffling variety. Artists, who cultivate openness in service of a vision that encompasses the world, must become particularly adept at this balancing act. Yet the mundane world of material survival—not to mention the ego—can sometimes mire an artist in a rut. The tempo of success can change again over time; it takes wisdom to move along with it.

At midlife, Tori Amos understands that she cannot rule life's tidal shifts, only navigate them. She is a rider of the waves, her sense of the future defined by an undiminished faith in music's power. Like Quan Yin, she learns from listening, and finds her power in leading those who listen to her back to the answers within themselves.

CONVERSATION BETWEEN TORI AND ANN:

One deep purpose of music is to present a holistic version of what has been broken. There is a tradition of this that goes back thousands of years. Writers and artists have gone deep, deep inside; some have been killed because of this work, because it is perceived by many as a threatening act. There has been a deep belief that the masses are controlled because they have been separated from themselves at the core. They have been separated from the voice in their own soul. This is how you control another person, and this control gets perpetuated by those who don't even know they're passing this behavior on to their children. And at some point in my life, I really believed this was a war artists waged, a battle between people separated from their wholeness and those who saw that the only way forward was to eliminate the curse, the hierarchy, and redefine power.

I've felt music's integrating effect throughout my own life. Music more than anything else is what keeps me on the planet. I don't know if in another life I would be given music. So I'm going to create with it as much as I can. It is the only universal language that's tangible. Love is a universal language, but that's a much more abstract concept than being able to communicate with anyone in the world because the two of you can dance to a rhythm that we all innately understand without having to say a word. Music is more than a privilege; without it, I really don't know how I would cope. It's one reason I haven't gone off the rails.

As I've grown older, I have realized what a debt I owe to creativity. I can't say it enough: this force is not something that I own, or generate by myself, and as I've learned to embrace its profundity, I have been able to let it guide me into new phases.

The Native American way of thinking says you have to move on the medicine wheel. Too many people, especially women, are trying to stay in a place that they can't sustain physically and emotionally and spiritually. Thinking in terms of the Four Directions—the south, realm of innocence; the west, seat of power; the north, territory of hard-earned experience, and the east, frontier of enlightenment—you cannot remain within a direction that has blown you out. The west has said, "That's all now." And you have to move to the north. You're approaching middle age.

I heard this message from certain wise people whom I met when I was thirty-five. They would say, "You have to see that middle age means midlife." I was saying, "No, no, no, I've only had a few records out," but these guides were being realistic. If I make it to seventy, which is a few years shy of the average life expectancy of an American woman today, then I'd hit my midlife at that point.

We're in a business and a culture that doesn't accept such changes for women. We're still supposed to be wearing our little midriff tops and staying perpetually twenty-five. Some of the men in my field have made the transition to midlife quite elegantly. Neil Young, for example, or Bruce Springsteen. But for those artists, it's always been about the content. So I shifted perspective in my musical career, too; I said, "Okay, let's go back to my content. Let's go back to the power of the pen."

There were other inspirations I could tap into for this transition, coming more from the world of visual art. Georgia O'Keeffe made it as an old lady. Dorothea Tanning is in her nineties and still painting and writing poetry. I found some examples in the jazz world—Ella Fitzgerald performed into her seventies, despite health problems; Rosemary Clooney made a comeback in her late sixties. Myself at thirty-five, I felt that though the business is so much about the image, there is still a place for the songwriters singing the songs and not just handing them over to the next ingenue.

A lot of younger women have said to me, "Looking at your generation is the scariest thing in the world. What we have to look forward to is very bleak if our so-called role models aren't happy with who they are and wish they were more like us." They want somebody to turn around and say, "Middle age is a great place to be; you will *want* to arrive at this place." The songs that have been coming to me lately, with their varied points of view, have been helping me to see how many different aspects of the self there are and that there is so much to work with, for each of us, at every stage.

I'm beginning to see myself less and less as the one going out with the ships and sailing the seven seas. I did that. Okay. I've breastfed pigs. Then there came a time when I had to realize that it's now for other women to traverse that particular territory. I think I'm in a place where I'm trying to realize again what my role is. And it's not sitting there half-naked with a guitar between my legs. When others try to tell you what your role should be, and you can't pull it off, it's a problem. After all, you've got to wake up with yourself in the morning.

The Native sages who came to see me gave me another message, which came true. It's a conversation about business. The message was, in the tribe, women realized certain benefits as they aged. They were then included in discussions they couldn't join when they were younger. The Western, capitalist worldview doesn't recognize the usefulness of women's experience. Imagine if we treated men the same way—we'd lose so many of our poets and visionaries. Popular music is so focused on the outer being that it's hard for everyone to survive and stay in the game. And if you think about it, the women who have lasted are the ones who've kept themselves looking a certain way—Cher, Tina Turner, Madonna. However they did it, they maintained their looks. But it's interesting to note none of those three women is a composer. They might play at it, but they're not writers like Neil Young or other rock males. The women who are great composers, like Joni Mitchell, but who maybe haven't tailored their image to the modern consumer, aren't out on the "circuit" as much. So for female composers about ready to turn forty, the industry is not banging down your door. Yes, if you're an icon you will be able to play Merriweather Post, but you may not be sitting alongside Dave Matthews on the playlists at radio. Herein lies the challenge: to be able to traverse pop culture's addiction to imaging, all the while infusing your pencil not with lead but with estrogen.

A lot of leading men are just happening at forty. By that age, they know how to be clever, they know how to listen, they supposedly have experienced life. They might not be as cute as younger guys, but they're often sexier and almost always more powerful. In rock, it's somewhat different, even for men. We are drawn to the young king. I think it's messianic. And it's also obviously sexual. Americans, especially, still aren't comfortable with adult sexuality. It's like, your mommy and daddy have sex—no, no, no, no. There's a general denial, even though some people may leak it, even mommies at playgroup.

What I've experienced in Europe is that there's a place for mature sexuality; there really, really is, and there has been historically. And it isn't necessarily trashy. There's dignity and elegance to sexuality, because it's part of your life. And because there's a place for it, sex is not just everywhere, randomly emerging, as it does in our popular culture now, which is what many parents are so afraid of.

Becoming a parent has helped me see the proper place of things in my own life. When you're a mommy you have the opportunity to get very clear. I can deal with the music business now and not lose too much energy over its obnoxious aspects, because I know where my priorities are. What matters, in terms of work, are the songs. That doesn't mean I'm not willing to do the other work that's necessary. But when difficult situations come up, now I can see that there's an inner working to it all. There was a time when I believed that making records was separate from life, and I began to hear from other people that it wasn't. Wiser people than I advised me that no, it's part of your life. That's why you need to have a studio close to where you live, really trust your collaborators, and integrate and balance all the elements.

Mark's father gave me some wisdom before he died, and I remember it most days. He said, "If I could be any age [he was in his midseventies at the time] I would want to be forty." I said, "Tell me why." I was really surprised. I wasn't forty yet; I think I was thirty-five. He said, "That was when I was old enough to know the what and the how of it all, and still young enough to do it."

Some people feel they've lost something as they get older. For me, I feel like I've gained a thing I was desperately looking for. I'm not saying there aren't days when I look in the mirror and say, "Jesus Christ, I look old." But there's a quality within me now that I was hungry for, starving for, looking for, in my midtwenties, and I didn't find it. I found it later, outside the music industry, when I started choosing my friends wisely. I made a choice not to stay in L.A.; I made a choice to leave London. And I knew that my relationships would develop with the people who should be part of my life, even if they lived six thousand miles away, not just those I ran across as I pushed my career. Friendships are based on being tested. Being backstage when the champagne is flowing because you have your hands on a huge success is not really the time when a friendship is tested.

The miscarriages—I wouldn't wish them on an enemy, but they really brought me to a place of bitterness and loss. And instead of wallowing in that, at a certain point I could begin to take the gall out of it. Nearly everyone is faced with some kind of health problem at some point, and when you are, that sense of immortality goes, that arrogance. Maybe there was a time when I thought I was immortal; I think a lot of people do. But certain physical struggles have come to me, and the best thing about them is that I have so much more compassion for what people go through physically, and for their losses. I'm beginning to accept that the body goes through changes. Lots of changes. Sometimes when I'm onstage in the middle of a show I feel better than I've ever felt in my life. When I turned forty I was doing a show and I thought to myself, "Why didn't anyone tell me how great you could feel at forty?" Then of course there are those days when I'm just trying to put one foot in front of the other.

SONG CANVAS: "Jamaica Inn"

I've always been drawn to fire. When I was seventeen I chased it, when I was twenty-seven I danced with it, and when I was thirty-seven I nursed it. Like women, fire changes. In one moment it can be warming, in another moment it can burn everything around you to the ground. These days I'm entertaining the idea of a flame contained. The idea of a lighthouse. When I was being told a bit of Cornish history I was fascinated with the stories of the wrecker. Wreckers did not bring accidental destruction upon a vessel. By holding up a light, wreckers gave ships the false signal that it was safe to come in. Daphne du Maurier's book *Jamaica Inn* goes into detail about the Cornish custom of wrecking. Apparently, even vicars would hold a false light up so that once a ship was wrecked they would be able to sustain the local village with the goods that were smuggled out of the water. When I was driving down the coast from Bude to Padstow, I was drawn into this modern-day idea of homewrecking. In my car I started to sing the chorus for the song "Jamaica Inn" after seeing a small boat through the gales that I found myself in. Could I have written this song in sunny Southern California? Probably not. After all, I was physically in the land of Daphne du Maurier's *Jamaica Inn*, which was a real place, as well as *Rebecca*, another one of her books that took place in Cornwall. I reference both of these books in the song because they are the antecedents. I still don't know to this day if my character survives the shipwreck that she is in . . .

With the gales my little boat was tossed. How was I to know that you'd send her with a lantern to bring me in? "Are you positive this is a friend?" the captain grimaced. "Those are cliffs of rock ahead, if I'm not mistaken." The sexiest thing is trust. I wake up to find the pirates have come, tying up along your coast. How was I to know the pirates had come? Between Rebecca's, beneath your firmaments, I have worshiped in the Jamaica Inn.

When I was younger I looked for lighthouses—as one of those wild ships on the sea in my twenties. I found a lot of other wild ships out there just like me. Some of us were trying to board one another's ships. But there weren't a lot of lighthouses.

If you look at it through the medicine wheel, my generation is moving slowly from west now to north. We're having to move because we're getting shoved out. You cannot always be the one with the blazing lights that no one has seen before. But a lighthouse is something you can depend on. You see land in the distance when you are that new ship, and little do you know that there are monstrous underwater cliffs with hooks that say "50 percent" on them, and boy, you could sure use a lighthouse.

There are women to whom I look for guidance, and they have been walking that dark walk. They have been around long enough. Having to carve out a path with just a little matchstick, in some instances. But still I could go have a cup of tea with these mentors; they had an open door. But that role has been so marginalized in our popular culture. To me, that's why you see so many people chasing youth. Yet these young ingenues who define our standards cannot be the high priestesses, because they haven't walked the road. They haven't gone to visit Persephone and faced their own reflection while on their knees.

A good way to think of it is, you're part of something. Not the center. You make choices to be effective, and telling stories is a way for people to step into different worlds with you without leaving our chairs. There are some days as a songwriter when you look out at five thousand people and say to yourself, "Well, I can either take them on a giant rollerskate ride or down the cave of a projectile-vomiting dragon." And you really don't want to do the latter. So I apologize in advance if you find yourself in this dragon's cave at any of my shows. But I also know some cute dragons . . .

There are artists who really feel they are the seductress. And some of them are. Some of them hold the codes to this archetype, and watching them move is akin to watching flowers turn themselves into liquid perfume. This is a delicious archetype to play with, but it can also be a double-edged sword if the seduction has blinded the performer to her own inner beauty. This eventually can become a nightmare and a painful place to be because of the lonely narcissism of it, and the risk. The fall is great. The chroniclers who first defined the role of the artist understood this. In ancient days, there was no confusion about whether the artist was the king or the subject. He was not. But the chronicler was sovereign as he tried to pinpoint what was going on in the village. I'm trying to get back to a sense of what it means to be an artist in a community. The storyteller brings forth what is hidden, and what is being erased.

ACKNOWLEDGMENTS

TORI:

First, a thanks to Husband for patience and perspective, and to Natashya for giving up "Tash Time." Ann, it's been a privilege. Chelsea, I could not have done this without our daily two-hour international brainstorming. Johnny, many thanks for dealing with all the headaches so I didn't have to. To Mel for being so giving of your art and vision for the cover. Rakesh, you warrior you . . . Gerry for believing and Sheri for the beauty you give.

To Mom and Dad as always for their sense of humor.

To those who have given good counsel—Phil, Jim, the Wolf, Jamie, John, and Heather.

To the Crew, near and far, and for those interviewed: Keith, Andy, Matt, Jon, Ali, Joel, Jen, Dunc, Marcel, Miss Karen, and Dan. To Cody and Hayley for book nitpicking in the nicest possible way. Hugs to Marie, Beenie (Nancy), Super-Debs, Kelsey, Helen, Adam, Loren, Mike, Neil, Manny, and everyone at Martian.

Ann:

Undying thanks to Eric Weisbard for incredible patience in a time of great craziness, and to Rebecca, simply for existing. Tori, your brilliance, curiosity, and heart made this experience more than I could have hoped for. I echo all of Tori's thank-yous, from Chelsea onward, to the family that has formed around Martian studios and on the road. A special thanks to Alison Evans—my pally on the bus.

Rakesh Satyal had the vision and Gerry Howard had the faith to make this unique project a reality. My agent, Sarah Lazin, is unparalleled in fighting for what her clients need; this is one of so many thanks I owe her. Catherine Mayhew helped with the details. Bob Santelli and my colleagues at Experience Music Project gave much-needed time and understanding, as did Craig Marks and Rob Tannenbaum at Blender. Kelley Guiney transcribed hours of conversation and offered important insights. Carrie Lehenbauer gave crucial support and feedback.

This book wasn't the only newborn to enter my life during this period. I thank the staff at Open Adoption and Family Services, especially Katie Ruprecht Stallman, for leading us through an extremely intense experience; their support allowed me to keep sane enough to work. More than anyone, I thank Mallory Blaschka, and her mom, Kelly, for their incredible strength and generosity in joining the gift circle that surrounds our daughter, Rebecca Brooklyn Weisbard, the spark that lights all my writing efforts now.

TORI AMOS is foremost among the artists who have redefined the role of women in pop in the last decade. Her piano-based music revived that instrument in rock and roll, and her complex yet accessible songs have pushed the parameters of pop writing. Since the double-platinum success of her solo debut, *Little Earthquakes*, in 1992, Amos's albums and tours have reached millions of listeners worldwide. She is the co-founder of the Rape, Abuse, and Incest National Network (RAINN). Her ninth recording, *The Beekeeper*, was released in February 2005.

ANN POWERS has been writing about popular music and society since the early 1980s. She is the author of *Weird Like Us: My Bohemian America* and co-editor of *Rock She Wrote: Women Write About Rock, Pop, and Rap*. She was a pop critic for the *New York Times* from 1997 until 2001 and an editor for the *Village Voice* from 1993 until 1996. She has written for most music publications and her work has been widely anthologized. She is currently a curator at the Experience Music Project, an interactive music museum in Seattle, Washington.